SCOTLAND

A-Z VISITORS' ATLAS and GUIDE

CONTENTS

Reference and Key to Tourist Information 2
Key to Map Pages 3
Road Maps (1:200,000) 4-59
Outer Hebrides (1:250,000)..60-63
Orkney Islands (1:250,000).....64-65
Shetland Islands (1:250,000) ..66-67
Towns and Holiday Resorts.....68-87
Index to Towns and Villages....88-96
Index to Places of Interest.....97-105

Geographers' A-Z Map Company Ltd
Fairfield Road, Borough Green,
Sevenoaks, Kent TN15 8PP
Enquiries & Trade Sales
01732 781000
Retail Sales
01732 783422
www.a-zmaps.co.uk

Edition 3 2007
Copyright © Geographers' A-Z Map Company Ltd.

MOTORWAY	M9	TOLL	TOLL
MOTORWAY UNDER CONSTRUCTION		MILEAGE BETWEEN MARKERS	8
MOTORWAY PROPOSED		RAILWAY AND STATION	
MOTORWAY JUNCTIONS WITH NUMBERS	6	LEVEL CROSSING AND TUNNEL	
Unlimited interchange	6	RIVER OR CANAL	
Limited interchange	7	7	COUNTY OR UNITARY AUTHORITY BOUNDARY	
MAJOR ROAD SERVICE AREA	DREGHORN	NATIONAL BOUNDARY	
with 24 hour Facilities	S	BUILT-UP AREA	
MOTORWAY SERVICE AREA	HARTHILL S	VILLAGE OR HAMLET	
with access from one carriageway only	S	WOODED AREA	
PRIMARY ROUTE	A82	SPOT HEIGHT IN FEET	• 813
PRIMARY ROUTE DESTINATION	PERTH		
DUAL CARRIAGEWAYS (A & B Roads)			
CLASS A ROAD	A701		
CLASS B ROAD	B7009		
NARROW MAJOR ROAD (Passing Places)		NATIONAL GRID REFERENCE (Kilometres)	100
MAJOR ROADS UNDER CONSTRUCTION		PAGE CONTINUATION	48
MAJOR ROADS PROPOSED			
GRADIENT 1:5 (20%) & STEEPER	«	AREAS COVERED BY TOWN AND HOLIDAY RESORT PLANS	
(Ascent in direction of arrow)			

HEIGHT ABOVE SEA LEVEL
- 400' - 1,000' — 122m - 305m
- 1,000' - 1,400' — 305m - 427m
- 1,400' - 2,000' — 427m - 610m
- 2,000'+ — 610m +

TOURIST INFORMATION

AIRPORT	✈	MOTOR RACING CIRCUIT	
AIRFIELD	✛	MUSEUM, ART GALLERY	
HELIPORT		NATIONAL PARK OR FOREST PARK	
BATTLE SITE AND DATE	✕ 1066	NATIONAL TRUST PROPERTY (Open)	NT
CASTLE (Open to Public)		(Restricted Opening)	NT
CASTLE WITH GARDEN (Open to Public)		(National Trust for Scotland)	NTS NTS
CATHEDRAL, ABBEY, CHURCH, FRIARY, PRIORY	✝	NATURE RESERVE OR BIRD SANCTUARY	
COUNTRY PARK		NATURE TRAIL OR FOREST WALK	
FERRY (Vehicular)		PLACE OF INTEREST Monument •	
Please contact ferry operator for crossing times (Foot only)		PICNIC SITE	⊼
GARDEN (Open to Public)	❀	RAILWAY, STEAM OR NARROW GAUGE	
GOLF COURSE 9 HOLE 18 HOLE		THEME PARK	
HISTORIC BUILDING (Open to Public)		VIEWPOINT	
HISTORIC BUILDING WITH GARDEN (Open to Public)		WILDLIFE PARK	
HORSE RACECOURSE		WINDMILL	
INFORMATION CENTRE	i	ZOO OR SAFARI PARK	
LIGHTHOUSE			

SCALE

1: 200,000

3.156 Miles to 1 inch (2.54 cm) / 2 Km (1.243 Miles) to 1 cm

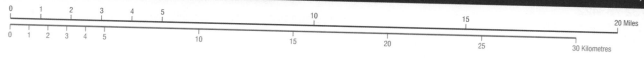

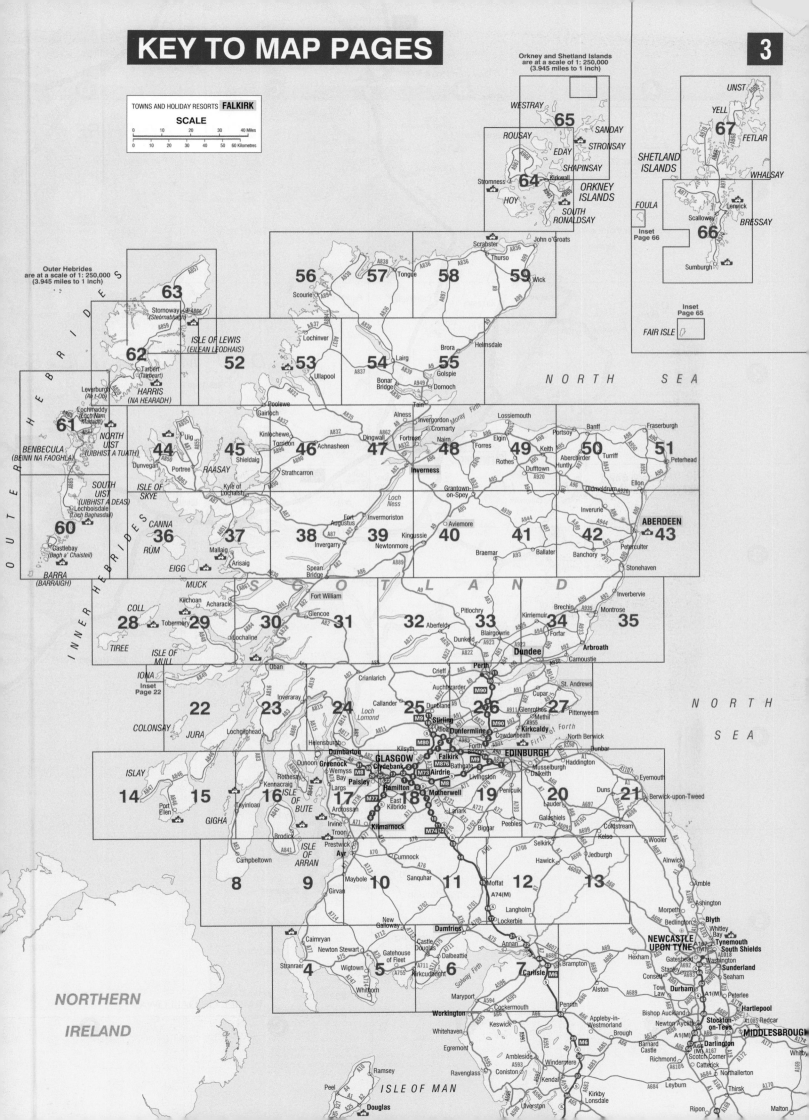

KEY TO MAP PAGES

TOWNS AND HOLIDAY RESORTS **FALKIRK**

SCALE

Orkney and Shetland Islands
are at a scale of 1: 250,000
(3.945 miles to 1 inch)

Outer Hebrides
are at a scale of 1: 250,000
(3.945 miles to 1 inch)

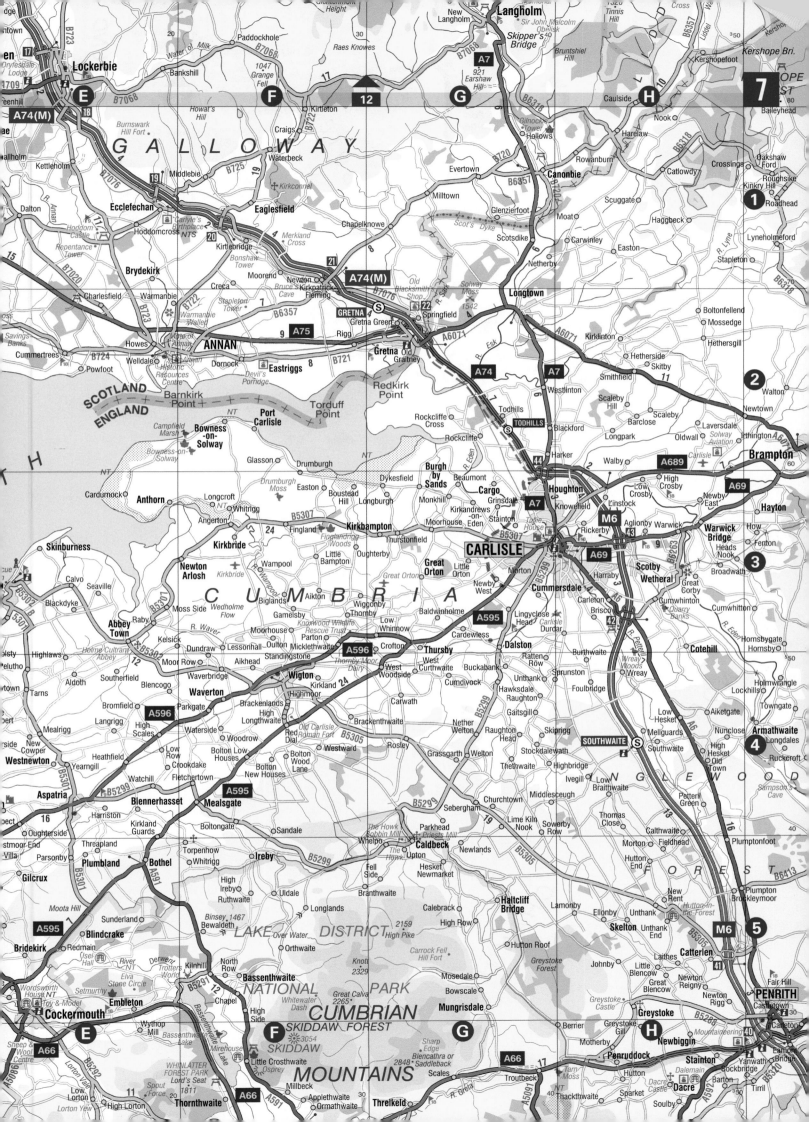

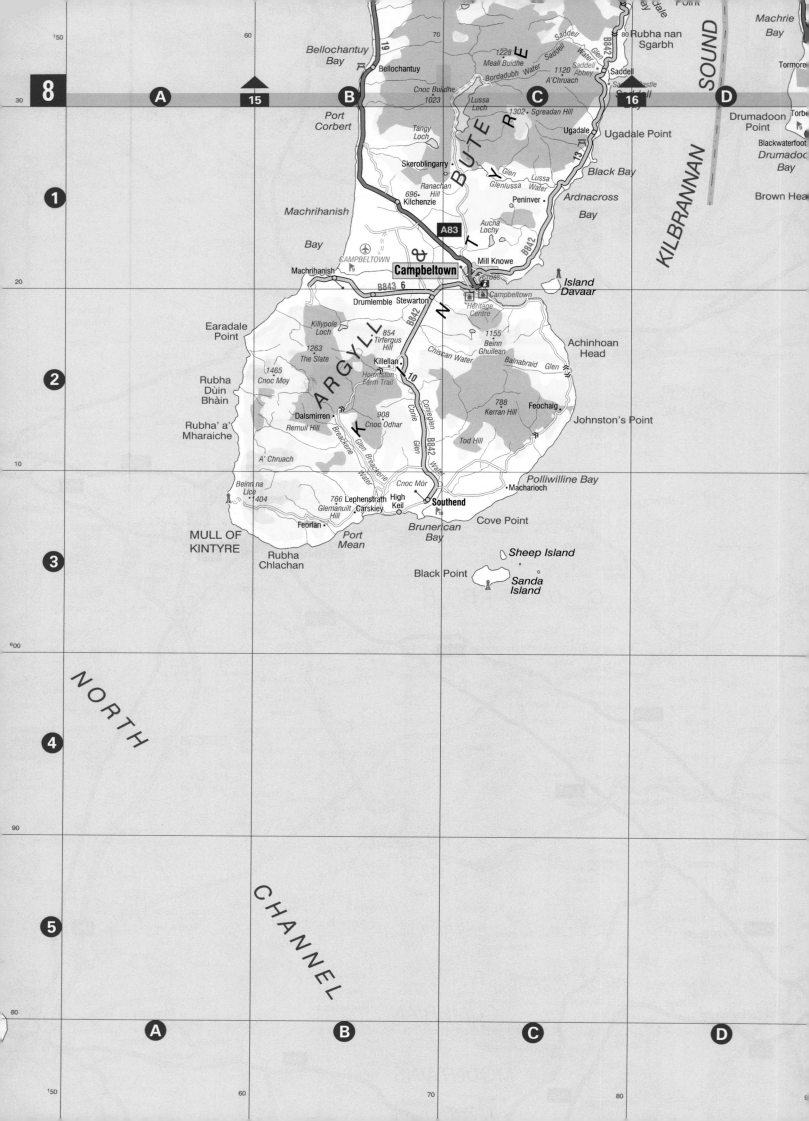

A **B** **C** **D**

1

2

3

4

5

Nave Island

Eilean
Beag

Ardnave
Loch

Tòn Mhór

Loch
Laingeadail Kilnave

Loch Còrr Sanaigmore Loch an
Fhir Mhór

Braigo

Rubha
Lamanais

Leckgruinart

Grulinbeg Loch
Gruinart

B8017

Saligo Bay

Saligo Gruinart

Coul
Point Loch Gorm

Loch Gorm
Castle

I S

B8018

ISLAY

Machir
Bay Kilchoman

Carraig
Dhubh

Cnoc Dubh Conisby

Bruichladdich

Kilchiaran Kilchiaran Loch
Bay Gearach

Bo
Dis

Islay Life

Octomore

Port Charlotte

760
Beinn Tart
Lossit a' Mhill

Loch

Laggan

Lossit
Bay

Neribus Laggan
Point

A8847

Octofad Lagg

RHINNS

Port Gleann
na Gaoidh

Portnahaven

Port Wemyss

Orsay RHINNS POINT

Bay

Slugaide
Glas

Dùn Mór Ghil T H E

Lower
Killeyan

American
Monument Loch
Kinnabus

MULL OF OA Beinn

A **B** **C** **D**

Oban to
Lochboisdale 5hrs.

Oban to
Castlebay 5hrs.

Cair

Eag na
Maoile

Eilea

Rubha Mór

Bousd

Cornaigmore   Sorisdale

Rubh'a' Bhinnein

COLL

Loch
Fada

Rubha Hogh

Grishipoll

Cliad Bay

Clabhach   B8071

Loch Cliad   Bagh Feisdlum

Hogh Bay   340   B8071

Ben
Nogh   Arinagour

Totronald   Loch nan
Cinneachan

Loch
Anlaimh   Acha   B8070

Feall
Bay   Coll   Uig   Eilean
Ornsay

Coll   Breachacha   5
Castle

Calgary Point   Port na
h-Eathar

Gunna   Port   Crossapol
a' Mhurain   Bay

Caolas Bàn   **Soa**

Gunna Sound   Coll to Tiree 1hr. 10mins.

Miodar

Vaul   Carnan
Bay

Hough   Balephetrish   Vaul   Salum   Caolas
Skerries   **Bay**   Rubha Dubh

Cornaigmore   Loch   B8069   Ruaig
Riaghain

Sraid Ruadh   Balephetrish   Gott   Kirkapol

Balevullin   B8068   Gott Bay

Hough   Kilmoluaig   Cornaigbeg   5

Kenovay
TIREE

Kilkenneth   Loch an   B8068   **Scarinish**
Eilein

Moss   Baugh
Sandaig   Heylipol   B8068   Crossapol   Heanish   Rubha Tràigh
Middleton   Barrapol   an Duin
Port Mor   2
Thatched House   Loch a'   **Hynish**
Port   Phuill   B8065   **Bay**   **TIREE**
Bharrapool   B8067   **Balemartine**

Balephuil   Mannal

Balephuil   West   Signal
Bay   Hynish   Tower
Hynish

Port Snoig

INNER   Treshnish Isles   Lunga

Bac Mor or
Dutchman's Cap

Bac Beag

Réidh   Eilean
Eilean   Annraidh

Abbey &
Nunnery

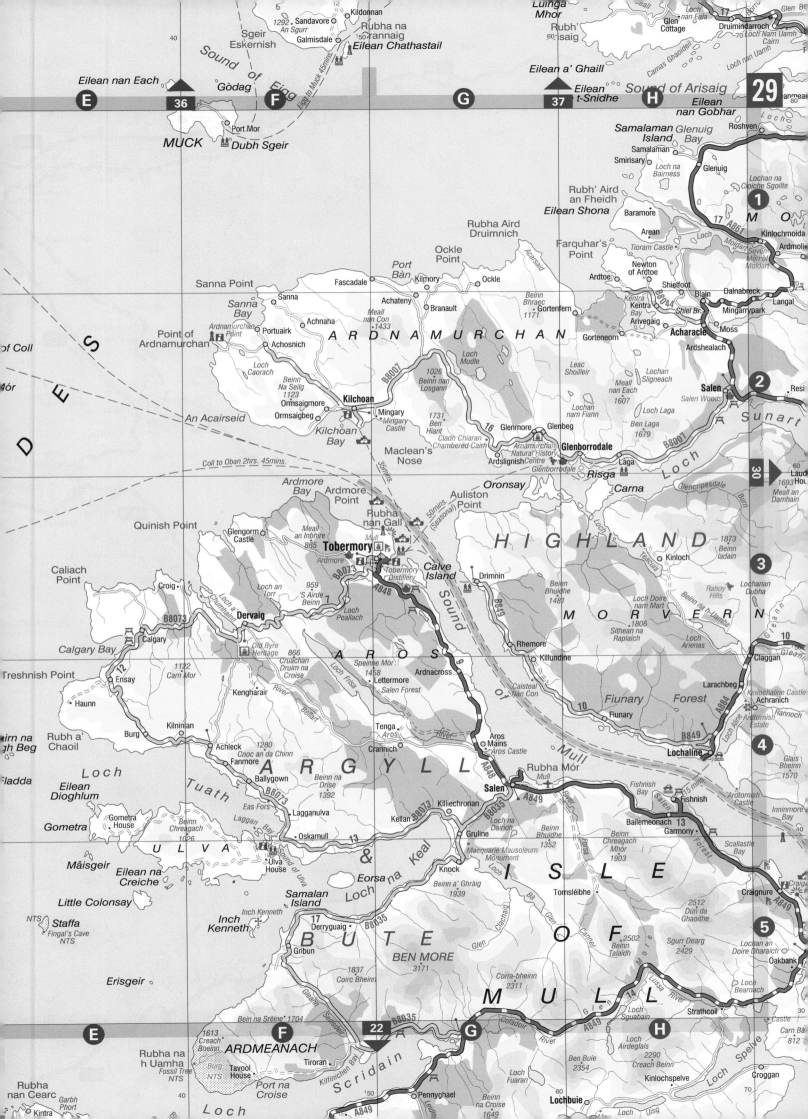

Map labels

Leachie Hill
Fetteresso Castle
Castle Haven
Dunnottar
Brae of Glenbervie
A90
Dunnottar Woodland Park
Thornyhive Bay
Fiddes Castle
Drumlithie
Herscha Hill 723
E
Glenbervie
42
Bruxie Hill 711
Milton of Barras
F
Fowlsheugh
Crawton
ty Forest
nfarquhar Lodge
Bervie Water
G
43
H
80

Bridge of Mondynes
Roadside of Catterline
Crawton Bay
uchenblae
chty Forest
17
Catterline
Braidon Bay
NSHIRE
Fordoun
Bridge of Kair
Parkneuk
Roadside of Kinneff
Fernieflatt
Fordoun
B967
Grassic Gibbon
Whistleberry Castle
Todhead Point
E
MEARNS
Arbuthnott House
Arbuthnott
Kinneff
Little John's Haven
Allardice Castle

ncekirk
Easter Tulloch
Knox Hill
Inverbervie
Bervie Bay
Haligreen Castle
Benholm Castle
Garvock
Gourdon

A90
Benholm
Mill

B9120
Chapelfield

Lauriston Castle
Johnshaven

Lochside
13
St. Cyrus
St. Cyrus
Pathhead

18
Montrose Air Station

18
MONTROSE
Montrose

Ferryden
ntrose Basin
irkton Craig
Usan
Dunninald House
Boddin Point

Lunan Bay

ie Haven
Red Head

N O R T H

S E A

Bell Rock

1
2
3
4
5

E
F
G
H

Maidens POINT *Oronsay*
Bracadale Portnalong

Rubha nan Clach Dun Ard An T-Sabhail Fiskavaig Fernilea B8009
Arnaval 1210 Talisker Distillery **Carbost**
Gleann Oraid Drynoch A863
A **B** Talisker Bay **44** **C** Merkadale River Drynoch **D** ISLE
Talisker Loch Sleadale Eynort River Beinn Bhreac A87
Beinn nan Cuithean Slig
Eynort
1468 Beinn Bhreac Eynort Glen Brittle Forest

1 Loch Eynort M I N G I N I S H 3167 Sgurr nan Gillean
An Dubh-sgeir Sgurr a' Ghreadaidh 3197 Harta Corrie
Stac an Tuill **CUILLIN** **HILLS**
Bualintur Glenbrittle Sgurr Alasdair 3257 Loch Coruisk
3037 Sgurr nan Eag
Loch Brittle Ceann na Beinne 736
2 Rudh An Dunain Chambered-Cairn Soay Sound 464 Beinn Bhreac Loch Scavai
Mol-chlach **SOAY** Eilean r

3 Garrisdale Point **CANNA** NTS 693 Carn a' Ghaill Castle Rùm to Canna 1hr. 5mins. Rubha Shamhnan Insir Mallaig to Canna 2hrs.
426 Ceann Creag-airighe A' Chill An Coroghon
Sanday Canna Harbour Camas Pliasgaig
Sound of Canna Kilmory Mullach Mór 997
Guirdil Bay Kinloch Mallaig to Rùm 1hr. 10mins.
Sgorr Mhór 1273 Rùm Kinloch Loch Scresort
4 Oigh-sgeir Schooner Point Orval 1874 Loch Gainmhich Rùm
Sgorr Reidh Long Loch
RÙM Glen Harris Loch Fiachanis Hallival Askival 2663
NATIONAL NATURE RESERVE Ruinsival 2552 Ainshval
Sgurr nan Gillean
Loch Papadil
Rubha nam Meirleach Cleadale
Bay of Laig
Eigg
Rubha an Fhasaidh Loch Beinn Tighe
5 1292 Sandavore An Sgurr Kil
Sgeir Eskernish Galmisdale
Eilean nan Each Gòdag Eil
Sound of Eigg Eigg to Muck 45mins.
Port Mor
A **28** **B** **C** **29** **D**
MUCK Dubh Sgeir

SEA OF INNER *T H E   H E B R I D E S* *H E B R I D E S* *H I G* *SOUND OF RÙM*

NORTH SEA

Port Erroll
Bay of Cruden
Whinnyfold

Ythanbank
Inverebrie
10
Yonderton
Broomfield
Ellon Castle
Kinharrachie
Esslemont Castle
Ellon NTS 5
Denhead
Meikle Loch
Old Slains Castle
Kirkton of Logie Buchan
B9003
Kirktown of Slains
Meikle Tarty
Sands of Forvie
Collieston
Tipperty
Knockhall Castle
Hackley Head or Forvie Ness
B9000
Hill of Fiddes
Newburgh
Udny Station
Foveran
Newburgh Bar
Tillery
Foveran Burn
Drums
14
Beauty Hill
Craigie
B979
Whitecairns
B977
Balmedie
Belhelvie
Balmedie
B977
Potterton
DANGER AREA
Corby Loch
Blackdog
Fowlershill
B999
B997
Scotstown Moor
eywood
A90
Aberdeen Exhibition & Conference Centre
Danestone
Woodside
Bridge of Don
Seaton Park
Donmouth
Hayton
Botanical Gs.
Old Aberdeen
Killybrewster
ABERDEEN
Maritime NTS
Footdee
Ferryhill
Torry
Nigg Bay
Ruthrieston
Blackhorse
Kincorth
Doonies Farm
Bridge of Dee
Loirston
Nigg
Souter Head
4
A956
A90
Cove Bay
Charlestown
A90
Hillside
Findon
Portlethen
10
Portlethen Village
Downies
Cammachmore Bay
Cammachmore
Newtonhill
Muchalls

Doonie Point

on Point

Aberdeen to:
Kirkwall 6hrs.
Lerwick 12hrs.

E A90 **F** A975 **G** **H** **43**
51
E 35 **F** **G** **H**

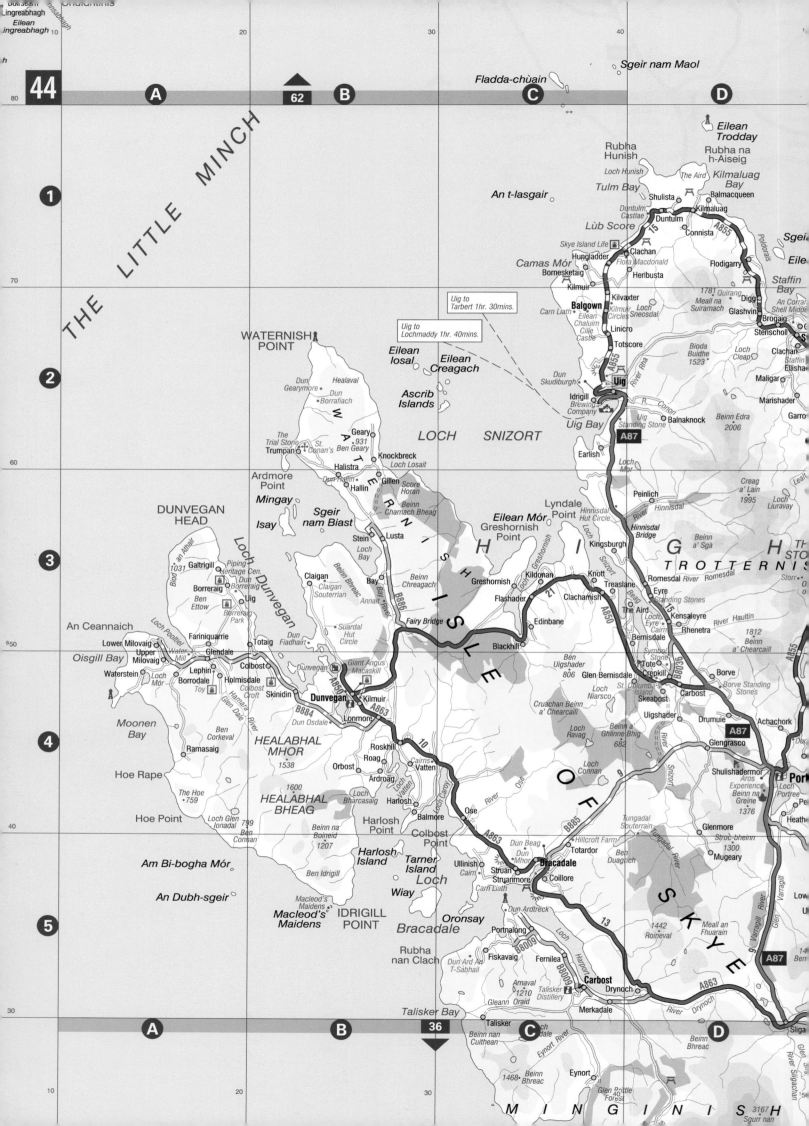

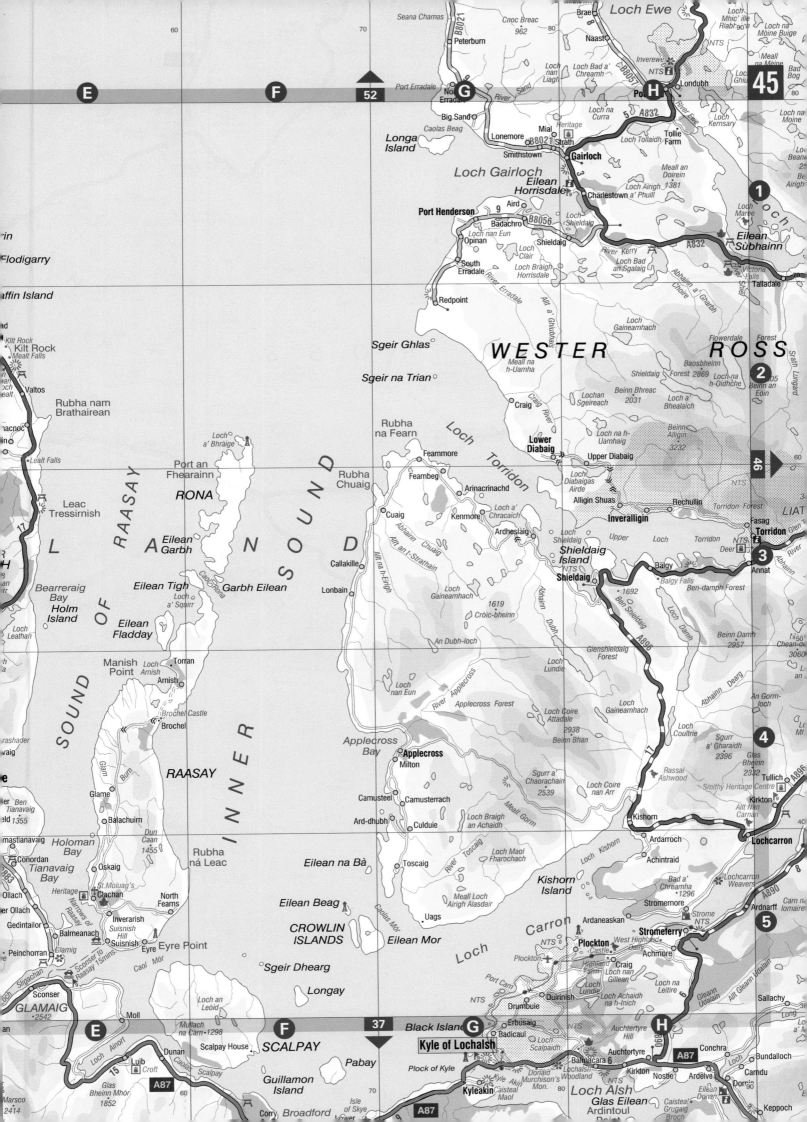

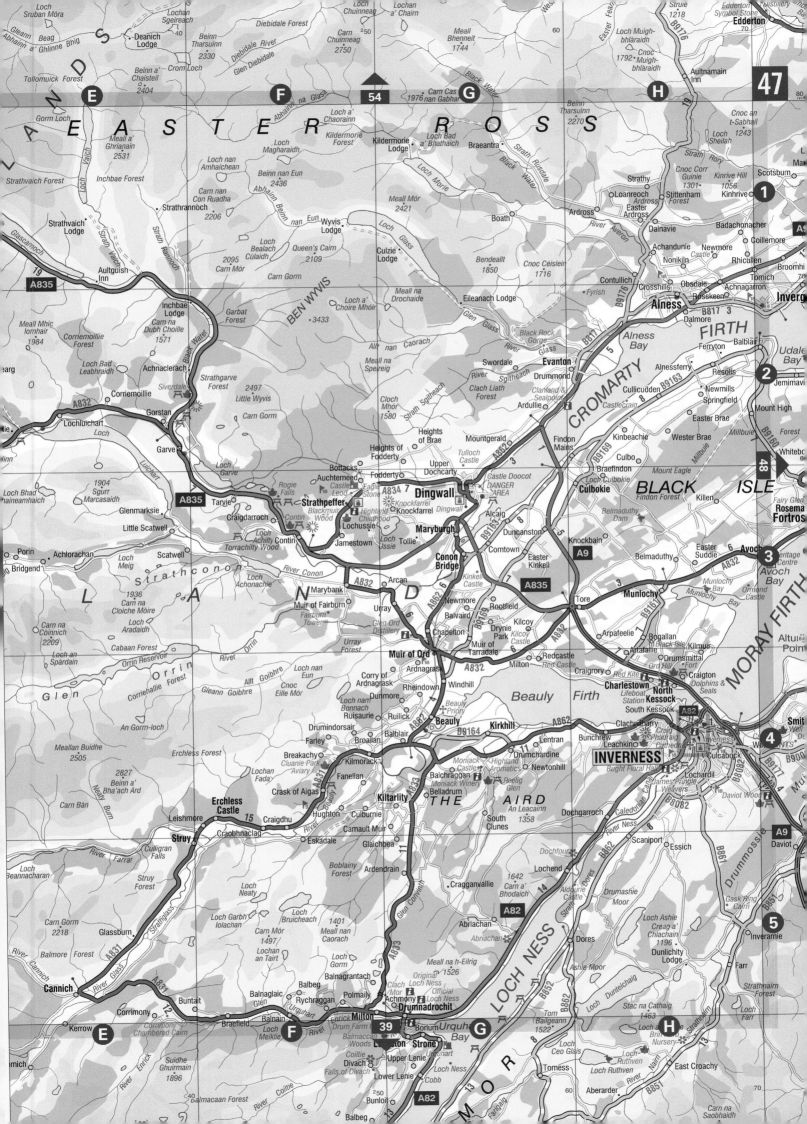

boist

Sulaisiadar

Aird

Gairsbost

EYE PENINSULA (AN RUBHA)

Seisiadar

Aiginis

An Choc

12

Pabail Uarach

52

Pabail Iarach

288 *Beinn Phabail*

Bagh Phabail Iarach

A **B** **C** **D**

60 70 80

1

20 ◀ **63**

2

10

Ullapool to Stornoway 2hrs. 40mins.

3

900

Pri

4

Greenstone Point

Loch na Doire Duinne **Opinan**

Loch nan Clachan Geala **Mellon Udrigle** *Loch a' Choire*

Slaggan Bay

Eilean Furadh Mór *Loch an t-Slagain* 513 *Beinn Dearg Nhor* **Achgarve**

Rubha Reidh *Camas Mór* **Rubha nan Sasan** **Mellon Charles**

90 *Loch an Draing* B8057 **Cove** **Ormiscaig** A832

An Cuaidh 972 *Loch Airigh an Eilein* **Mellangaun** **Aultbea** *Loch na B* **Drumchork**

Loch Sguod **Isle of Ewe**

Melvaig *Loch a' Bhaid-luachraich*

Aultgrishan B8021 **Midtown** **Loch Ewe** *Loch Mhic' ill Riabhaich*

5

Seana Chamas *Cnoc Breac 962* **Brae**

Peterburn **Naast** **Inverewe** NTS

Loch nan Liagh *Loch Bad a' Chreamh* NTS **Londubh** *Loch Ghiu*

Port Erradale **North Erradale** *River Sand* **Poolewe** *River Ewe*

30

A **B** **45** **C** *Loch na Curra* 5 **D** *Loch Kernsary*

Big. **Tollie Farm** *Loch Tollaidh*

▼ *Caolas Beag* **Lonemore** **Mial** *Heritage*

Longa Island **Smithstown** B8021 **Strath**

150 60 70 **Gairloch**

Loch Gairloch 80 *Meall an Doirein*

Eilean Horrisdale *Loch Airigh 1381*

Charlestown a' Phuill

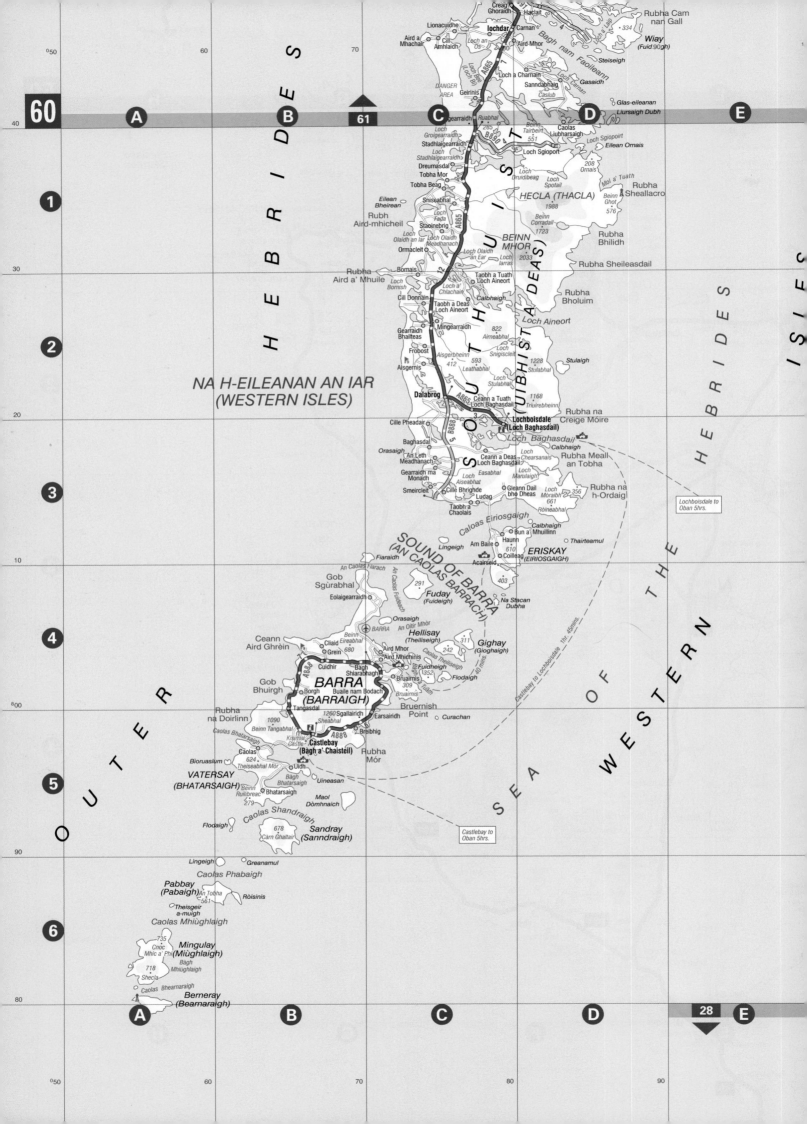

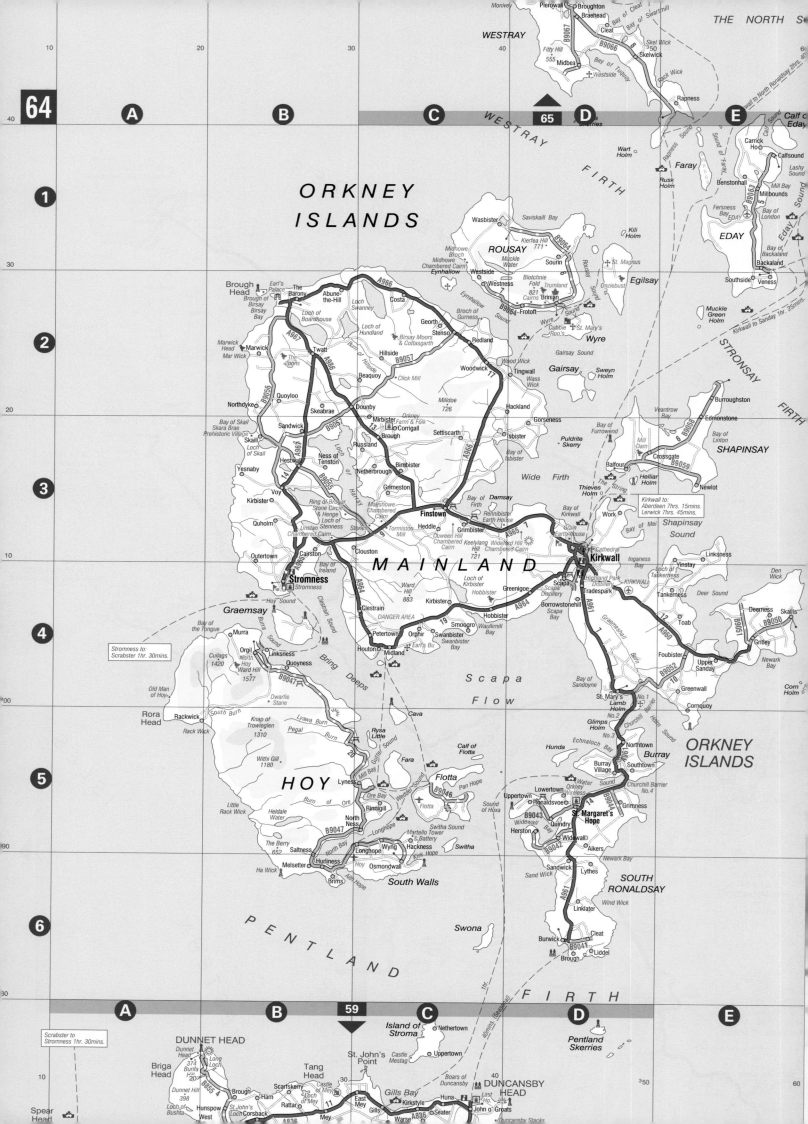

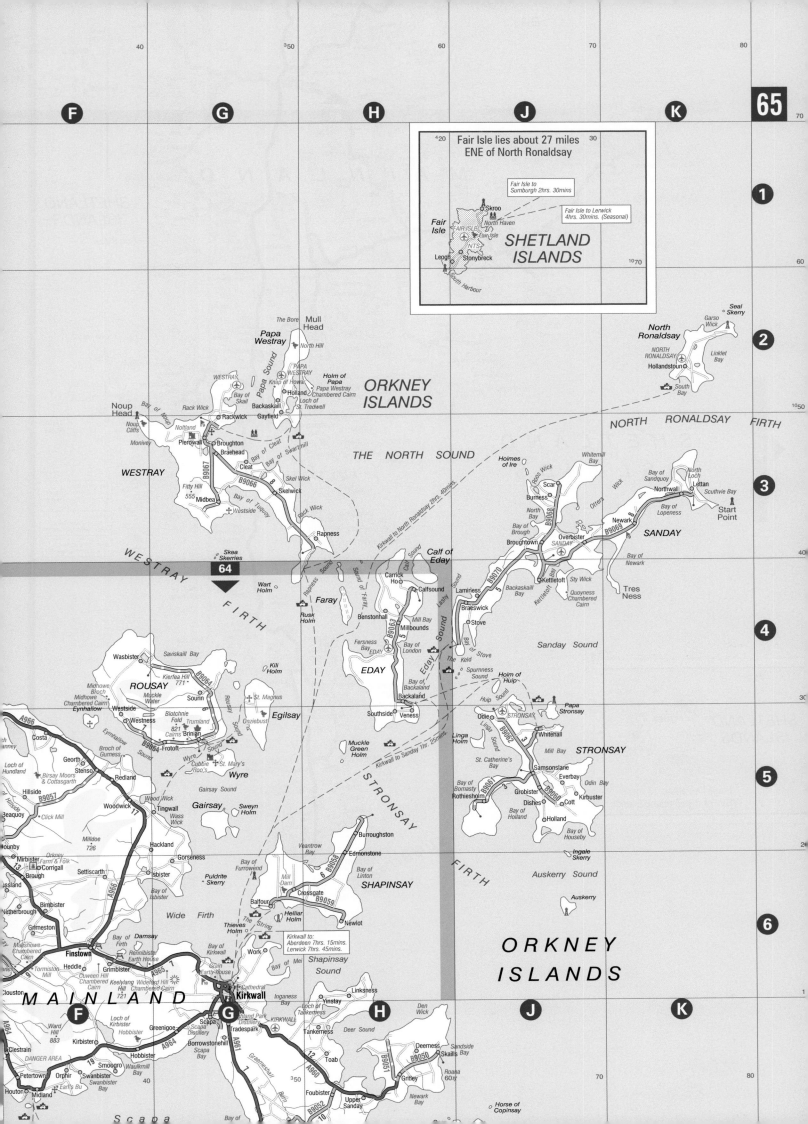

TOWN PLAN PAGES

Aberdeen	....	page69
Aviemore	....	page70
Ayr	....	page70
Dumfries	....	page71
Dundee	....	page72
Dunfermline	....	page73
Edinburgh	....	page74-77
Glasgow	....	page78-80
Falkirk	....	page81
Fort William	....	page81

Hamilton	....	page82
Inverness	....	page82
Kilmarnock	....	page83
Kirkcaldy	....	page83
Motherwell	....	page84
Oban	....	page84
Paisley	....	page85
Perth	....	page85
St Andrews	....	page86
Stirling	....	page87

REFERENCE

MOTORWAY	M8
MOTORWAY UNDER CONSTRUCTION	
MOTORWAY PROPOSED	
MOTORWAY JUNCTIONS WITH NUMBERS	4 5
Unlimited Interchange 4	
Limited Interchange 5	
PRIMARY ROUTE	A92
DUAL CARRIAGEWAYS	
CLASS A ROAD	A804
CLASS B ROAD	B700
MAJOR ROADS UNDER CONSTRUCTION	
MAJOR ROADS PROPOSED	
MINOR ROAD	
RESTRICTED ACCESS	
PEDESTRIANIZED ROAD & MAIN FOOTWAY	
ONE WAY STREET	→ →
TOLL	TOLL
RAILWAY AND STATION	
LEVEL CROSSING AND TUNNEL	
BUILT-UP AREA	
ABBEY, CATHEDRAL, PRIORY ETC.	†
AIRPORT	✈

BUS STATION	
CAR PARK (Selection of)	P
CHURCH	†
CITY WALL	
FERRY (Vehicular)	
(Foot only)	
GOLF COURSE	
HELIPORT	
HOSPITAL	H
INFORMATION CENTRE	i
LIGHTHOUSE	
MARKET	
NATIONAL TRUST PROPERTY (Open)	NTS
(Restricted opening)	NTS
PARK & RIDE	P+
PLACE OF INTEREST	■
POLICE STATION	▲
POST OFFICE	★
SHOPPING PRECINCT	
SHOPMOBILITY	
TOILET	▽
VIEWPOINT	

ABERDEEN

Built almost entirely from granite, Aberdeen is the third largest city in Scotland. However, it is not only famed for its splendid granite architecture, Aberdeen has been a Royal Burgh since the 12th century, it is home to one of the oldest universities in Britain and it has an important maritime history and even today remains one of Britain's busiest harbours. To the north of the city is Old Aberdeen and though it has been incorporated with the main part of the city since 1891, it maintains its own ambience. Old Aberdeen is primarily associated with the university and the distinctive crown spire of Kings College, founded in 1495 by Bishop Elphinstone during the reign of King James IV. Later in 1860 King's college would combine with Marischal College in the main part of the city (see below) to form the University of Aberdeen. Today, most visitor attractions centre on the main part of the city along Union Street and its environs. From here it is a short walk to the harbour that has played a significant role in shaping Aberdeen's prosperity since the 12th century when shipping tithes were first introduced. Ferries to Orkney and the Shetlands leave from the quay and the largest fish market in Scotland can be visited Monday to Friday. The Aberdeen International Youth Festival takes place each year usually at the beginning of August and attracts many young performers from around the world who descend on the city for ten days to showcase their talents. Aberdeen is a diverse city with a wide spectrum of attractions that make it an attractive tourist destination throughout the year.

PLACES OF INTEREST
Tourist Information Centre (All Year) - Broad Street. Tel: (01224) 288828
◆ ABERDEEN ART GALLERY - This popular attraction houses an important fine art collection with particulary good examles of 19th, 20th and 21st century works, a rich and diverse applied art collection, an exciting programme of special exhibitions, a gallery shop and café. Schoolhill.
◆ ABERDEEN ARTS CENTRE - Small gallery exhibiting contemporary arts and crafts. 33 King Street. ◆ ABERDEEN CATHEDRAL - Perpendicular Gothic style episcopal church dating from 1817. Within the cathedral is an exhibition that reflects the history of Christianity in the north east of Scotland. King Street.
◆ ABERDEEN MARITIME MUSEUM - The museum highlights the history of the North Sea using models, paintings and computer interactives. The offshore oil industry is brought to life using the world's largest oil platform model. This attraction includes Aberdeen's oldest building, Provost Ross's House, built in 1593. Shiprow. ◆ ABERDEEN MERCAT CROSS - Dating from 1686, Aberdeen's mercat cross is regarded as the finest example in Scotland. It depicts a unicorn mounted on a hexagonal base on which are panels with medallion heads of the ten Stuart monarchs together with heraldic coats-of-arms. Union Street. ◆ ABERDEEN RC CATHEDRAL - Gothic revival Victorian cathedral dating from 1860-80. 20 Huntly Street.
◆ KIRK OF ST NICHOLAS - Dating from the 12th century, this is the original parish church of Aberdeen. Only the transepts remain of the original structure and modifications have continued into the 20th century with the addition of Scottish stained glass. Back Wynd. ◆ MARISCHAL COLLEGE - Famed as the world's second largest granite building, Marischal College was founded in 1593 as a Protestant University by the Earl of Marischal. The present buildings date predominantly from the 19th century and the neo-Gothic west front is regarded as one of the world's finest architectural achievements in granite. Broad Street.
◆ MARISCHAL MUSEUM - Housed in the University of Aberdeen's impressive Marischal College (noted for being the second largest structure in the world), the diverse collection of exhibits have been gathered by generations of university graduates from around the world. The displays illustrate the arts and customs of different cultures from ancient to modern times and include fine examples of Egyptian and Classical antiquities. Broad Street.
◆ PEACOCK VISUAL ARTS - Contemporary art exhibitions and events. Digital, photography and printmaking workshops. 21 Castle Street.
◆ PROVOST SKENE'S HOUSE - This 16th century house captures the grandeur of earlier times with a stunning series of period room settings and Painted Gallery. Changing displays highlight local history and the Costume Gallery features fashions. Broad Street.
◆ UNION TERRACE GARDENS - Sunken Victorian gardens with outdoor draughts board and a floral display of the City's crest 'Bon Accord.' (Bon Accord can be found on the city's Coat of Arms and is linked to the toast "Happy to meet, sorry to part, happy to meet again."). Union Terrace.

ENTERTAINMENT
◆ Cinemas - 10 Ship Row. 49 Belmont Street. Queen's Link Leisure Park, East Aberdeen.
◆ Concerts - Aberdeen Exhibition and Conference Centre, Bridge of Don, North of Aberdeen. Aberdeen Music Hall, Union Street. Lemon Tree, West North Street.
◆ Theatres - Aberdeen Arts Centre, King Street. His Majesty's Theatre, Rosemount Viaduct. Lemon Tree, West North Street.

SPORT & LEISURE
◆ Ice Rink - Linx Ice Arena, Beach Promenade, East of Aberdeen.
◆ Sports Centres - Beach Leisure Centre, Beach Promenade. Bon Accord Baths, Justice Mill Lane. Bon Accord Sports Centre. (Within the Bon Accord Centre), George Street. Chris Anderson Stadium, Linksfield Road. Vida Sports Centre, Balgownie Road, Bridge of Don, North of Aberdeen.
◆ Swimming Pools - Beach Leisure Centre, Bon Accord Baths (as above).
◆ Ten-Pin Bowling - Cosmic Bowling, Codonas Amusement Park, Beach Boulevard. Vida Sports Centre, Balgownie Road, Bridge of Don, North of Aberdeen.

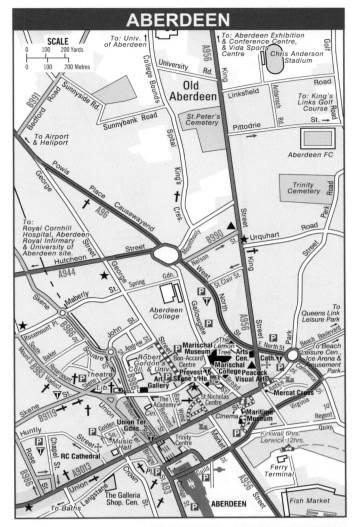

Aberdeen

Crathes Castle

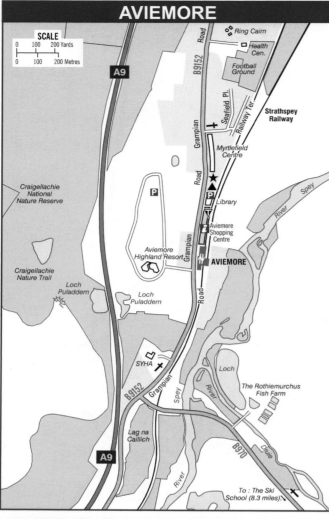

AVIEMORE

32 miles South of Inverness on the A9 lies the Highland resort of Aviemore, a picturesque village renowned for its spectacular mountain scenery. In close proximity to Britain's premier ski area, the Cairngorm Mountains, Aviemore is an ideal base from which to tour the Highlands offering the tourist a diverse range of quality accommodation along with leisure facilities and visitor attractions. To maintain its continued popularity as a UK holiday destination, Aviemore has embarked upon an ambitious programme of regeneration in order to reaffirm its status as a world class centre for tourism throughout the year.

PLACES OF INTEREST

Tourist Information Centre (All year) - Aviemore Shopping Centre, Grampian Road. Tel: (01479) 810363 ◆ CRAIGELLACHIE NATURE RESERVE & NATURE TRAIL - (SNH) 260 hectare National Nature Reserve containing a mixture of birchwood and moorland.
◆ STRATHSPEY RAILWAY - 9.5 mile standard gauge railway running between Aviemore, Boat of Garten and Broomhill passing within sight of some of the highest and most spectacular mountains in Scotland. Aviemore Station.

SPORT & LEISURE

◆ Skiing Facilities - Cairn Gorm Ski School , 8.3 miles south east of Aviemore.

AYR

Ayr is a busy shopping centre and commercial seaport. With its long stretches of sandy beach, backed by pleasant lawns behind the esplanade, it is also one of Scotland's premier coastal resorts. The town is centred around Alloway Street and High Street. Famous for its associations with Burns (born in Alloway immediately to the south and who described Ayr as the town of 'honest men and bonnie lasses'), the Tam O'Shanter Inn on the High Street & 'Twa Brigs' (Auld Brig, described below, and New Bridge built in 1788, rebuilt in 1877-9) feature in his works. Burns statue is near the railway station in Burns Statue Square. Of architectural interest are the restored 16th century Loudoun Hall on Boat Vennel off New Bridge Street, the oldest building in the town, and the Town Buildings surmounted by a slender spire built in the early 1820s, off the same road. Ayr Racecourse (in the east of the town) is Scotland's top horse racing centre.

PLACES OF INTEREST

Tourist Information Centre (All year) - 22 Sandgate. Tel: (01292) 678100
◆ AULD BRIG - Bridge over River Ayr dating from c1491, subject of Burns' 'Twa Brigs'. For 300 years Ayr's only bridge, now pedestrianized. High Street / River Street. ◆ AULD KIRK - Fine church, also known as the New Church of St John, built in 1655 with money given by Cromwell to replace the 'Old Church' (see below) incorporated in his fort. Burns was baptised here. Kirk Port, High Street. ◆ CRAFT DAFT - Decorate your own ceramic ornament, mug or plate. Glass and silk painting plus many other crafts. 2 Cow Wynd, Alloway Street. ◆ JOHN MACADAM MONUMENT - Monument to John Macadam, the road builder, born in Ayr in 1756, who gave his name to the word 'tarmacadam'. Wellington Square.
◆ NEWTON STEEPLE - Georgian (rare in this district) steeple of 1795, formerly at entrance to parish church. King Street. ◆ PIRATE PETE'S - Scotland's biggest indoor children's play centre. Toddlers area, ball pools, slides, cinema and much more. Ayr Pavillion, Pavillion Road.
◆ ST JOHN'S TOWER - Restored tower of Old Church of St John where the Scottish Parliament met after Bannockburn in 1315 to confirm the succession after Bruce. Later absorbed into a large Cromwellian fort built in 1652. Views to island of Arran from top. By appointment. Eglinton Terrace.
◆ WALLACE TOWER - Early 19th century neo-gothic tower, with statue of William Wallace in niche, built on site where Wallace, a Scottish patriot, is reputed to have been imprisoned in the early 1300s. High Street.

ENTERTAINMENT

◆ Cinemas - Burns Statue Square.
◆ Concerts - Town Hall, New Bridge Street. Gaiety Theatre, Carrick Street. Citadel Leisure Centre, South Harbour Street.
◆ Theatres - Gaiety Theatre (as above).

SPORT & LEISURE

◆ Ice Rink - Ayr Ice Rink, Limekiln Road.
◆ Parks & Gardens - Belleisle Park, Belleisle (S Ayr). Craigie Park, Craigie Road. Rozelle Park, Monument Road (S Ayr).
◆ Sports Centres - Citadel Leisure Centre, South Harbour Street.
◆ Swimming Pools - Citadel Leisure Centre (as above).
◆ Ten-Pin-Bowling - L A Bowl, Miller Road.

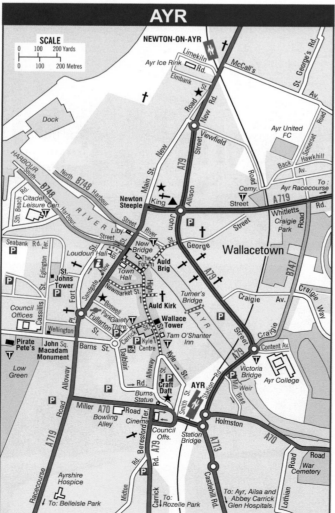

DUMFRIES

Dumfries is an attractive border town situated on the picturesque River Nith that divides it from Maxwelltown, with which it was amalgamated in 1929. With many of the houses painted in pastel colours or built of red sandstone and a modern shopping centre, it is the main centre for the region being given the status of a royal burgh as early as the 12th century. The town was the scene of the murder of 'the Red' Comyn by Robert Bruce in 1306 (marked by a plaque on a building in Castle Street), an event that started a change in the course of Scottish history that culminated with the defeat of the English at the battle of Bannockburn in 1314. Dumfries has been sacked many times, notably by the retreating Bonnie Prince Charlie in 1745 after his march on England, and consequently there is little from the medieval period to see, however a walk along the High Street and the waterfront at Whitesands is recommended. The Academy on Academy Street educated the playwright and novelist James Matthew Barrie, author of 'Peter Pan' whilst Robert Burns, Scotland's national poet lived here between 1791 and his death in 1796 during which time he wrote many of his poems and songs. The town contains many Burns sites of interest including (in addition to those listed below) a plaque marking his first home in Bank Street (then called Wee Vennel or 'Stinking Vennel' by Burns because of an open sewer which ran down the street to the river), a marble statue in front of Greyfriars church, Castle Street (built in 1867) and his family pew in St Michael's church, St Michael Street. Burns' favourite walk (now called 'Burns' Walk'), is on the east bank of the river off Nunholm Road in the north of the town.

PLACES OF INTEREST

Tourist Information Centre (All year) - 64 Whitesands Tel: (01387) 253862

◆ BURNS MAUSOLEUM - Built in 1815 in the style of a domed Grecian temple. Burns, his wife & several of his children are buried here. St Michael's Churchyard, St Michael Street.

◆ DEVORGILLA BRIDGE (OLD BRIDGE) - Six arched sandstone bridge of 1431, rebuilt in the 17th century after severe flood damage, now pedestrianized. Last in a succession of bridges here; the first wooden structure was built by Lady Devorgilla Balliol in the 13th century. Mill Road / Whitesands.

◆ DUMFRIES CAMERA OBSCURA - Astronomical instrument (one of only three in Scotland) installed in 1836 on the top floor of the old windmill tower at Dumfries Museum. Moving panoramic images are projected onto a table top screen allowing visitors to enjoy magnificent views of Dumfries & the surrounding countryside in a unique way. Dumfries Museum, The Observatory, Rotchell Road.

◆ DUMFRIES MUSEUM - History of South West Scotland. Exhibitions trace the history of the people of Solway, Dumfries & Galloway, early Christianity, prehistory, natural history & Victorian life. The Observatory, Rotchell Road.

◆ GLOBE INN - 17th century working inn; Burns' favourite tavern. Rooms are unchanged since the 1790s including the poet's chair & other relics. 56 High Street.

◆ GRACEFIELD ARTS CENTRE - Large collection of Scottish paintings. Monthly exhibitions of contemporary art & craft. 28 Edinburgh Road.

◆ MID STEEPLE - Old Town Hall (or tolbooth) built between 1707 & 1708 marking the town centre. A table shows distances to important Scottish towns & to Huntingdon in England. High Street.

◆ OLD BRIDGE HOUSE MUSEUM, THE - Museum of local life in sandstone building built in 1660 (the oldest house in Dumfries) adjoining Devorgilla Bridge. Period rooms include a Victorian nursery, kitchens from the mid 19th century & dentist's surgery. Devorgilla Bridge, Mill Road.

◆ ROBERT BURNS CENTRE - Set in an 18th century watermill, audio-visual presentations, exhibitions, original manuscripts & relics recount Burns' last years in Dumfries. The centre also includes a model of Dumfries in Burns' time, museum trails, activities for children, plus an award-winning café-restaurant. In the evenings the centre is home to the regional film theatre for Dumfries & Galloway. Mill Road.

◆ ROBERT BURNS HOUSE - Refurbished 18th century sandstone house, Burns' second home which he moved to in 1793 (& where he died in 1796 at the age of thirty-seven), containing his writing desk & chair, manuscripts & relics connected with the poet. Burns Street.

ENTERTAINMENT

◆ Cinemas - Robert Burns Film Theatre, Robert Burns Centre (see above).
◆ Concerts - Easterbrook Hall, The Crichton Site, Bankend Road, South East Dumfries.
◆ Theatres - Easterbrook Hall (as above). Theatre Royal, Shakespeare Street.

SPORT & LEISURE

◆ Parks & Gardens -Castledykes Park, Glencaple Road (S Dumfries).
Deer Park, Mill Road.
Dock Park, St Michael's Bridge Road.
Goldie Park, Glasgow Street.
Greensands, Park Lane.
Hamilton Stark Park, Moat Road (S Dumfries).
King George V Park, Glasgow Street.
Mill Green, Mill Road.
Noblehill Park, Annan Road (E Dumfries).
◆ Swimming Pools -Dumfries Swimming Pool, Park Lane.
◆ Sports Centres - David Keswick Athletic Centre, Marchmount (NE Dumfries).
Dumfries Ice Bowl Leisure Complex, King Street.
King George V Astro Arena, King George V Park, Glasgow Street.

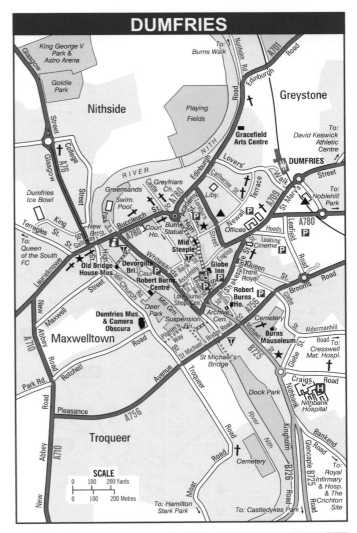

Devorgilla Bridge

Loch Ken

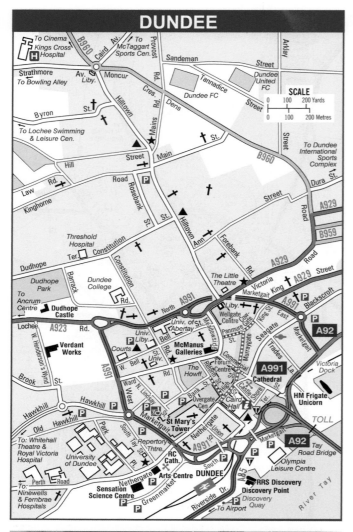

DUNDEE

DUNDEE

With its picturesque setting on the River Tay, Dundee is the fourth largest city in Scotland. The history and fortunes of Dundee are inextricably linked to its maritime heritage. Dundee was once the United Kingdom's leading whaling port and maritime trading meant that goods from around the world were available. The emphasis on sea trading meant that ship construction was an important industry and today great vessels such as the RRS Discovery and HM Unicorn Frigate survive to reflect a vital part of Dundee's heritage. By the early 19th century the textile industry was thriving and Dundee became renowned as the jute capital of the world. Of historical interest Dundee has much to offer, The Howff, which was for three centuries until 1857 the city's primary burial ground, was given to the town in 1564 by Mary Queen of Scots. However, originally it was an adjoining orchard to a Franciscan monastery founded in 1270 by Devorguilla Balliol and destroyed in 1548.

Wishart Arch located on Cowgate is thought to date from 1548 and is the only surviving city gate. It is named in memory of George Wishart, a reformer who was burnt at St Andrews in 1546. During 1544, when Dundee was stricken by plague, Wishart preached from this gate in two directions; to those affected who were excluded from the town and those within whom remained unaffected. 1878 saw the construction of the Tay Rail Bridge, which at two miles long was the longest bridge in the world. However, it was not to be long before disaster struck and on the evening of December 28th the following year during a severe storm, the centrepiece of the bridge collapsed while a train was crossing it which resulted in the death of the 75 passengers on board. Engineering faults and poor construction were blamed for the disaster but this did not deter from reconstructing it, a project that commenced three years after the tragedy.

Today Dundee is a lively city to explore where industrial heritage has laid the foundations for an exciting range of modern tourist attractions. It is a popular University City, with a large percentage of students it offers a vibrant nightlife.

PLACES OF INTEREST

Tourist Information Centre (All Year) - 7-21 Castle Street. Tel: (01382) 527527

◆ DISCOVERY POINT - Attraction centres around Captain Scott's famous Antarctic exploration ship, the RRS Discovery which was built in Dundee in 1901. Dramatic visual presentations recreate the events in the Discovery story and other exhibitions reveal what happened to the ship following the exploration. Discovery Quay.

◆ DUDHOPE CASTLE - Dating from the 13th century, the castle was once the hereditary home of the Constables of Dundee. The town bought the castle and park in 1983, but the castle can only be viewed from the outside. Barrack Road

◆ DUNDEE CATHEDRAL - Dating from 1853, this Scottish Episcopal Church was designed by Sir George Gilbert Scott. The Cathedral's 64 m (210 ft) high tower and spire is a renowned landmark. High Street.

◆ DUNDEE CONTEMPORARY ARTS - Opened in March 1999, the DCA houses five floors of galleries, cinemas, artists facilities, education resources, the University of Dundee visual research centre and the Café Bar. 152 Nethergate.

◆ DUNDEE ROMAN CATHOLIC CATHEDRAL - This Cathedral church dedicated to St Andrew dates from the 1830s. Nethergate.

◆ DUNDEE ST MARY'S TOWER - The 15th century tower known also as the Old Steeple is the only surviving part of the pre-Reformation Church of St Mary. Nethergate.

◆ HM FRIGATE UNICORN - The Unicorn is the oldest British built warship still afloat and is Scotland's only example of a wooden warship. Today the ship houses a museum that offers a fascinating insight into naval life of the period through models and explanatory displays. Victoria Dock.

◆ MCMANUS GALLERIES - Housed in a Victorian Gothic building dating from 1867 is Scotland's main museum with a fine array of exhibits including collections of silver, glass and furniture. There are displays on local history and a fine art collection which includes the work of Scottish artists from the 19th and 20th centuries. Albert Square. Closed until 2007.

◆ SENSATION SCIENCE CENTRE - Dundee's newest visitor attraction, this innovative science visitor centre offers an insight into the perception of the senses.- Greenmarket.

◆ VERDANT WORKS - This restored 19th century jute mill is one of a few surviving examples of the industry. Exhibitions reveal how Dundee became the jute capital of the world and the effect that the industry had in shaping the town's history. West Henderson's Wynd.

ENTERTAINMENT

◆ Cinemas - Harefield Road, North West Dundee. Kingsway West, North West Dundee. Contemporary Arts Centre, Nethergate.

◆ Concerts - Caird Hall, City Square.

◆ Theatres - Dundee Repertory Theatre, Tay Square. The Little Theatre, Victoria Road. Whitehall Theatre, Bellfield Street, West Dundee.

SPORT & LEISURE

◆ Parks & Gardens - Dudhope Park, Dudhope Terrace.

◆ Ski Slope - The Ancrum Centre for the Environment, Ancrum Road, North West Dundee.

◆ Sports Centres - Dundee International Sports Complex, Mains Loan, North East Dundee. Lochee Swimming and Leisure Centre, Lochee, West Dundee. Mc Taggart Sports Centre, Old Glamis Road, North Dundee. Olympia Leisure Centre, Riverside Drive.

◆ Swimming Pools - Lochee Swimming and Leisure Centre (as above).

◆ Ten-Pin Bowling - Dundee Megabowl, Harefield Road, North West Dundee.

Dundee Museum

Arbroath Cliffs

Forth Bridge

Loch Lomond

DUNFERMLINE

Scotland's ancient capital for over 500 years, Dunfermline was one of the early settlements of the Celtic Church and a favoured stronghold of the warrior King Malcolm Canmore. In 1070 King Malcolm married the saintly Saxon princess, Margaret whom while fleeing from the Normans was shipwrecked in the Forth and taken to Dunfermline. Together they founded their palace and later built a priory. In 1270 following her death, Margaret was proclaimed a saint and Dunfermline became one of the great centres of pilgrimage in Europe. The town is associated with the birth of numerous kings and queens and is the final resting place of Robert the Bruce. Aside from royalty, Dunfermline has benefited significantly from the generosity of Andrew Carnegie, the great philanthropist who did much to improve facilities available to the people of his native town. Today Dunfermline is a bustling town with a wealth of history to be discovered and a diverse range of visitor attractions.

PLACES OF INTEREST

Tourist Information Centre (All Year) - 1 High Street. Tel: (01383) 720999
◆ ABBOT HOUSE HERITAGE CENTRE - Located in the historic Maygate, the award-winning Abbot House takes the visitor through 1000 years of history from the Picts to the present day. Café, gift shop and garden. Maygate.

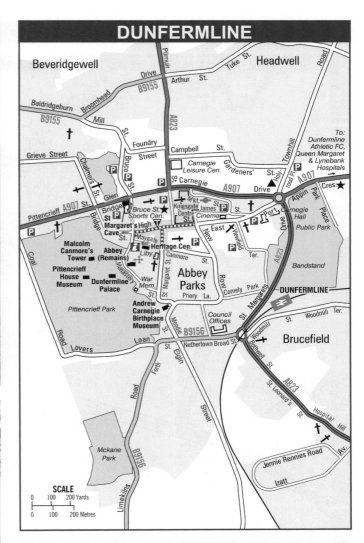

DUNFERMLINE

◆ ANDREW CARNEGIE BIRTHPLACE MUSEUM - Located in the house where Carnegie was born in 1835, the museum tells the extraordinary story of his rise from poverty to prominence when he emigrated to the United States and created the country's largest steel works. On the first Friday of every month visitors are able to enjoy demonstrations of a working Jacquard handloom reminiscent of the one used by Carnegie's father. The Memorial Hall, endowed by Mrs Louise Carnegie, adjoins the birthplace cottage and charts her husband's astounding business career from bobbin boy to the world's richest steel magnate. Moodie Street.
◆ DUNFERMLINE ABBEY - (HS) Remains of a Benedictine abbey founded by Margaret I in the 11th century. The foundations remain under the present Romanesque style nave built during the 12th century. A brass in the choir marks the grave of King Robert the Bruce. Pittencrieff Park.
◆ DUNFERMLINE PALACE & VISITOR CENTRE - (HS) Royal Palace developed out of the original abbey guest house. The palace was destroyed by fire in 1304 but was rebuilt by James IV in 1500. It was the birthplace of Charles I, the last monarch born in scotland in 1600. Pittencrieff Park.
◆ MALCOLM CANMORE'S TOWER - Ruin of a fortified tower alongside the burn where King Malcolm Canmore held court after the death of Macbeth. Pittencrieff Park.
◆ PITTENCRIEFF HOUSE MUSEUM - 17th century mansion house situated in Pittencrieff park was given to the town by Andrew Carnegie. Exhibits in the house include an important costume collection and displays illustrating the history of the house and park. Pittencrieff Park.
◆ ST MARGARET'S CAVE - 84 steps below the Glen Bridge Car Park is the cave where Margaret, an 11th century queen and saint sought refuge for prayer and meditation. Glen Bridge Car Park.

ENTERTAINMENT
◆ Cinemas - East Port.
◆ Concerts - Carnegie Hall, East Port.
◆ Theatres - Carnegie Hall (as above).

SPORT & LEISURE
◆ Parks & Gardens - Dunfermline Public Park, Appin Crescent. Mc Kane Park, Limekilns Road. Pittencrieff Park, Pittencrieff Street.
◆ Sports Centres - Bruce Street Sports Centre, Bruce Street. Carnegie Leisure Centre, Pilmuir Street.
◆ Swimming Pools - Carnegie Leisure Centre (as above).

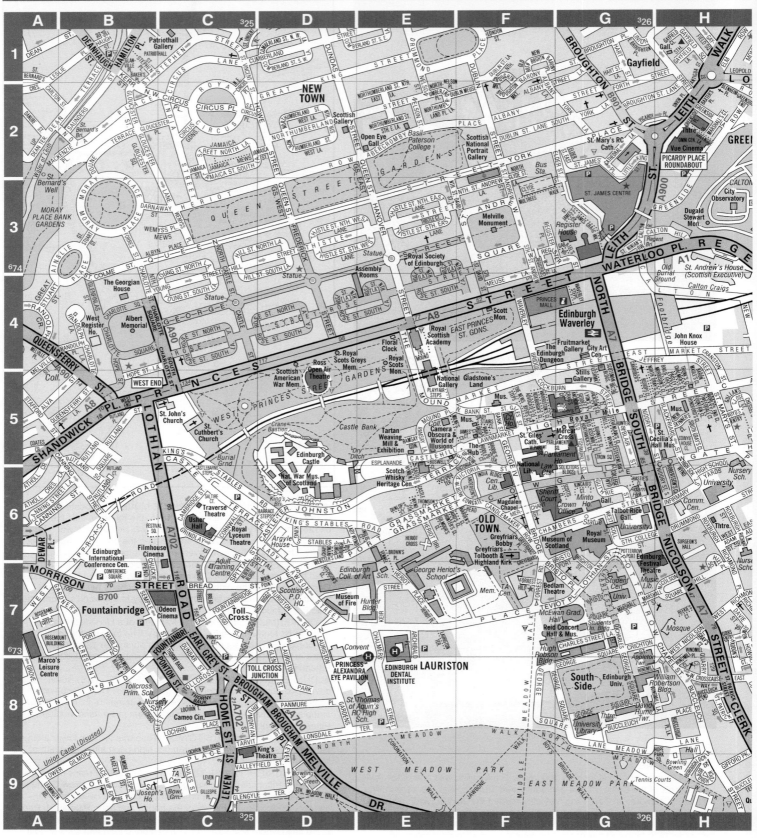

INDEX

Abbeyhill. -4L
Abbeyhill Cres. -4K
Abbeymount. -3L
Abbey Strand. -4L
Abercromby Pl. -2E
Advocate's Cl. -5F
Ainslie Pl. -3A
Aird's Cl. -6E
Aitchison's Cl. -7D
Albany La. -2F
Albany St. -2F
Albany St. La. -2F
Albert Bldgs. -7C
Albyn Pl. -3B
Alva St. -2M
Alva St. -5A
Anchor Cl. -5G
Anderson's Cl. -6F

Antigua St. -1H
Archibald Pl. -7E
Atholl Cres. -6A
Atholl Cres. La. -6A

Bailie Fife's Cl. -5H
Bakehouse Cl. -5J
Baker's Pl. -1B
Bank St. -5F
Baron Maule's La. -5H
Barony Pl. -1F
Barony St. -1F
Barrace Steps. -6D
Baxter's Pl. -2H
Bell's Wynd. -5G
Bernard Ter. -9J
Bishops Cl. -5H
Blackfriars St. -5H
Blair St. -5G

Blenheim Pl. -2H
Boroughloch. -9H
Boroughloch Sq. -9H
Borthwick's Cl. -5G
Boswell's Cl. -5E
Bowmont Pl. -8J
Boyd's Entry. -5H
Boy's Brigade Wlk. -8F
Brand Pl. -2M
Bread St. -7C
Bread St. La. -7C
Breidwood Ga. -7J
Briery Bauks. -7J
Brightons St. -6G
Bristo Pl. -7F
Bristo Port. -6G
Bristo Sq. -7G

Brougham St. -8C
Broughton Mkt. -1F
Broughton Pl. -1G
Broughton Pl. La. -1G
Broughton St. -1G
Broughton St. La. -2G
Brown's Cl. -4K
Brown's Ct. -4K
Brown's Pl. -6E
Brown's Pl. -7J
Brown St. La. -7J
Brunswick St. -1J
Brunswick St. La. -1J
Brunton Gdns. -1L
Brunton Pl. -2K
Brunton Ter. -2L
Buccleuch Pend. -8H
Buccleuch Pl. -8G
Buccleuch St. -8H
Buccleuch Ter. -9H

Buccleuch Pl. La. -8H
Bull's Cl. -4K
Burnet's Cl. -5G
Byer's Cl. -5F

Calton Hill. -3G
Calton Hill Stairs. -4J
Calton Rd. (EH1) -3G
Calton Rd. (EH7) -4G
Calton Rd. (EH8) -4G
Cambridge St. -6C
Campbell's Cl. -4K
Candlemaker Row. -6F
Canning. -5B
Canning St. -5B
Canning St. La. -6A
Canongate. -4G
Canongate Tolbooth. -4J
Carlton St. -2A
Carlton Ter. -2K

Carlton Ter. Brae. -2L
Carlton Ter. La. -2K
Carlton Ter. M. -2K
Carnegie St. -7J
Carnegie St. -7J
Carrubber's Cl. -4G
Castlehill. -5E
Castle St. -4C
Castle Ter. -5C
Castle Wynd Nth. -6E
Castle Wynd Sth. -6E
Cathedral La. -2G
Chalmers Bldgs. -8B
Chalmer's Cl. -5H
Chalmers St. -7E
Chapel St. -7H
Chap Wynd. -6D

Charlesfield. -7G
Charles St. -7G
Charles St. La. -7G
Charlotte La. -4B
Charlotte Sq. -4B
Chessel's Ct. -5H
Chuckie Pend. -7B
Circus Gdns. -2C
Circus La. -2C
Circus Pl. -2C
Clerk St. -8H
Clyde St. -3F
Coates Cres. -5A
Cockburn St. -5F
Coinyie Ho. Cl. -5H
College Wynd. -5H
Conference Sq. -7B
Cooper's Cl. -4J
Cornwall St. -6C

Coronation Wlk. -8E
Cowan's Cl. -8H
Cowgate. -5F
Cowgatehead. -6F
Craig's Cl. -5G
Cranston St. -4H
Crichton's Cl. -4K
Crichton St. -7G
Croft-an-Righ. -3L
Cumberland St. -1D
Cumberland St. Nth. W.
La. -1D
Cumberland St. Sth. E.
La. -1D
Cumberland St. Sth. W.
La. -1D

Danube St. -2A
Darnaway St. -3B

Darroch Ct. -5J
Davie St. -7H
Deanhaugh St. -1B
Dean St. -1A
Dean Ter. -2A
Doune Ter. -2B
Drumdryan St. -8C
Drummond Pl. -1E
Drummond St. -6H
Dublin Meuse. -2E
Dublin St. (EH1) -1F
Dublin St. (EH3) -1F
Dublin St. La. Nth. -1F
Dublin St. La. Sth. -2F
Dumbiedykes Rd. -6K
Dunbar's Cl. -4J
Dunbar St. -7C
Dundas St. -1D
Dunlop's Ct. -6E

Earl Grey St. -7C
E. Adam St. -6H
E. Broughton Pl. -1G
E. Crosscauseway. -8H
Easter Rd. -2L
E. Fountainbridge. -7C
E. Market St. -4G
E. Norton Pl. -2K
E. Parkside. -9L
Elder St. -2G
Elder St. E. -2G
Elm Row. -1H
Esplanade. -5E

Festival Sq. -6B
Flesh Mkt. -5G
Forbes St. -8J

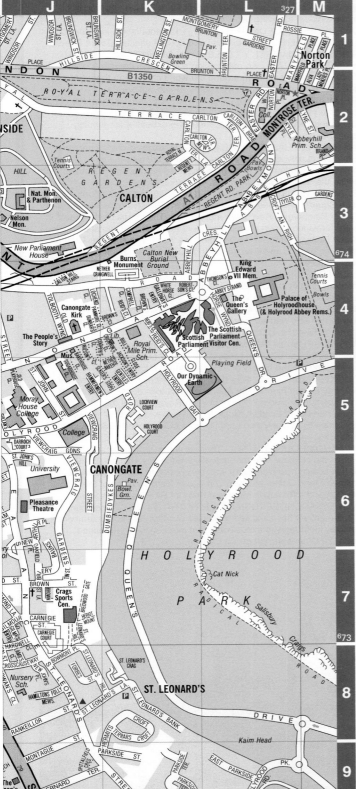

REFERENCE

One Way Street — Traffic flow on A Roads is also indicated by a heavy line on the driver's left.	
Junction Name	PICARDY PLACE ROUNDABOUT
Restricted Access	
Pedestrianized Road	
Track & Footpath	
Residential Walkway	
Railway	Station / Tunnel
Built-up Area	
Car Park (Selected)	P
Church or Chapel	†
Fire Station	■
Hospital	H
Information Centre	i
Police Station	▲
Post Office	★
Toilet: without facilities for the Disabled	▽
with facilities for the Disabled	▽
Educational Establishment	
Hospital or Hospice	
Industrial Building	
Leisure or Recreational Facility	
Place of Interest	
Public Building	
Shopping Centre or Market	
Other Selected Buildings	

SCALE : 1:9504 **(6.66 inches to 1 mile)**

0 — ¼ — ½ MILE
0 — 250 — 500 — 750 Metres

Hunter Sq. -5G
Hyndford's Cl. -5H

India Bldgs. -6F
India Pl. -2B
India St. -2C
Infirmary St. -6H
Inglis Ct. -6E

Jackson's Cl. -5G
Jackson's Entry. -4K
Jamaica M. -2C
Jamaica St. -2C (not continuous)
Jamaica St. Nth. La. -2C
Jamaica St. Sth. La. -2C
James' Ct. -5F
James Craig Wlk. -3G
Jawbone Wlk. -9F
Jeffrey St. -4G
Johnston Ter. -6D

Keir St. -7E
Kerr St. -1B
Kincaid's Ct. -6G
King's Stables La. -6D
King's Stables Rd. -5C
Kyle Pl. -2L

Lady Lawson St. -6D
Lady Menzies Pl. -2M
Lady Stairs Cl. -5F
Lady Wynd. -6D
Lamb's Cl. -7H
Lauriston Gdns. -7D
Lauriston Pk. -7D
Lauriston Pl. -7B
Lauriston St. -7D
Lauriston Ter. -7E
Lawnmarket. -5F
Leamington Rd. -9A
Leith St. -3G
Leith Wlk. -2H
Leopold Pl. -1H
Leslie Pl. -1A
Leven Cl. -9C
Leven St. -9C
Leven Ter. -8D
Lit. King St. -2G
Lochend Cl. -4J
Lochrin Bldgs. -8C
Lochrin Pl. -8C
Lochrin Ter. -8C
Lochview Ct. -5K
London Rd. -1H
London St. -1F
Lonsdale Ter. -8D
Lothian Rd. (EH1) -5B
Lothian Rd. (EH3) -5B
Lothian St. -7G
Lwr. Gilmore Pl. -9A
Lyne St. -2M
Lyon's Cl. -5G

Mackenzie Pl. -2A
Main Point. -7C
Market St. -5F
Marshall's Ct. -2H
Marshall St. -7G

Maryfield. -2L
Maryfield Pl. -2L
Meadow La. -8G
Melville Dr. -9D
Melville Pl. -4A
Melville St. -4A
Merchant St. -6F
Meuse La. -4F
Middle Mdw. Wlk. -9F
Milne's Ct. -5E
Montague St. -9J
Montgomery St. -1L
Montgomery St. La. -1H
Montrose Ter. -2L
Moray Pl. -3B
Morrison's Cl. -5H
Morrison St. -7A
Mound, The. (EH1) -5E
Mound, The. (EH2) -4E
Mound Pl. -5E
Multrees Wlk. -3F

Nelson Pl. -2E
Nelson St. -1E
Nether Bakehouse. -5K
Nether Craigwell. -4K
New Arthur Pl. -6J
New Broughton. -1F
New John's Pl. -8J
New Skinner's Cl. -5H
New St. -4H
News Steps, The. -5F
Nicolson Sq. -7H
Nicolson St. -6H
Niddry St. -5G
Niddry St. Sth. -6H
Nth. Bank St. -5F
North Bri. -4G
Nth. Bridge Arc. -5G
Nth. Castle St. -3C
Nth. Charlotte St. -4B
Nth. Clyde St. La. -2F
North E. Circus Pl. -2C
Nth. Gray's Cl. -5G
North Mdw. Wlk. -8D
Nth. Richmond St. -6H
Nth. St Andrew La. -3F
Nth. St Andrew St. -2F
Nth. St David St. -3E
Northumberland Pl. -2E
Northumberland Pl. La. -2E
Northumberland St. -2D
Northumberland St. Nth. E. La. -2E
Northumberland St. Nth. W. La. -2D
Northumberland St. Sth. E. La. -2E
Northumberland St. Sth. W. La. -2D
North W. Circus Pl. -2C

Oakfield Pl. -6J
Old Assembly Cl. -5G
Old Broughton. -1F
Old Fishmarket Cl. -5G
Old Playhouse Cl. -5J
Old Tolbooth Wynd. -4J

Omni Cen. -2H

Paisley Cl. -5H
Panmure Cl. -4J
Panmure Pl. -8D
Parkside St. -9K
Parkside Ter. -9K
Parliament Sq. -5F
Patriothall. -1B
Picardy Pl. -2G
Playfair Steps. -5E
Pleasance. -5H
Ponton St. -8C
Port Hamilton. -7B
Portsburgh Sq. -6D
Potterrow. -7G
Potterrow Port. -6G
Princes St. -7C
Princes Mall. -4F
Princes St. -5B

Quarry Cl. -8H
Queen's Dr. -4L
Queensferry St. -4A
Queensferry St. La. -5A
Queen St. -3C
Queen St. Gdns. E. -2F
Queen St. Gdns. W. -3D

Radical Rd. -6L
Ramsay Gdn. -5E
Ramsay La. -5E
Randolph Cres. -4A
Randolph La. -4B
Randolph Pl. -4B
Rankeillor St. -8J
Reekies Ct. -7H
Regent Rd. -3H
Regent Ter. -3K
Regent Ter. M. -3K
Register Pl. -3F
Reid's Cl. -4K
Reid's Ct. -4K
Richmond La. -7H
Richmond Pl. -6H
Riddle's Ct. -5F
Riego St. -7C
Robertson's Cl. -6H
Robertson's Ct. -4K
Rosebank Cotts. -7A
Rosemount Bldgs. -7A
Rose St. -4C
Rose St. Nth. La. -4C (not continuous)
Rose St. Sth. La. -4C (not continuous)
Rossie Pl. -1L
Roxburgh Pl. -6H
Roxburgh's Cl. -5F
Roxburgh St. -6H
Royal Cir. -2C
Royal Ter. -2H
Royal Ter. M. -2K
Rutland Ct. La. -6B
Rutland Pl. -5B
Rutland Sq. -5B
Rutland St. -5B

St Andrew Sq. -3F
St Bernard's Cres. -1A

St Colme St. -4B
St Giles St. -5F
St James Cen. -3G
St James Pl. -2G
St James's Sq. -3G
St John's Hill. -6J
St John St. -5J
St Leonard's Bank. -8K
St Leonard's Crag. -8K
St Leonard's Hill. -7J
St Leonard's La. -8J
St Leonard's St. -8J
St Mary's St. -5H
St Ninian's Row. -3G
St Patrick Sq. -8H
St Patrick St. -8H
St Stephen Pl. -1B
St Stephen St. -1B
St Vincent St. -1C
Saltire Ct. -6C
Saunders St. -2B
Scotsman Bldgs. -4G
Semple St. -7B
Shandwick Pl. -5A
Simon Sq. -7H
Slater's Steps. -5J
Solicitors Bldgs. -6G
South Bri. -5G
Sth. Charlotte St. -4C
Sth. College St. -6G
Sth. E. Circus Pl. -2C
Sth. Gayfield La. -1H
Sth. Gray's Cl. -5G
South Mdw. Wlk. -9D
Sth. St Andrew St. -3F
Sth. St David St. -3F
Spittalfield Cres. -9J
Spittal St. -7C
Spittal St. La. -6D
Stafford St. -5A
Stevenlaw's Cl. -5G
Sugarhouse Cl. -5J
Surgeon's Hall. -6H

Tarvit St. -8C
Terrars Cft. -8K
Teviot Pl. -7F
Thistle Ct. -3E
Thistle St. -3D
Thistle St. Nth. E. La. -3E
Thistle St. Nth. W. La. -3D
Thistle St. Sth. E. La. -3E
Thistle St. Sth. W. La. -3D
Thomson's Ct. -6E
Thorny Bauk. -7C (not continuous)
Tron Sq. -5G
Trunk's Cl. -5H
Tweeddale Ct. -5H
Tytler Gdns. -3L

Union Pl. -2H
Union St. -1G
Up. Bow. -5F
Up. Dean Ter. -2A
Up. Gilmore Pl. -9B

Up. Greenside La. -2H

Valleyfield St. -9C
Veitch's Sq. -1B
Vennel. -6E
Victoria St. -6F
Victoria Ter. -6E
Viewcraig Gdns. -5F
Viewcraig St. -5J

Warden's Cl. -6F
Wardrop's Ct. -5F
Warriston's Cl. -5F
Waterloo Pl. -3G
Waverley Bri. -4F
Waverley Steps. -4G
Webster's Land. -6D
Wellington St. -1K
Wemyss Pl. -3C
Wemyss Pl. M. -3B
W. Adam St. -6H
W. Approach Rd. -7A
West Bow. -6F
W. College St. -6G
W. Crosscauseway. -8H
West End. -5B
W. Nicolson St. -7H
W. Norton Pl. -2L
W. Parliament Sq. -5F
West Port. (EH1) -7D
West Port. (EH3) -7D
W. Register St. -3F
W. Register St. La. -3F
W. Richmond St. -7H
W. Tollcross. -8C
White Horse Cl. -4K
Wilson's Ct. -4J
Windmill St. -8H
Windmill La. -8G
Windmill Pl. -7H
Windmill St. -8G
Windsor St. -1J
Windsor St. La. -1J
World's End Cl. -5H

York La. -2G
York Pl. -2F
Young St. -4C
Young St. Nth. La. -4C
Young St. Sth. La. -4C

Forres St. -3B
Forrest Hill. -7F
Forrest Rd. -7F
Forth St. -2G
Fountainbridge. -8A
Fountain Cl. -5H
Frederick St. -3D

Gabriel's Rd. -3G
Galloway's Entry. -4K
Gardner's Cres. -7B
Gayfield La. -1H
Gayfield Sq. -1H (not continuous)
Geddes E. -5G
Gentiles Entry. -5K
George IV Bri. -5F
George Sq. -8G
George Sq. La. -8F

George St. -4C
Gibbs Entry. -7H
Gifford Pk. -9H
Gillespie Pl. -9C
Gillespie St. -9B
Gilmore Pl. -9B
Gilmore Pl. La. -9B
Gilmour's Cl. -6E
Gilmour's Entry. -7J
Gilmour St. -7J
Glanville Pl. -1B
Glenfinlas St. -4B
Glengyle Ter. -9C
Glen St. -7D
Gloucester La. -2B
Gloucester Pl. -2B
Gloucester Sq. -2B
Gloucester St. -2B
Grassmarket. -6E

Gray's Ct. -7H
Gt. King St. -2D
Gt. Stuart St. -4A
Greenside End. -2H
Greenside La. -2H
Greenside Pl. -2H
Greenside Row. -3H
Greyfriars. -6F
Greyfriars Pl. -6F
Grindlay St. -6C
Grindlay St. Ct. -7C
Grove St. -8A
Gullan's Cl. -5H (not continuous)
Guthrie St. -6G

Haddon's Ct. -7H
Hailes St. -9C
Hamilton Folly M. -8J

Hamilton Pl. -1B
Hammermen's Entry. -5J
Hanover St. -3E
Hardwell Cl. -7J
Hart St. -1G
Hart St. La. -1G
Hastie's Cl. -6G
Haugh St. -1B
Heriot Bri. -6E
Heriot Cross. -6E
Heriot Mt. -7J
Heriot Pl. -7E
Heriot Row. -3C
Hermits Cft. -8K
High Riggs. -7C
High School Wynd. -5H
High School Yards. -6H
High St. -5F

Hill Pl. -7H
Hillside Cres. -1J
Hillside St. -1K
Hill Sq. -6H
Hill St. -3C
Hill St. Nth. La. -3C
Hill St. Sth. La. -4C
Holyrood Ct. -5K
Holyrood Gait. -5K
Holyrood Pk. Rd. -9L
Holyrood Rd. -5J
Home St. -8C
Hope Pk. Sq. -8H
Hope St. -5B
Hope St. La. -5B
Horse Wynd. -4L
Howden St. -7H
Howe St. -2D
Hunter's Cl. -6E

EDINBURGH

Referred to as the 'Athens of the North', Edinburgh is a flourishing city renowned for its history, style, diversity and prestigious annual festival, which is considered to be the most important and successful event of its kind in Britain. During the month of August, the city becomes a magnet for thousands of people from around the world intent on participating in the festival scene.

Edinburgh divides itself between the Old and New Town areas. The Old Town includes the ancient city centre, where the famous Royal Mile links the Castle and Holyrood, and the historical districts of Grassmarket and Greyfriars. The New Town, dating mainly from the 18th century extends north from Princes Street, Edinburgh's main shopping street, and comprises a continuous development of grand streets, squares, circuses and green spaces regarded as a masterpiece of urban architecture.

PLACES OF INTEREST

Tourist Information Centre (All year) - 3 Princes Street.
Tel: 0845 22 55 121. www.edinburgh.org

◆ BRASS RUBBING CENTRE (74, 5H) - Housed in Trinity Apse, the only remaining part of the collegiate church founded in 1462. The centre holds a fine collection of replica brasses and Pictish stones from which rubbings can be made. Chalmers Close.

◆ BURNS MONUMENT (75, 4K) - A monument dedicated to Scotland's most beloved poet Robert Burns (1759-1796) built in 1830 by architect Thomas Hamilton. Regent Road.

◆ CAMERA OBSCURA & WORLD OF ILLUSIONS (74, 5E) - This Victorian 'Eye in the Sky' has fascinated visitors for 150 years with its live moving panorama of the city. Enjoy access to free telescopes showing a spectacular 360º rooftop panorama and listen to your guide recount tales of Edinburgh's exciting past. In World of illusions you can immerse yourself in three floors of mind-boggling hands-on exhibits from shadow walls to bendy mirrors, seeing in 3D to shaking hands with your ghost. Castlehill.

◆ CHILDHOOD, MUSEUM OF (74, 5H) - This museum houses an extensive collection of childhood memorabilia including toys, games, books and dolls. For the adult visitor there are exhibitions relating to the history of child welfare including health, education and upbringing. 42 High Street.

◆ CITY ART CENTRE (74, 5G) - A rich collection of fine art, almost entirely by Scottish artists, is housed within the City Art Centre. Since opening in 1980, the six exhibition galleries have displayed work dating from the 17th century, encompassing a wide range of media. 2 Market Street.

◆ EDINBURGH CASTLE (74, 5D) - The imposing fortress of Edinburgh Castle has dominated the cityscape since the Middle Ages, defiantly rooted to the ancient volcanic outcrop upon which it stands. Its strategic positioning and defensive structures have withstood countless sieges and provided successive Kings and Queens with refuge. The castle is home to the Scottish Crown Jewels, the Stone of Destiny and the famous 15th century siege gun Mons Meg. Of particular note is the remarkable St Margaret's Chapel, which has remained perfectly intact for 900 years, making it Edinburgh's oldest surviving building. Castlehill

◆ EDINBURGH DUNGEON, THE (74, 4F) - Experience life in barbaric times through reconstructions, exhibits and special effects. Market Street.

◆ EDINBURGH UNIVERSITY COLLECTION OF HISTORIC MUSICAL INSTRUMENTS (74, 7G) - An outstanding and diverse collection of over 1000 musical instruments from around the world chronicling the art of instrument making over the past 400 years. Bristo Square.

◆ FIRE, MUSEUM OF (74, 7D) - Displays illustrate the history of the oldest municipal fire brigade in the UK. Other exhibits include fire engines dating from 1806 and information relating to the development of fire fighting. Lauriston Place.

◆ FRUITMARKET GALLERY, THE (74, 4G) - Exhibiting contemporary art of the highest quality, the gallery is committed to bringing the work of artists with both established and emerging international reputation to Scotland and presenting the work of Scottish artists. 45 Market Street.

◆ GEORGIAN HOUSE, THE (74, 4B) - (NTS) Situated on the north side of Charlotte Square, designed by Robert Adam in1791, this house exemplifies the style of Edinburgh's New Town architecture. The rooms of No.7 (built in 1796) are furnished in period style and there is a video presentation "Living in a Grand Design" that reflets life in the New Town. The National Trust for Scotland also owns 5 and 6 on the north side and 26 to 31 on the south. Charlotte Square.

◆ GLADSTONE'S LAND (74, 5F) - (NTS) Built in 1620, this six-storey tenement building in the Old Town is furnished in period style with unusual tempera paintings on the ceilings and walls. 477B Lawnmarket.

◆ GREYFRIARS BOBBY (74, 6F) - Statue in memory of Greyfriars Bobby, the skye terrier who watched over his master's grave for 14 years after his death from 1858-1872. Candlemaker Row.

◆ HBOS MUSEUM ON THE MOUND (74, 5F) - The museum has recently been refurbished and displays recount the history of various banks and companies, and the the history of money. North Bank Street.

◆ HOLYROOD ABBEY (75, 4L) - (HS) The ruined nave is all that remains of this Abbey church founded for Augustinian canons during the late 12th early 13th centuries. Beneath the Abbey the Royal Vault is the final resting place for a number of Scottish Kings, including David II (son of Robert the Bruce), James II, James V and Lord Darnley, Mary Queen of Scot's second husband. Canongate.

◆ JOHN KNOX HOUSE (74, 5H) - There is some contention as to whether John Knox, the religious reformer actually lived in this 15th century town house. It is known however, that it was once inhabited by James Mossman, goldsmith to Mary, Queen of Scots.The house features relics of the Reformation and information regarding Knox's Life. 43-45 High Street.

◆ MATTHEW ARCHITECTURE GALLERY, THE (74, 6G) - Since opening in 1992, the gallery has exhibited examples of historical and contemporary architecture, together with expositions from internationally acclaimed architects. 20 Chambers Street.

Edinburgh View

Edinburgh Tattoo

Princes Street

◆ MUSEUM OF EDINBURGH, THE (75, 4J) - Huntly House, a beautifully well-preserved 16th century building, provides the setting for exhibitions devoted to the local history of Edinburgh. The diverse range of artefacts include pottery, silverware, street signs and treasures of national importance. 142 Canongate.

◆ NATIONAL GALLERY OF SCOTLAND (74, 5E) - Located in the heart of the city, the gallery has been open to the public since 1859. The collection comprises a comprehensive catalogue of work from the Renaissance era to the Post Impressionist period. The Mound.

◆ NATIONAL LIBRARY OF SCOTLAND (74, 6F) - Founded in 1682, the library is one of the largest in Britain and since 1710 has been able to claim a copy of every book published in Britain. George IV Bridge.

◆ NATIONAL MONUMENT (75, 3J) - Built in 1822 to honour the Scottish who perished in the Napoleonic wars, this monument was designed to emulate the Parthenon, (temple dedicated to Athena, the Greek goddess of war). Unfortunately, it was never completed due to a collapse in funding and remains today unfinished. Calton Hill.

◆ NATIONAL WAR MUSEUM OF SCOTLAND (74, 5D) - This absorbing museum reflects the experience of war, sourced from personal diaries, photographs and official documents. Other exhibits include uniforms, insignia and equipment, medals, decorations, weapons, paintings, ceramics and silverware. Edinburgh Castle.

◆ NELSON MONUMENT (75, 3J) - Built between 1807 and 1815, this was one of the first monuments to Admiral Nelson. The climb to the top is rewarded with splendid panoramic views across the city. 32 Calton Hill.

◆ OUR DYNAMIC EARTH (75, 5K) - Discover our planet's past, present and future. Be shaken by volcanoes, fly over glaciers, feel the chill of polar ice, get caught in a tropical rainstorm and debate the planet's future in the Futuredome. 107 Holyrood Road.

◆ PALACE OF HOLYROODHOUSE & HOLYROOD PARK (75, 4L) - At the end of Edinburgh's historic Royal Mile stands the Palace of Holyroodhouse, the Queen's official Scottish residence. Today, tourists can visit the Royal apartments, the Throne room, the Royal Dining Room and the Great Gallery to experience the grandeur of this Royal residence. Canongate, Royal Mile.

◆ PEOPLE'S STORY, THE (75, 4J) - Housed in the 16th century Tolbooth, this museum reflects working class life in Edinburgh since the 18th century. Sounds, sights, smells and reconstructed rooms combine to evoke an atmosphere of a bygone era. Canongate Tolbooth.

◆ ROYAL MUSEUM (74, 6G) - Housed in an impressive Victorian building designed by Capt. Francis Fowkes, the architect of the Royal Albert Hall in London, the museum's diverse collection covers natural history, geology, decorative arts, science and technology. Chambers Street.

◆ ROYAL SCOTTISH ACADEMY (74, 4E) - Presenting the cream of Scottish contemporary art through an ongoing programme of exciting exhibitions including painting, sculpture, printmaking, installation, photography, arcitecture, new media, film and performance art. The Mound.

◆ ST. GILES' CATHEDRAL (74, 5F) - Founded in 1120, most of the remaining architecture dates from the 14th and 15th centuries including the famous crown spire that dominates the city skyline. Royal Mile.

◆ ST. MARY'S RC CATHEDRAL (74, 2G) - This Cathedral church of St. Mary was designed by Gillespie Graham and dates from 1814 and 1890. The St. Andrews Altar contains the National Shrine to Scotland's patron saint. Broughton Street.

◆ SCOTCH WHISKY HERITAGE CENTRE, THE (74, 6E) - An award winning attraction that takes the visitor on a ride through history in a whisky barrel to discover the ancient traditions and origins of whisky production. 345 Castlehill.

◆ SCOTT MONUMENT (74, 4F) - One of Edinburgh's most famous landmarks, this monument to Sir Walter Scott was designed by George Kemp and erected between 1840 and 1844. The statue itself depicts Scott with his dog and incorporates characters from his novels. East Princes Street Gardens.

◆ SCOTTISH NATIONAL PORTRAIT GALLERY (74, 2F) - Visual history of Scotland from the 16th century to the present day depicted through portraits of figures who shaped it: royalty, philosophers, poets and rebels are included. The gallery also houses the National Collection of Photography. 1 Queen Street.

◆ STILLS GALLERY (74, 5G) - Scotland's premier photographic gallery exhibits a comprehensive collection of contemporary photography. 23 Cockburn Street.

◆ TALBOT RICE GALLERY (74, 6G) - The gallery exhibits Edinburgh University's 'Old Master' collection alongside a changing programme of temporary displays. South Bridge.

◆ TARTAN WEAVING MILL AND EXHIBITION (74, 5E) - Housed in the former Castlehill Reservoir Cistern, this working mill allows visitors to view the entire production process of tartan from sheep to shop. 555 Castlehill.

◆ WRITERS' MUSEUM, THE (74, 5F) - Located in the historic Lady Stair's House dating from 1622, the museum houses an exhibition that revolves around Scotland's three great writers; Robert Burns, Sir Walter Scott and Robert Louis Stevenson. Lady Stair's Close.

ENTERTAINMENT
◆ Cinemas - Lothian Road (2). Home Street .
◆ Concerts - Assembly Rooms, George Street. Ross Open Air Theatre, Princes Street Gardens. Usher Hall, Lothian Road.
◆ Theatres - Edinburgh Festival Theatre, Nicolson Street. Edinburgh Playhouse, Greenside Place. King's Theatre, Leven Street. Royal Lyceum Theatre, Grindlay Street. Traverse Theatre, Cambridge Street.

SPORT & LEISURE
◆ Parks & Gardens - East Meadow Park, Meadow Lane. East Princes Street Gardens, Princes Street, Regent Road Park, Abbeymount. Royal Terrace Gardens, Royal Terrace. West Meadow Park, Melville Drive. West Princes Street Gardens, Princes Street.

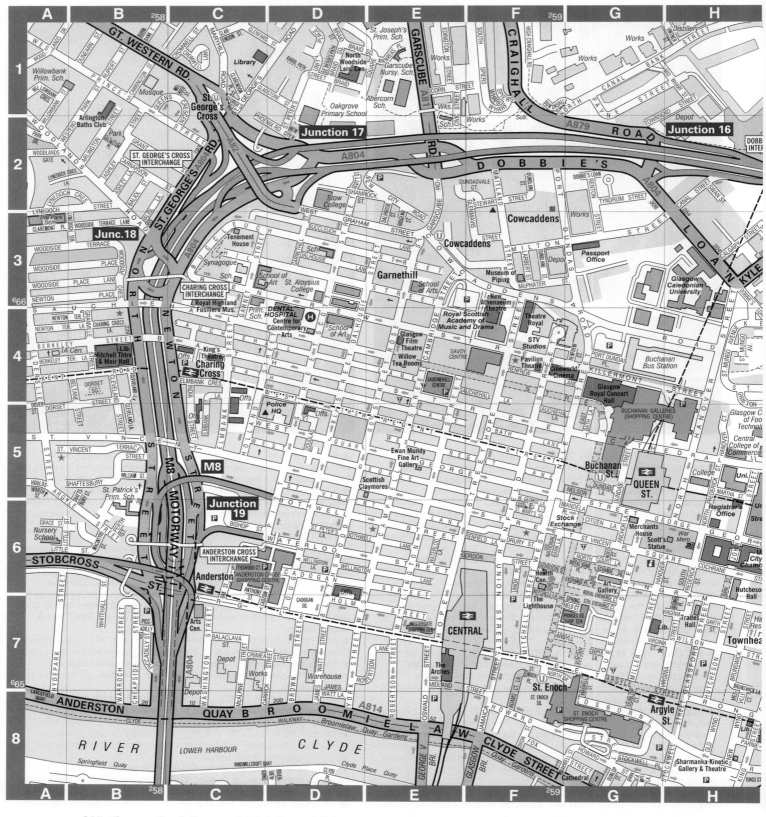

INDEX

Adams Ct. La. -8F
Albion Ga. -7J
Albion St. -8J
Alexandra Pde. -4M
Anchor La. -6G
Anderston Cross Shop.
 Cen. -6C
Anderston Quay. -8A
Anthony St. -6C
Argyle St. (G1) -7G
Argyle St. (G2) -7C
Argyle St. (G3) -5A
Argyll Arc. -7F
Arlington Pl. -2B
Arlington St. -2B
Ashley La. -2B
Ashley St. -2B

Baird St. -3J
Balaclava St. -7C

Baliol La. -3B
Baliol St. -2B
Barrack St. -8M
Bath La. -4C
 (not continuous)
Bath La. -4C
Bell St. -7J
Beltane St. -4B
Berkeley St. -4A
Berkley Ter. La. -4A
Bishop St. -6C
Blackfriars St. -7J
Black St. -3K
Blythswood Ct. -6C
Blythswood Sq. -5D
Blythswood St. -7D
Bothwell La. -6C
Bothwell St. -6D
Braid Sq. -1D
Braid St. -1D
Broomielaw. -8C

Brown St. -8D
Brunswick La. -7H
Brunswick St. -7H
Buccleuch La. -3C
Buccleuch St. -3C
Buchanan Galleries
 (Shop. Cen.). -5G
Buchanan St. -7F
Burnbank Ter. -8B
Burrell's La. -6K

Cadogan Sq. -7D
Cadogan St. -6D
Cadzow St. -7C
Calgary St. -3H
Cambridge St. (G2) -4E
Cambridge St. (G3) -4E
Canal St. -2H
Candleriggs. -8J
Carnarvon St. -2B
Carrick St. -8D

Carrington St. -1B
Castle St. -3M
Cathedral Sq. -6L
 (not continuous)
Cathedral St. -5G
Charing Cross La.
 -4B
Charles St. -2M
Cheapside St. -8B
Chisholm St. -8J
Citizen La. -6G
Civic St. -2H
Claremont Pl. -3A
Clarendon Pl. -1C
Clarendon St. -1C
Cleveland La. -4B
Cleveland St. -4B
Clyde Pl. -8D
Cochrane St. -6H
College La. -7K
College St. -7J

Collins St. -6L
Corn St. -1E
Couper Pl. -3J
Couper St. -3J
Cowcaddens Rd. -3E
Craighall Rd. -1F
Crimea St. -7C
Cromwell La. -1C
Cromwell St. -1C

Dalhousie La. -3D
Dalhousie St. -4D
 (not continuous)
Dixon St. -8F
Dobbie's Loan. -2F
Dobbie's Loan La. -4J
Dorset Sq. -5A
Dorset St. -5A
Douglas La. -5D
Douglas St. -7D
Dover St. -5A

Drury St. -6F
Drygate. -6L
Duke St. -6K
Dunblane St. -2F
 (not continuous)
Dundas La. -5G
Dundas St. -5G
 (not continuous)
Dundasvale Ct. -2F
Dunearn St. -1B
Dunlop St. -8G
 (not continuous)

E. Bath La. -5G
E. Campbell St. -8L
Edington St. -1E
Elderslie St. -4A
Elmbank Cres. -4C
Elmbank St. -5C
Elmbank St. La. -5C

Exchange Pl. -6G

Fountainwell Rd. -1K
Fox St. -8F

Gallowgate. -8J
Garnethill St. -3D
Garnet St. -4C
Garscube Rd. -1E
Garth St. -7H
George V Bri. -8E
George Sq. -6G
George St. -6H
Gibson Hgts. -6L
Gladstone St. -1C
Glasgow Bri. -8F
Glassford St. -7H
Glebe Ct. -4K
Glebe St. (G4) -3K
Glebe St. (G4) -4L
 (not continuous)

Glenfarg St. -1C
Glenmavis St. -2F
Gordon La. -6F
Gordon St. -6F
Grace St. -6A
Grafton Pl. -4H
Grant St. -2B
Granville St. -4B
Gt. Dovehill. -8K
Gt. Western Rd. -1B

Hanover Ct. -5H
Hanover St. -6G
High Craighall Rd.
 -1F
High St. -8J
Hill St. -3C
Holland St. -5C
Holm St. -7D
Hope St. -7E
Houldsworth St. -5A

Howard St. -8F
Hunter St. -8L
Hutcheson St. -7H
Hydepark St. -7A

India St. -4C
Ingram St. -7G
Inner City Trad. Est.
 -3J

Jamaica St. -8F
James Watt La. -8D
James Watt St. -8D
John Knox St. -6M
John St. -6H

Karol Path. -1D
Kennedy Path. -4J
Kennedy St. -4H
Kent Rd. -4A
Killermont St. -4G

King St. -8H
Kyle St. -3H

Ladywell St. -6M
Lancefield Quay. -8A
Larbert St. -3F
Lister Hgts. -6L
Lister St. -3K
Lit. Dovehill. -8K
Little St. -6A
London Rd. -8J
Lynedoch Cres. -2A
Lynedoch Cres. La.
 -2A
Lynedoch St. -2A
Lynedoch Ter. -3B

McAlpine St. -8C
McAslin Ct. -4K
McAslin St. -4L
McFarlane St. -8L

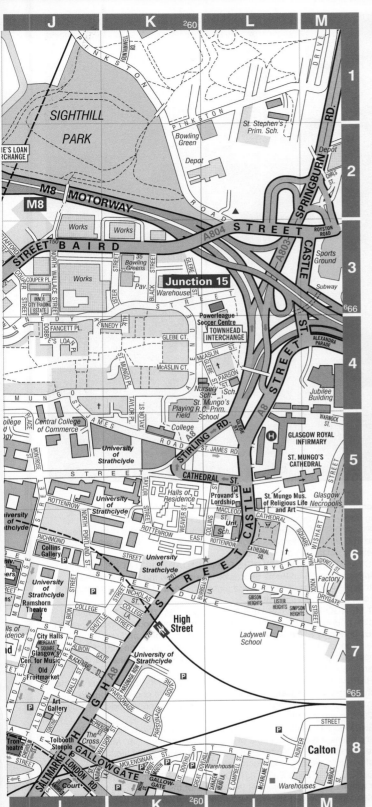

REFERENCE

One Way Street — Traffic flow on A Roads is also indicated by heavy line on the driver's left.	→
Junction Name	DOBBIE'S LOAN INTERCHANGE
Restricted Access	
Pedestrianized Road	
Track & Footpath	
Residential Walkway	
Railway	Station — Tunnel
Underground Station	Ⓤ
Built-up Area	MAY / PL
Car Park (Selected)	Ⓟ
Church or Chapel	†
Fire Station	■
Hospital	Ⓗ
Information Centre	ℹ
Police Station	▲
Post Office	★
Toilet	▽
Educational Establishment	
Hospital or Hospice	
Industrial Building	
Leisure or Recreational Facility	
Place of Interest	
Public Building	
Shopping Centre or Market	
Other Selected Buildings	

SCALE : 1:9504 (6.66 inches to 1 mile)

0 ¼ ½ MILE

0 250 500 750 Metres

George Square

Macintyre St. -6B
Macleod St. -6L
McPhater St. -3F
McPherson St. -8J
Maitland St. -2F
Manresa Pl. -1E
Martha St. -5H
Maryhill Rd. -1C
Maxwell St. (G1) -7G
Maxwell St. (G1) -8G
Melrose St. -1C
Melville Ct. -8H
Metropole La. -8G
Midland St. -7E
Mid Wharf St. -1H
Miller St. -7G
Milton St. -3F
Mitchell La. -7G
Mitchell St. -7F
Moir St. -8K
Molendinar St. -8K

Montrose St. -6J

National Bank La. -6F
Nelson Mandela Pl. -5G
New City Rd. -2D
   (not continuous)
Newton Pl. -3A
Newton St. -4C
Newton Ter. -4A
Newton Ter. La. -4A
New Wynd. -8H
Nicholas St. -6K
Nth. Canal Bank St.
   -1G
Nth. Ct. -6G
North Ct. La. -6G
North Dr. -7F
Nth. Frederick St. -6H
Nth. Hanover St. -6H
Nth. Portland St. -6J
North St. -3B

Nth. Wallace St. -3J

Oak St. -6C
Old Wynd. -8H
Osborne St. -8G
Oswald St. -8E

Park Dr. -2A
Parnie St. -8H
Parsonage Row. -7K
Parsonage Sq. -7K
   (not continuous)
Parson St. -4L
Payne St. -1G
Perth St. -6B
Phoenix Rd. -2C
Picadilly St. -7B
Pinkston Dr. -2K
Pinkston Rd. -1J
Pitt St. -6D
Port Dundas Pl. -4G

Port Dundas Rd. -2F
Princes Sq. Shop. Cen.
   -7G

Queen's Cres. -1B
Queen St. -7G

Renfield La. -6F
Renfield St. -6F
Renfrew Ct. (G1) -4J
Renfrew Ct. (G2) -4G
Renfrew La. -4F
Renfrew St. -3C
Renton St. -2G
Richmond St. -6J
Riverview Gdns. -8D
Robertson La. -7D
Robertson St. -8E
Ropework La. -8G
Rose St. -4E
Rottenrow. (G1) -5J

Rottenrow. (G4) -6L
Rottenrow E. -6K
Royal Bank Pl. -6G
Royal Exchange Ct.
   -7G
Royal Exchange Sq.
   -7G
Royston Rd. -3M
Rupert St. -1B

St Andrew's La. -8J
St Andrew's St. -8J
St Enoch La. -7F
St Enoch Pl. -7F
St Enoch Shop. Cen.
   -7G
St Enoch Sq. -8F
St George's Pl. -1C
St George's Rd. (G3)
   -3B
St George's Rd. (G4)
   -1C

St James Rd. -4J
St Mary's Ct. -6F
St Mary's La. -6F
St Mungo Av. -4H
St Mungo Pl. -4K
St Mungo's Cathedral.
   -5L
St Peters La. -6D
St Peter's Path. -1D
St Peter's St. -2D
St Vincent La. -5D
St Vincent Pl. -6G
St Vincent St. (G2) -5A
St Vincent St. (G3) -5A
St Vincent Ter. -5A
Saltmarket. -8J
Saracen Head La. -8L
Sauchiehall Cen. -4C
Sauchiehall La. -4C
   (not continuous)
Sauchiehall St. -4A

Savoy Cen. -4E
Scott St. -4D
Shaftsbury St. -5B
   (not continuous)
Shamrock St. -2D
Shuttle St. -7J
Simpson Hgts. -7M
Sth. Exchange Ct. -7G
Sth. Frederick St. -6H
Sth. Spiers Wharf. -1F
Spiers Wharf. -1F
Spoutmouth. -8K
Springburn Rd. -2M
Springfield Ct. -7G
Stafford St. -3J
Stewart St. -2F
Stirling Rd. -5K
Stobcross St. -6A
Stock Exchange. -6G
Stockwell Pl. -8G
Stockwell St. -8H

Swan St. -2H

Taylor Pl. -4K
Taylor St. -5K
   (not continuous)
Tenement Ho. -3C
Tontine La. -8J
Townsend St. -2G
Trongate. -8H
Tyndrum St. -2G

Union Pl. -6F
Union St. -6F
Unity Pl. -1D

Vintner St. -1H
Virginia Ct. -7G
Virginia Pl. -7H
Virginia St. -7H

Walls St. -7J

Warnock St. -5M
Warroch St. -8B
Washington St. -8C
Waterloo La. -6E
Waterloo St. -6D
Watson St. -8J
Weaver St. -6K
Wellington La. -6D
   (not continuous)
Wellington St. -7E
W. Campbell St. -7D
Westend Pk. St. -2A
Westgate Shop. Cen.
   -7E
W. George La. -5C
W. George St. -5D
   (not continuous)
W. Graham St. -2D
W. Nile St. (G1) -6F
W. Nile St. (G2) -6F
W. Prince's St. -1A

W. Regent La. -5E
W. Regent St. -4D
   (not continuous)
Whitehall St. -7B
William St. -5B
Willowbank Cres. -1A
Willowbank St. -2A
Wilson St. -7H
Wishart St. -6M
Woodlands Dr. -1A
Woodlands Ga. -2A
Woodlands Rd. -2A
Woodside Cres. -3B
Woodside Pl. -3A
Woodside Pl. La. -3A
Woodside Ter. -3A
Woodside Ter. La. -3B

York St. -8D

GLASGOW

The history of Glasgow can be dated from the 6th century when a settlement developed around the church built by St Mungo on the banks of the Molendinar burn. His popularity earned him the name 'dear one' and to this day is the patron saint of the city. These first inhabitants named their settlement 'Glas Ghu' (dear green place) and with the city and its environs boasting no less than 70 parks and green spaces it certainly lives up to its name. In the period between the death of St Mungo and the granting of a charter in 1175 by William the Lion, little is known of the city's history, but from this date the city became a prosperous centre. In 1451 the university was founded which after St Andrew's is Scotland's oldest University and the 4th oldest in the UK and in 1611 Glasgow became a Royal Burgh. The city prospered through its ability to trade in tabacco, sugar and cotton with the American colonies but when the American Revolution affected this in 1775 the city turned to industry. With the advent of Industrialisation in the 19th century, Glasgow concentrated upon ship building and soon established a reputation for quality throughout the world that earned the city its reputation as 'Second City of the British Empire.' However, the onset of economic depression in post war England would contribute to the decline of industrial prestige. Depression of the industry was slowed down by the need for naval re-armament in the 1930s but by the 1950s demand was dwindling and combined with cheap foreign competition, Glasgow could no longer compete in the industrial arena.

With a rich heritage of cultural splendour, Glasgow realised that this was the key to renewed prosperity. Splendid Victorian architecture lay beneath the grime of an industrial age and once restored would revive the city as a cultural centre. Many of the city's buildings reflect the style of the talented Glasgow born architect, Charles Rennie Mackintosh (1868-1928) whose influential style contributed significantly to shaping the distinctive forms of Art Nouveau throughout Europe. Architecture became a focus for his artistic expression and in the city there is an abundance of public buildings, private buildings and tea rooms that display the familiar Mackintosh style. The Willow Tea Rooms on Sauchiehall Street, designed for Kate Cranston in 1903 have been restored to reflect Mackintosh's original design and the School of Art on Renfrew Street, architecturally one of Mackintosh's greatest achievements is still in use as an art school. In 1990 Glasgow was awarded the prestigious title of Cultural Capital of Europe and in 1999 was designated UK City of Architecture and design. Today, Glasgow is one of the UK's most visited cities offering visitors a wealth of cultural heritage and visitor attractions.

Glasgow University

PLACES OF INTEREST

Tourist Information Centre (All Year) - 11 George Square.
Tel: (0141) 204 4400

◆ COLLINS GALLERY (79, 6J) - Affiliated to the University, the gallery mounts various exhibitions including contemporary, fine and applied art and photography. 22 Richmond Street.

◆ GALLERY OF MODERN ART (78, 6G) - Elegant, neo-classical building situated in the heart of the city, the gallery offers a range of contemporary exhibitions and activities, displaying work by Scottish and International artists as well as addressing contemporary social issues. Queen Street.

◆ GLASGOW CITY CHAMBERS (78, 6H) - Built in 1883-88 by William Young, the imposing City Chambers is a magnificent example of 19th century architecture that occupies the east side of George Square. Today, the building is home to the headquarters of Glasgow City Council.

◆ GLASGOW NECROPOLIS (79, 5M) - Adjacent to the Cathedral, this cemetery dating from 1883 is modelled on the famous Pere la Chaise in Paris and is renowned for its elaborate tombs. Castle Street.

◆ GLASGOW RC CATHEDRAL (78, 8G) - The earliest part of this structure dates from the 1790s and the remains that can be seen today date predominantly from 1866. Duke Street.

◆ GLASGOW ST MUNGOS CATHEDRAL (79, 5L) - (HS) Dating predominantly from the 15th century, the cathedral is regarded as one of Glasgow's most important buildings both architecturally and historically. Castle Street.

◆ HUTCHESON'S HALL (78, 6H) - (NTS) Designed by David Hamilton during the 19th century, this A listed building was originally founded by George and Thomas Hutcheson in 1641 as a hospice for men and orphan boys. Today the hall houses a visitor centre and Gallery of Contemporary Design. 158 Ingram Street.

◆ LIGHTHOUSE, THE - SCOTLAND'S CENTRE FOR ARCHITECTURE, DESIGN & THE CITY (78, 6F) - Heralded as the flagship project of Glasgow's 1999 UK City of Architecture & Design, the centre has attracted national and international recognition for its exhibition programmes. Also within the complex is the Mackintosh Interpretation Centre, which provides an insight into the work of the great Scottish artist. 11 Mitchell Lane.

◆ MARTYRS' SCHOOL (79, 4L) - One of the earliest buildings designed by Charles Rennie Mackintosh just after completing his apprenticeship with Honeyman and Keppie. Parts of the building are open to the public by appointment. Parson Street.

◆ MITCHELL LIBRARY (78, 4B) - Founded in 1874, this is the largest public reference library in Europe. Contained within its 1.5 million volumes can be found a wide range of literature relating to the culture and history of Glasgow and Scotland. North Street.

◆ PIPING, MUSEUM OF (78, 3F) - Museum houses an outstanding collection of bagpipes and exhibitions that trace the origins and history of piping through innovative displays. 30-34 McPhater Street.

◆ PROVAND'S LORDSHIP (79, 5L) - Dating from 1471, this is the oldest house in Glasgow which was originally built as a manse to the adjacent St Nicholas Hospital. 3 Castle Street.

◆ ROYAL HIGHLAND FUSILIERS REGIMENTAL MUSEUM (78, 3C) - Displays of medals, uniforms and records relating to the history of The Royal Scots Fusiliers, The Highland Light Infantry and the Royal Highland Fusiliers. 518 Sauchiehall Street.

◆ ST MUNGO RELIGIOUS LIFE & ART MUSEUM (79, 5L) - Innovative museum offering an insight into religious faiths throughout the world through various art forms which aspire to promote understanding and respect between people of different faiths and of none. After exploring the world's six main religions visitors can relax in contemplation in the peaceful Zen garden, the first of its kind in Britain. 2 Castle Street.

◆ SHARMANKA KINETIC GALLERY & THEATRE (78, 8H) - Unique kinetic sculptures made from pieces of old scrap perform live choreography to music and synchronised light. 64 Osborne Street (temporary address from July 2006 to early 2008).

◆ TENEMENT HOUSE, THE (78, 3C) - (NTS) Dating from the late 19th century, this is a typical example of a Victorian tenement flat. Many of the original furnishings remain to create a fascinating insight of life in the early part of the 20th century. 145 Buccleuch Street.

◆ TOLBOOTH STEEPLE (79, 8J) - Dating from 1626, this seven storey tower with its distinctive crown at the summit of the 34 m (113ft) high steeple marked the centre of Glasgow until Victorian times. Glasgow Cross.

ENTERTAINMENT

◆ Cinemas - Renfrew Street.
◆ Concerts - Arches, The, 253 Argyle Street / 30 Midland Street. Glasgow Royal Concert Hall, Sauchiehall Street. Mitchell Theatre & Moir Hall, Granville Street. Old Fruitmarket, (within City Hall), Albion Street.
◆ Theatres - Arches, The, (as above). Mitchell Theatre & Moir Hall,, (as above). King's Theatre, Bath Street. New Athenaeum Theatre, (within Academy of Music & Drama), Renfrew Street. Pavilion Theatre, Renfield Street. Ramshorn Theatre, Ingram Street. Theatre Royal, Hope Street. Tron Theatre, Trongate.

SPORT & LEISURE

◆ Parks & Gardens - Sighthill Park, Pinkston Road.
◆ Sports Centres - North Woodside Leisure Centre, Braid Square.
◆ Swimming Pools - North Woodside Leisure Centre (as above).

FALKIRK

A historic town with an important industrial heritage, Falkirk today offers the visitor a diverse range of attractions and interesting places steeped in history to explore. Falkirk was once an area of strategic importance and this is illustrated by the construction of the Antonine Wall, the route of which (albeit predominantly obliterated) ran through the centre of Falkirk. Built in 140AD and named after the Roman Emperor of the time, Antonius Pius, who ordered its construction as a defence against the Northern tribes, the Antonine Wall stretched for 36 miles from Old Kirkpartrick on the Clyde to Carriden on the Firth with forts interposed every 2 miles. The wall itself was a turf rampart on a stone base with a ditch to the north and a military road running parallel along the south side. The most significant remains around Falkirk can be viewed at Kemper Avenue (see below) and to the west of the town on Anson Avenue a short section of embankment can be viewed.

PLACES OF INTEREST

Tourist Information Centre (All year) - 2-4 Glebe Street.
   Tel: (01324) 620244
◆ FALKIRK FORT - Site of a Roman fort on the Antonine Wall with interpretative display panels which provide information on the location. Kemper Avenue.

ENTERTAINMENT

◆ Cinemas - Princes Street.
◆ Concerts - Town Hall, West Bridge Street.
◆ Theatres - Town Hall (as above).

SPORT & LEISURE

◆ Parks & Gardens - Bellsmeadow Park, Bellsmeadow Road. Blinkbonny Park, Gartcows Road. Callendar Park, Callendar Road. Dollar Park, Camelon Road. Victoria Park, Thornhill Road.
◆ Sports Centres - Coasters Arena, Grangemouth Road. Mariner Leisure Centre, Glasgow Road (approximately 1 mile from centre of Falkirk off A803).
◆ Swimming Pools - Mariner Leisure Centre (as above).
◆ Ten-Pin Bowling - G X Superbowl, Glasgow Road (approximately 1 mile from centre of Falkirk off A803).

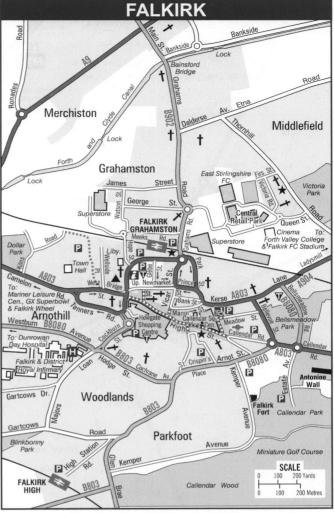

FORT WILLIAM

The history of Fort William can be dated from 1655 when General Monk built an earthwork fort here, the purpose of which to quote Johnson was to keep "savage clans and roving barbarians" at bay. This was later rebuilt under William III and, for a short time the town was renamed Maryburgh in honour of his queen. In both 1715 and 1745, the Jacobites failed to capture the fort and it was eventually pulled down during the late 19th century. For today's visitor, Fort William is synonymous to Ben Nevis and the town has become a popular holiday resort and base for the many people who wish to climb Britain's highest mountain.

PLACES OF INTEREST

Tourist Information Centre (All Year) - Cameron Square.
   Tel: (01397) 703781
◆ JACOBITE, THE (FORT WILLIAM TO MALLAIG STEAM SERVICE) - Considered to be one of the 'greatest railway journeys of the world' the train travels 50 miles from Fort William to the West Coast fishing port of Mallaig. Steeped in history, the route encompasses breathtaking scenery with views of Ben Nevis, Neptune's Staircase and the magnificent 21 arch Glenfinnan Viaduct. Fort William Station.
◆ WEST HIGHLAND MUSEUM - Founded in 1922, exhibitions illustrate the history of traditional Highland life. The museum also houses a world famous Jacobite collection. Cameron Square.
◆ WEST HIGHLAND WAY - Long distance footpath covering 95 miles between Glasgow and Fort William.

ENTERTAINMENT

◆ Cinemas - Cameron Centre, Cameron Square.
◆ Concerts - The Nevis Centre, An Aird.
◆ Theatres - The Nevis Centre, (as above).

SPORT & LEISURE

◆ Other - Shinty Pitch, An Aird.
◆ Sports Centres - Lochaber Leisure Centre, Belford Road. The Nevis Centre, An Aird.
◆ Swimming Pools - Lochaber Leisure Centre (as above).
◆ Ten Pin Bowling - The Nevis Centre (as above).

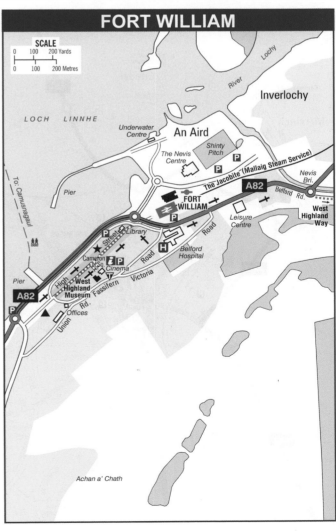

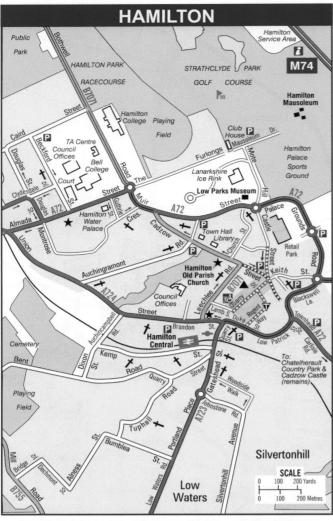

HAMILTON

There has been a settlement at Hamilton since prehistoric times, which was known as Cadzow, a name derived from the Celtic "Cadihou" meaning "beautiful castle." It was in 1445, that a charter granted by James II to the first Lord Hamilton gave permission for the official name of the town to be changed to that of his family. The town was once one of the main stopping places for the stagecoach that ran between England and Scotland and the towns museum (see below) is housed in a former coaching inn. With the rise of industrialisation, the town became the centre of a mining district, but closure of the pits forced diversification and today Hamilton is a thriving town that offers a wide range of visitor attractions and leisure facilities.

PLACES OF INTEREST

Tourist Information Centre (All Year) - Road Chef Services (M74 Northbound) Tel: (01698) 285590

◆ HAMILTON MAUSOLEUM - Built in 1850 for the 10th Duke of Hamilton as a family chapel and crypt at an estimated cost of £150,000 the mausoleum is a spectacular structure designed by David Bryce. C/o Chatelherault, Carlisle Road.

◆ HAMILTON OLD PARISH CHURCH - Dating from 1732-34, this church was designed by William Adam. Strathmore Road.

◆ HAMILTON PARK RACECOURSE - Considered to be one of the most picturesque racecourses in Britain, it once formed part of the Royal forest of Cadzow. The inaugural race meeting at Hamilton was held in August 1782 and today the racecourse offers a varied fixture list throughout the season that includes some evening meetings during the summer months. Bothwell Road.

◆ LOW PARKS MUSEUM - Museum was created through the amalgamation of the former District Museum with the Cameronians Regimental Museum and is housed in the towns oldest building, once a coaching inn which dates from 1696. Exhibitions include displays on the Clyde Valley and Hamilton Estate. 129 Muir Street.

ENTERTAINMENT

◆ Concerts - Town Hall, Cadzow Street.
◆ Theatres - Town Hall (as above).

SPORT & LEISURE

◆ Ice Rink - Lanarkshire Ice Rink, Mote Hill.
◆ Parks & Gardens - Public Park, Bothwell Road.
◆ Sports Centres - Hamilton Palace Sports Ground, Mote Hill. Hamilton Water Palace, Almada Street.
◆ Swimming Pools - Hamilton Water Palace (as above).
◆ Ten-Pin Bowling - Cosmic Bowl, M & D's Theme Park, North East of Hamilton, junction 5 off the M74.

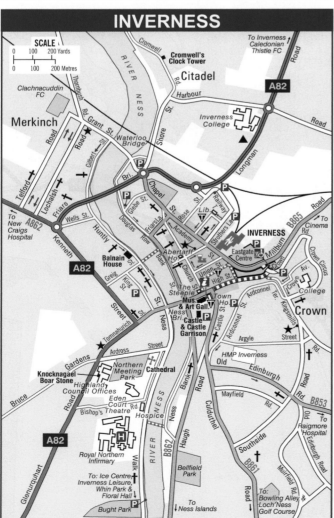

INVERNESS

Referred to as the 'Capital of the Highlands', Inverness is a bustling town centre with a rich heritage and though the emphasis today lies with administration, commerce and industry, Inverness is still a worthy tourist destination. Lying on the shores of the Moray Firth and divided by the River Ness, the main part of the town occupies the right bank. Notable buildings include the Town House, a Victorian Gothic building dating from 1880, Abertarff House, built in 1592 which was restored by the National Trust for Scotland in 1963 and is now used as their Highland office and Dunbar's Hospital which was built in 1688 as an almshouse. Across the river to the west of the town lies the Caledonian Canal, which runs from Fort William to Inverness and dates from 1822.

PLACES OF INTEREST

Tourist Information Centre (All Year) - Castle Wynd. Tel: (01463) 252401

◆ BALNAIN HOUSE - Georgian House built around 1726, Balnain House was originally used as a hospital for soldiers following Culloden and is now home to the Scottish Music Centre. 40 Huntly Street.

◆ CASTLE GARRISON ENCOUNTER - Historical reconstruction set in 1745; the Black Watch has been recalled to Flanders and recruits are needed to form a new regiment. Potential recruits to this innovative attraction experience the enlisting procedure from signing up to being in the intimidating presence of The Sergeant of the Guard who will be responsible for their training. Inverness Castle.

◆ CROMWELL'S CLOCK TOWER - Site of Cromwell's Fort which was destroyed during the Restoration, the clock tower is all that remains. Cromwell Road.

◆ FLORA MACDONALD STATUE - This statue dedicated to the Highland heroine dominates the grounds of Inverness Castle. Inverness Castle.

◆ INVERNESS CASTLE - Once a formidable Canmore stronghold dating from the 12th century and later occupied by the Jacobites in 1715 and again in 1745 by the Young Pretender who destroyed the castle. The site was cleared in 1834 and today the building is home to the law courts and local government offices. The Drum Tower recounts the story of the castle and can be visited by the public in the summer.

◆ INVERNESS CATHEDRAL - Built between 1866 & 1869, this Gothic style cathedral was the first to be completed in Britain since the Reformation. Ardross St.

◆ INVERNESS MUSEUM & ART GALLERY - Displays of human and natural history are combined to reflect the history of Inverness and the Highlands. The collection also includes silver, weapons and period costume. Castle Wynd.

◆ KNOCKNAGAEL BOAR STONE - Preserved within the Council Offices, the stone is inscribed with Pictish symbols which depict a mirror case and wild boar. Glenurquhart Road.

ENTERTAINMENT

◆ Cinemas - Eden Court Theatre, Bishops Road.
◆ Concerts - Eden Court Theatre (as above).
◆ Theatres - Eden Court Theatre (as above).

SPORT & LEISURE

◆ Ice Rink - Inverness Ice Centre, Bught Park.
◆ Parks & Gardens - Bellfield Park, Island Bank Road. Bught Park, South of Inverness. Northern Meeting Park, Ardross St. Whin Park, South of Inverness.
◆ Sports Centres - Inverness Leisure, Bught Park.
◆ Swimming Pools - Leisure Waters, Inverness Leisure, (as above).
◆ Ten-Pin Bowling - Rollerbowl, Culduthel Road, South of Inverness.

KILMARNOCK

Kilmarnock, a commercial town noted for its pedestrian friendly town centre, is reputed to have derived its name from the early Christian missionary St Marnock but the town only started to grow after receiving a Royal Charter in 1592. It was here that John Wilson (buried in Old High Kirk churchyard) published the first edition of Burns' poems in 1786, the site of his printing shop being marked by a plaque in Burns Precinct off The Cross. Other associations include Laigh Kirk, the former tower remaining with the rebuilt nave of 1802, situated off Bank Street in the oldest surviving part of the town.

PLACES OF INTEREST

◆ BURNS MONUMENT - Monument to the poet with statue erected in 1879. Kay Park, Strawberrybank Road.
◆ DEAN CASTLE COUNTY PARK - 200 acre park with visitor centre, walks, rivers, children's playground. Contains Dean Castle, built around a 14th century tower house, containing armour, tapestries, musical instruments & Burns manuscripts. Dean Road.
◆ DICK INSTITUTE - Geology, archaeology & natural history collections. Local history. Art gallery. Elmbank Avenue.
◆ NISBET STONE - Stone recalling the hanging here of John Nisbet in 1683 for supporting the Covenanters at the battle of Bothwell Bridge. The Cross.
◆ REFORMERS MONUMENT - Corinthian column erected in 1885 to commemorate Scottish pioneers of Parliamentary Reform. Kay Park, Strawberrybank Road.

ENTERTAINMENT

◆ Cinemas - Queen's Drive, South East Kilmarnock off A735.
◆ Concerts - Palace Theatre, Green Street.
◆ Theatres - Palace Theatre, (as above).

SPORT & LEISURE

◆ Ice Rink - Galleon Leisure Centre, Titchfield Street.
◆ Parks & Gardens - Dean Park, Dean Road. Howard Park, Dundonald Road. Kay Park, Strawberrybank Road.
◆ Sports Centres - Galleon Leisure Centre (as above). Hunter Sports Centre, Ardbeg Avenue.
◆ Swimming Pools - Galleon Leisure Centre, (as above).
◆ Ten-Pin Bowling - The Garage, Grange Street.

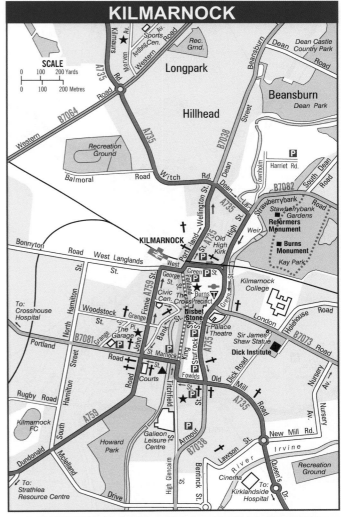

KIRKCALDY

With a historical past dating back to the 11th century, Kirkcaldy is today a thriving visitor destination with an important industrial heritage. During the 19th century, Kirkcaldy was the first town to use the power loom which would revolutionise the textile industry and it was world renowned for its manufacture of linoleum. Though little remains of this era there is still much to discover around the town. The main street that extends along the waterfront for over 4 miles gave rise to Kirkcaldy becoming known as the 'Lang toun of Fife' and even today it is still referred to as this. In the town centre the Town House dating from 1939-56 is topped by Kirkcaldy's patron, St Bryce. Near the harbour is Sailor's Walk, a row of 17th century houses restored by the National Trust for Scotland. The town has numerous famous associations; it was the birth place of the architect, Robert Adam in 1728 and Adam Smith was born here in 1723, returning later to write his influential work, 'Wealth of Nations'. Thomas Carlyle is also associated with the town for the period he spent teaching at the burgh school. In April Kirkcaldy hosts the famous Links Market along the Esplanade. Incorporating over a mile of fairground attractions and rides, the market dates from 1304 and is considered to be the longest street fair in Britain.

PLACES OF INTEREST

Tourist Information Centre (All Year)- 19 Whytescauseway. Tel: (01592) 267775
◆ BEVERIDGE PARK - Attractive park with rose gardens, children's play park, boating pond and mini farm. Abbotshall Road.
◆ KIRKCALDY MUSEUM & ART GALLERY - Exhibits a fine collection of 19th & 20th century Scottish paintings, including works by William McTaggart and the Colourist artist S J Peploe. There are also fascinating displays of local and natural history, a changing programme of exhibitions, café and shop. War Memorial Gardens.

ENTERTAINMENT

◆ Cinemas - Adam Smith Theatre, St Brycedale Avenue.
◆ Concerts - Adam Smith Theatre (as above).
◆ Theatres - Adam Smith Theatre (as above).

SPORT & LEISURE

◆ Ice Rink - Fife Ice Arena, Rosslyn Street, North East of Kirkcaldy.
◆ Parks & Gardens - Ravenscraig Park, North East of Kirkcaldy off A955. War Memorial Gardens, Kirkcaldy Station.
◆ Sports Centres - Kirkcaldy Swimming Pool, Esplanade.
◆ Swimming Pools - Kirkcaldy Swimming Pool, (as above).

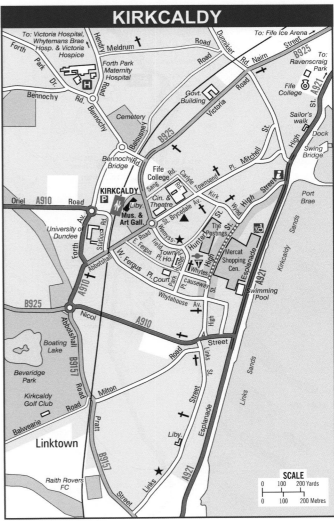

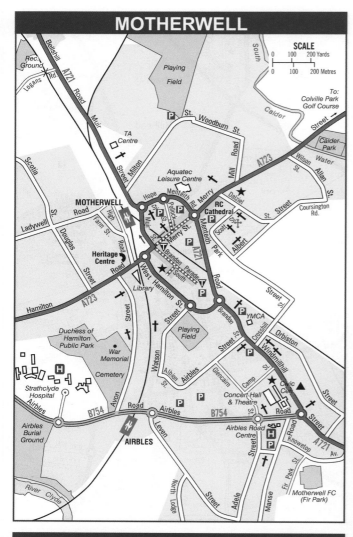

MOTHERWELL

SCALE

0 100 200 Yards

0 100 200 Metres

MOTHERWELL

Located at the head of the Clyde Valley, Motherwell is well situated to discover a remoter part of Scotland that is becoming increasingly popular as a tourist destination. The town was once famous for its iron, steel and engineering works and was home to the great Dalzell works, founded in 1871 by David Colville.

PLACES OF INTEREST

◆ MOTHERWELL HERITAGE CENTRE - Multi-media exhibition illustrates the history of Motherwell and the effects of industry on the area from the 19th century to the present day. High Road.

◆ MOTHERWELL RC CATHEDRAL - Dates from the 1870s but only became a cathedral in 1947. Coursington Road.

ENTERTAINMENT

◆ Concerts - Motherwell Concert Hall & Theatre, Windmillhill Street.

◆ Theatres - Motherwell Concert Hall & Theatre, (as above).

SPORT & LEISURE

◆ Ice Rink - Aquatec Leisure Centre, Menteith Road.

◆ Parks & Gardens - Calder Park, Merry Street. Duchess of Hamilton Public Park, Avon Road.

◆ Sports Centres - Aquatec Leisure Centre (as above).

◆ Swimming Pools - Aquatec Leisure Centre (as above).

Oban Bay

OBAN

Well situated on the shore, flanked by the island of Kerrera which provides protection against Atlantic storms, Oban is regarded as the 'unofficial capital of the West Highlands.' The town revolves around its busy port with fishing craft and leisure boats filling the harbour with colour and activity. Cruises are an important part of Oban's tourist industry and it is the main port for ferries bound for the Inner Hebrides with numerous other trips available to the islands of Coll, Tiree, Barra, South Uist, Colonsay and Islay. Returning to land, other attractions include McTavish's Kitchens on George Street which combines a restaurant with traditional Scottish entertainment including dancing and piping and an annual Seafood Festival is held in the town at the end of September. Obscured from view from the bay, the remains of Dunollie Castle to the north of Oban affords stunning views to the harbour by way of a short, but steep walk along a partially hidden path.

PLACES OF INTEREST

Tourist Information Centre (All Year) - Argyll Square. Tel: (01631) 563122

◆ MCCAIG'S TOWER - This folly dating from 1897 was commissioned by a local banker who aspired to alleviate unemployment whilst simultaneously perpetuating his own name. Though never completed, the tower stands as a monument to the McCaig family and the short walk up Jacobs Ladder to the viewing platform offers an excellent vantage point with outstanding views across the Bay to the Isle of Kerrera. Laurel Road.

◆ OBAN DISTILLERY & VISITOR CENTRE - Built in 1794, the distillery combines guided tours which reveal the ancient craft of distilling with exhibitions and an audio-visual presentation reflecting the history of Oban. Stafford Street.

◆ OBAN ROMAN CATHOLIC CATHEDRAL - Modern granite building dating from 1922, built by Sir Giles Scott. Corran Esplanade.

◆ WAR & PEACE MUSEUM - Collection of artefacts and memorabilia dating predominantly from the Second World War. North Pier.

ENTERTAINMENT

◆ Cinemas - Highland Theatre, George Street.

◆ Concerts - The Corran Halls, Corran Esplanade.

◆ Theatres - The Corran Halls (as above).

SPORT & LEISURE

◆ Parks & Gardens - Dungallan Park, Gallanach Road.

◆ Sports Centres - Atlantis Leisure, Dalriach Road.

◆ Swimming Pools - Atlantis Leisure (as above).

◆ Ten-Pin Bowling - Pro-Bowl, Shore Street.

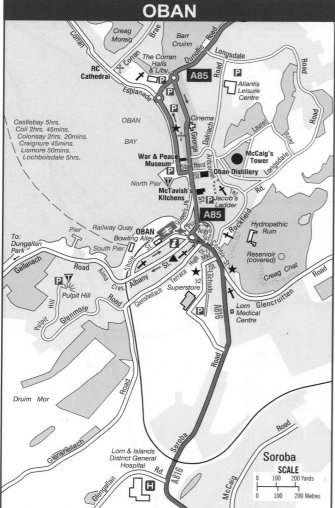

OBAN

Castlebay 5hrs.
Coll 2hrs. 45mins.
Colonsay 2hrs. 20mins.
Craignure 45mins.
Lismore 50mins.
Lochboisdale 5hrs.

SCALE

0 100 200 Yards

0 100 200 Metres

PAISLEY

With the White Cart Water flowing through the town centre, Paisley is a constantly developing town that is far more than a satellite of nearby Glasgow. Like so many other towns, Paisley flourished during the 19th century with the Industrial Revolution acting as a catalyst to providing prosperity for the town. British and French soldiers returning from India at the end of the 18th century brought with them fine Kashmir shawls which provided the inspiration for the development of a flourishing industry. The Kashmir designs were copied and Paisley soon became world renowned for its distinctively woven shawls.

PLACES OF INTEREST
Tourist Information Centre (All Year) - 9A Gilmour Street. Tel: (0141) 889 0711
◆ COATS OBSERVATORY - Dating from 1883 the displays in the centre offer an insight into the history of astronomy, astronautics and meteorology. 49 Oakshaw Street West. ◆ PAISLEY ABBEY CHURCH - A Cluniac Abbey Church originally founded in 1163, though destroyed by the English in 1307. The remaining structure dates mainly from the 15th century and within the church is displayed the Barochan Cross, a 10th century Celtic cross which is under the care of Historic Scotland. Abbey Close. ◆ PAISLEY MUSEUM & ART GALLERIES - The museum is home to the world's largest paisley shawl collection. Other exhibitions include displays on local industry and natural history. The exhibition programme in the art gallery specialises in reflecting the work of 19th century Scottish artists. High Street.
◆ PAISLEY RC CATHEDRAL - Dating from the 1870s, this cathedral church is dedicated to St Mirin, a 17th century Irish abbot who worked, died and was laid to rest here. Incle Street. ◆ PAISLEY THREAD MILL MUSEUM - Housed in part of the Mile End Mill, the collection includes artefacts and photographs of the mills from the 19th and 20th centuries. Seedhill Road. ◆ PLACE OF PAISLEY, THE - This building was originally an adjoining part of the abbey dating from 1475. Following the dissolution, it was converted to a mansion which belonged first to the Hamiltons and then to the earls of Dundonnald. After a long period of neglect, the building returned to the ownership of the church in 1903 and has since been extensively restored. Abbey Close. ◆ SMA' SHOT COTTAGES - Restored 18th century weaver's cottage furnished in period style and containing the original looms. 11-17 George Place.

ENTERTAINMENT
◆ Cinemas - Phoenix Business Park, West of Paisley.
◆ Concerts - Perth Concert Hall, Mill Street. Town Hall, Abbey Close.
◆ Theatres - Paisley Arts Centre, New Street. Town Hall (as above).
SPORT & LEISURE
◆ Ice Rink - Lagoon Leisure Centre, Mill Street.
◆ Parks & Gardens - Barshaw Park, Glasgow Road, East of Paisley. Brodie Park, Braids Road. East End Park, Seedhill Road. Fountain Gardens, Love Street. Saucehill Park, Patrick Street.
◆ Sports Centres - Lagoon Leisure Centre (as above). St Mirren Sport & Leisure Complex, Love Street located under football stands.
Swimming Pools - Lagoon Leisure Centre (as above).
◆ Ten-Pin Bowling - X S Superbowl, Wallneuk Road.

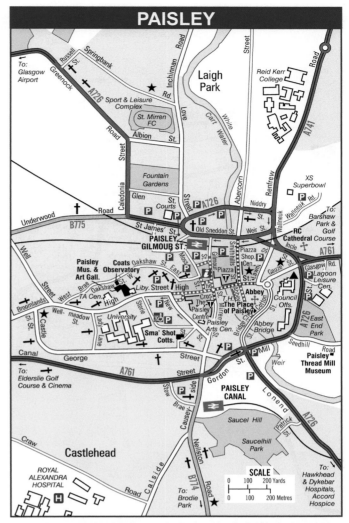

PERTH

Lying on the west bank of the River Tay, the Royal burgh of Perth is thought to have originated from a Roman camp and though there is dispute as to the validity of this, the rectangular street patterns seem to suggest that it may have been. Once the capital of Scotland, Perth was an important centre and coupled with its favourable location on the navigable River Tay, has maintained its pre-eminence as both a favourable tourist destination and busy harbour. There is a rich heritage to be discovered around the town with a diverse range of visitor and recreational attractions. The riverside North Inch Park is the notorious location of the 1936 'Battle of the Clans' when the Chattan and Kay clans fought each other to the death as a result of King Robert III unsuccessful attempt to curtail feuding between Highlanders. It was this battle that inspired Sir Walter Scott's novel, 'The Fair Maid of Perth.' The annual Perth Festival of the Arts held at the end of May encompasses the whole spectrum of performing arts and is considered to be one of the finest festivals of its kind in Scotland.

PLACES OF INTEREST
Tourist Information Centre (All Year) - Lower City Mills. Tel: (01738) 450600
◆ BLACK WATCH REGIMENTAL MUSEUM - Exhibition illustrates the history of the 42nd / 73rd Highland regiment from 1740 to the present day. Displays include silver, colours, uniforms and medals. Hay Street. ◆ FERGUSSON GALLERY - Gallery devoted to exhibiting the work of Scottish colourist painter, John Fergusson (1874-1961) who was an influential figure in the development of 20th century art in Scotland. Three galleries exhibit changing thematic displays of his work. Marshall Place. ◆ LOWER CITY MILLS - The only surviving Victorian mill in Perth that once produced porridge for prisons across Britain. West Mill Street.
◆ PERTH CATHEDRAL - Episcopal Cathedral founded in 1850 to serve the diocese of St Andrews, Dunkeld and Dunblane. North Methven Street.
◆ PERTH MUSEUM & ART GALLERY - Diverse range of displays covering fine and applied art, local and social history, natural history and archaeology. A changing programme of temporary exhibitions runs throughout the year. 78 George St.
◆ ST JOHN'S KIRK - Founded in 1126 by David I, however, much of the remaining building dates from the 15th century. Extensive restoration took place during the 19th century and in 1926 further modifications allowed for the church to house the County's war memorial. St John Street.

ENTERTAINMENT
◆ Cinemas - Murray Street.
◆ Concerts - Perth City Halls, King Edward St. St Johns Kirk, St John Street.
◆ Theatres - Perth City Halls (as above), Perth Theatre, High Street.

SPORT & LEISURE
◆ Ice Rink - Dewars Ice Rink, Glover Street.
◆ Parks & Gardens - Bellwood Park, Dundee Road. North Inch Park, Hay Street. South Inch Park, King's Place.
◆ Sports Centres - Bells Sports Centre, Hay Street.
◆ Swimming Pools - Perth Leisure Pool, Glasgow Road.

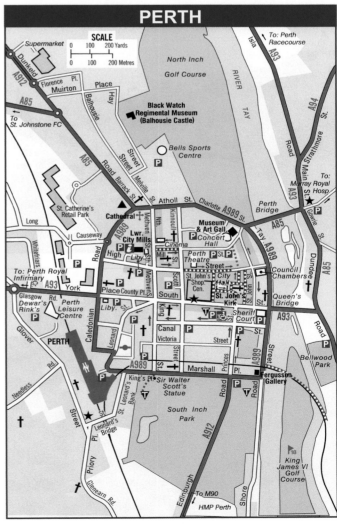

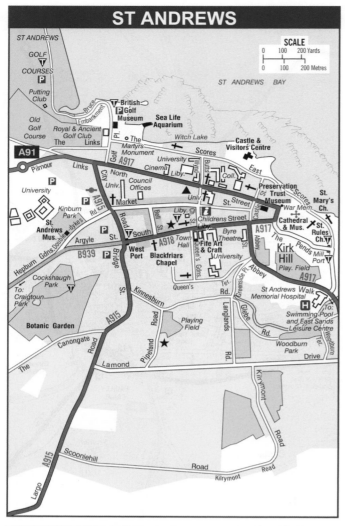

ST ANDREWS

SCALE

0   100   200 Yards
0   100   200 Metres

ST ANDREWS

According to legend, the town of St Andrews derives its name from the namesake saint whose remains were brought to this place by St Rule, a Greek monk. It was from here that a settlement developed with Celtic monks building St Mary's Church. The town became an important pilgrimage site with many people making the journey to visit the shrine of St Andrew, who became the patron saint of Scotland.

It is not only as a religious centre that St Andrews is worldly famous; it is heralded as the golfing capital of the world with numerous premier courses interspersed around the area. The game prospered in St Andrews and the Society of St Andrews Golfers was founded in 1754 to organise an annual competition, this later became known as the Royal and Ancient Golf club and today it is recognised as the governing body for the games rules in most countries. A annual golf week is held in April, which is organised by Links Golf in conjunction with the Fife Tourist Board attracting golfers from around the world.

Originally a market town, St Andrews was appointed a Royal Burgh in 1620 and is home to the oldest University in Scotland, founded in 1412 by Bishop Henry Wardlaw. St Salvator's on North Street was founded in 1450 and St Leonards dates from 1512 with the two being merged in 1747. St Mary's College founded in 1537 is home to the theology faculty. West Sands, one of Scotland's best beaches and location for some of the scenes in the film Chariots of Fire is also popular with visitors.

PLACES OF INTEREST

Tourist Information Centre (All Year) - 70 Market Street. Tel: (01334) 472021

◆ BLACKFRIARS CHAPEL - A vaulted side apse is all that remains of this 1525 chapel that was formerly part of a Dominican friary founded in 1274. South Street.

◆ BRITISH GOLF MUSEUM - The museum presents a chronological exploration of the development of golf spanning over the last 500 years. An extensive collection of golfing memorabilia is combined with explanatory displays and innovative exhibitions covering all golfing aspects including tournaments, players and the evolution of golfing equipment. Bruce Embankment.

◆ FIFE CONTEMPORARY ART & CRAFT - Formerly Crawford Art Centre located on North Street and now in a new home within the Town Hall, visitors can still enjoy a diverse range of arts activities. Exhibitions will be held at St Andrews Museum and occcasionally at the Byre Theatre. The Town Hall, Queen's Gardens.

◆ ST ANDREWS BOTANIC GARDEN - Discover a hidden treasure of almost 8000 species of ferns, herbaceous plants, shrubs and trees laid out in different areas including the Water Garden, Rock Garden and Peat Garden. The Cannongate.

◆ ST ANDREWS CASTLE & VISITOR CENTRE - (HS) Overlooking the sea are ruins of the 13th century stronghold, once belonging to the Archbishops of St Andrews. Today, notable features that remain include a 24 ft deep bottle dungeon hollowed out of solid rock from which death was the only escape, a mine and counter mine remain from a seige in 1546. The visitor centre incorporates a fascinating multi-media exhibition that illustrates the history of the castle. The Scores.

◆ ST ANDREWS CATHEDRAL & MUSEUM - (HS) Founded in 1160 by Bishop Arnold, this was once the largest cathedral in Scotland. The Cathedral museum houses an important collection of Early Christian and medieval artefacts found on the site. The Pends.

◆ ST ANDREWS MUSEUM - Housed in Kinburn House, a Victorian mansion, the museum traces the history of the St Andrews area from the Bronze Age to the present. Doubledykes Road.

◆ ST ANDREWS PRESERVATION TRUST MUSEUM - Collection reflects the social history of the burgh and includes a 1950's reconstruction of a grocery shop with period furniture, photographs and paintings. 12 North Street.

◆ ST ANDREWS SEA LIFE AQUARIUM - Over 30 aquatic habitats are incorporated to display a diverse range of native sea creatures including starfish, crabs, sharks, octopus and rays. There is a special 'Kingdom of the Seahorse' exhibition along with a seal pool and observation quay. The Scores.

◆ ST ANDREWS WEST PORT - Dating from 1589, with renovations in 1843, this is one of the few remaining city gates in Scotland. Exterior view only. South Street.

◆ ST MARY'S CHURCH - Perched on the cliff edge behind the cathedral, little remains of this cruciform church which was the earliest collegiate church in Scotland. East Scores.

◆ ST RULE'S CHURCH - Dating from the 12th century and precursor to the cathedral, St Rules Church is renowned for its 108ft tower. A small part of the chancel together with the tower is all that remains today. The Pends.

ENTERTAINMENT

◆ Cinemas - New Picture House, North Street.
◆ Concerts - Town Hall, South Street and University of St Andrews.
◆ Theatres - Byre Theatre, Abbey Street. Crawford Centre, North Street.

SPORT & LEISURE

◆ Parks & Gardens - Cockshaugh Park, Hepburn Gardens. Craigtoun Park, 2 miles South West of St Andrews.via B939. Kinburn Park, Doubledykes Road. Woodburn Park, Glebe Road.
◆ Sports Centres - East Sands Leisure Centre, St Mary Street off A917.
◆ Swimming Pool - East Sands Leisure Centre (as above).

St Andrews

St Andrews 18th Green

STIRLING

Situated on the River Forth, Stirling 'The Gateway to the Highlands' has from Medieval times been strategically regarded as the most important place in Scotland. Through time, the centrality of its location ensured that whoever held Stirling controlled the nation and it is therefore inevitable that much of Scotland's history intrinsically revolves around the ancient capital. The 13th & 14th century Wars of Independence, Wallace's victory over the English at Stirling Bridge in 1297 when he outmaneuvered the English by taking advantage of the river as a natural defence to divide the English army and force their retreat and numerous other battles were fought in close proximity to the Burgh. It was the victory at Stirling Bridge that inspired the fight for autonomy from English domination and though Wallace was later defeated at Falkirk in 1298, betrayed and brutally executed in London, his determination to free Scotland would live on. It was in 1314 that the reward came when King Robert the Bruce led his nation to freedom at the Battle of Bannockburn. An uneasy peace was born out of the 1314 victory and slowly the castle made the transition from fortification to Royal residence. Today, much of Stirling's heritage is still visible, the old town centering around Broad Street and St John's Street retains its charm with cobbled streets and numerous historic buildings. The Back Walk offers a scenic route through the town to Gowan Hill and during the summer months open top heritage bus tours operate which provide a fascinating insight into this historic town.

PLACES OF INTEREST

Tourist Information Centre (All Year) - 41 Dumbarton Road.
  Tel: (08707) 200620
Tourist Information Centre (All Year) - Castle Esplanade. Tel: (08707) 200622

◆ ARGYLL & SUTHERLAND HIGHLANDERS REGIMENTAL MUSEUM - Reflects history of the Regiment from 1794 to the present day. Displays include uniforms, paintings, a collection of medals dating from Waterloo and a realistic model of a World War 1 trench. Stirling Castle.

◆ ARGYLL'S LODGING - (HS) Built in 1630, this renaissance mansion is regarded as one of Scotland's most impressive buildings of this period. Castle Wynd.

◆ BEHEADING STONE, THE - This former execution site reflects a bygone era of gruesome capital punishment. Many important figures were slain at this site, amongst whom were Murdoch, Duke of Albany and several members of the family in 1425. Gowan Hill.

◆ KING'S KNOT - (HS) The remaining octagonal mound once formed part of a magnificent 17th century formal knot garden below the castle. King's Park.

◆ LADIES ROCK - Once a popular vantage point for the ladies of the court to watch the Royal Tournaments, the rock allows panoramic views across to the Trossachs and Ben Lomond. Valley Cemetery.

◆ MARS WARK - (HS) Standing at the head of the town, this renaissance building was commisioned by the Earl of Mar in 1569 and would have been built using stone from the ruined Cambuskenneth Abbey. It was damaged by cannon fire during the 1740's and the shell is all that remains. Castle Wynd.

◆ STAR PYRAMID - Monument in memory of Martyrs seeking religious freedom. Castle Wynd.

◆ STIRLING CASTLE - (HS) Perched 250ft on a rocky precipice commanding a dominant position over the burgh, Stirling Castle is the grandest of all Scottish castles both in location and architecture. Favoured Royal residence of the Stuart Monarchs, it stands as the focal point of Stirlings turbulent history. Upper Castle Hill.

◆ STIRLING CHURCH OF THE HOLY RUDE - Church where coronation of James VI was conducted in 1567. St John Street.

◆ STIRLING GUILDHALL - Known also as Cowane's Hospital, the guildhall was built between 1634 & 1649 by John Cowane to provide for the aged members of the Guild of Merchants. Outside is a statue of its founder.

◆ STIRLING MERCAT CROSS - The Mercat Cross in Broad Street was once the focal point of the town's trading activity. The unicorn figure on top of the cross is known locally as 'the puggy'. Broad Street.

◆ STIRLING OLD BRIDGE - (HS) Dating from 1400, this bridge was once of strategic importance as the most southerly crossing point across the River.

◆ STIRLING OLD TOWN JAIL - An authentic Victorian jail with fascinating tours where you can meet all the characters of prison life including Stirling's fearsome executioner! Prison Life exhibition, audio tour, souvenir and gift shop. St John Street.

◆ STIRLING SMITH ART GALLERY & MUSEUM - Award winning museum & gallery presents a diverse exhibition programme along with a permanent collection of fine art. Dumbarton Road.

◆ STIRLING VISITOR CENTRE - Exhibitions reflect the history of Stirling from the Wars of Independence through to the modern day. Castle Esplanade.

ENTERTAINMENT
◆ Cinemas - Allan Park.
◆ Concerts - Albert Halls, Dumbarton Road.
◆ Theatres - Tolbooth Theatre, Broad Street.

SPORT AND LEISURE
◆ Ice Rink - Williamfield, south of stirling.
◆ Parks & Gardens - Royal Gardens, Dumbarton Road. King's Park (Stirling Golf Club),Queens Road.
◆ Sports Centres - Rainbow Slides Leisure Centre, Goosecroft Road.
◆ Swimming Pool & Leisure Centre - Rainbow Slides Leisure Centre (as above).
◆ Ten Pin Bowling - AMF Bowling, Forth Street.

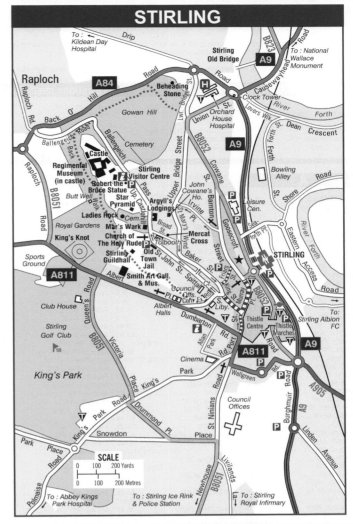

View from Stirling Castle

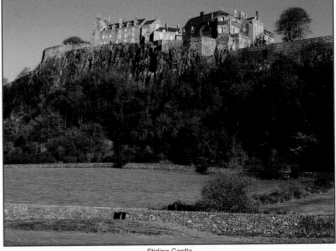
Stirling Castle

INDEX TO CITIES, TOWNS, VILLAGES, HAMLETS & LOCATIONS

(1) A strict alphabetical order is used e.g. Bailemeonach follows Baile Glas but precedes Baile Mhanaich.

(2) The map reference given refers to the actual map square in which the town spot or built-up area is located and not to the place name.

(3) Where two or more places of the same name occur in the same County or Unitary Authority, the nearest large town is also given; e.g. Achiemore. *High* . . . 2E **57** (nr. Durness) indicates that Achiemore is located in square 2E on page **57** and is situated near Durness in the Unitary Authority of Highland.

(4) Major towns are shown in bold, i.e. **Aberdeen.** *Aber* . . . . 3E **43** & **69**. Where they appear on a Town Plan a second page reference is given.

COUNTIES AND UNITARY AUTHORITIES with the abbreviations used in this index

Aberdeen : *Aber*
Aberdeenshire : *Abers*
Angus : *Ang*
Argyll & Bute : *Arg*
Clackmannanshire : *Clac*
Cumbria : *Cumb*
Dumfries & Galloway : *Dum*
Dundee : *D'dee*
East Ayrshire : *E Ayr*
East Dunbartonshire : *E Dun*
East Lothian : *E Lot*
East Renfrewshire : *E Ren*
Edinburgh : *Edin*
Falkirk : *Falk*
Fife : *Fife*
Glasgow : *Glas*
Highland : *High*
Inverclyde : *Inv*
Midlothian : *Midl*
Moray : *Mor*
North Ayrshire : *N Ayr*
North Lanarkshire : *N Lan*
Northumberland : *Nmbd*
Orkney : *Orkn*
Perth & Kinross : *Per*
Renfrewshire : *Ren*
Scottish Borders : *Bord*
Shetland : *Shet*
South Ayrshire : *S Ayr*
South Lanarkshire : *S Lan*
Stirling : *Stir*
West Dunbartonshire : *W Dun*
Western Isles : *W Isl*
West Lothian : *W Lot*

A

Abbey St Bathans. Bord 2E 21
Abbey Town. Cumb 3E 7
Aberarder. High 1H 39
Aberargie. Per 2C 26
Aberchalder. High 3E 39
Aberchirder. Abers 3B 50
Abercorn. W Lot 1F 19
Abercrombie. Fife 3G 27
Aberdalgie. Per 1B 26
Aberdeen. Aber 3E 43 & 69
Aberdeen (Dyce) Airport. Aber 2D 42
Aberdour. Fife 5C 26
Aberfeldy. Per 4D 32
Aberfoyle. Stir 3E 25
Aberlady. E Lot 1B 20
Aberlemno. Ang 3C 34
Abernethy. Per 2C 26
Abernyte. Per 5H 33
Aberuthven. Per 2A 26
Abhainn Suidhe. W Isl 4B 62
Abington. S Lan 1G 11
Aboyne. Abers 4A 42
Abriachan. High 5G 47
Abronhill. N Lan 1C 18
Abune-the-Hill. Orkn 2B 64
Acairseid. W Isl 4C 60
Acha. Arg 3C 28
Achachork. High 4D 44
Achahoish. Arg 1A 16
Achaleven. Arg 5C 30
Achallader. Arg 4G 31
Acha Mor. W Isl 2E 62
Achanalt. High 2D 46
Achandunie. High 1H 47
Ach'an Todhair. High 1D 30
Achany. High 3C 54
Achaphubuil. High 1D 30
Acharacle. High 2H 29
Acharn. Ang 1H 33
Acharn. Per 4C 32
Acharole. High 3F 59
Achateny. High 2G 29
Achavanich. High 4E 59
Achdalieu. High 1D 30
Achduart. High 3F 53
Achentoul. High 5B 58
Achfary. High 5D 56
Achfrish. High 2C 54
Achgarve. High 4D 52
Achiemore. High 2E 57 (nr. Durness)
Achiemore. High 3B 58 (nr. Thurso)
A'Chill. High 3B 36
Achiltibuie. High 3F 53
Achina. High 2A 58
Achinahuagh. High 2G 57
Achindarroch. High 3D 30
Achinduich. High 3C 54
Achinduin. Arg 5B 30
Achininver. High 2G 57
Achintee. High 4A 46
Achintraid. High 5H 45
Achleck. Arg 4F 29
Achlorachan. High 3E 47
Achluachrach. High 5D 38
Achlyness. High 3D 56
Achmelvich. High 1F 53
Achmony. High 5G 47
Achmore. High 5H 45 (nr. Stromeferry)
Achmore. High 4F 53 (nr. Ullapool)
Achnacarnin. High 5B 56
Achnacarry. High 5C 38
Achnaclerach. High 2F 47
Achnacloich. High 3E 37
Achnaconeran. High 2F 39
Achnacroish. Arg 4B 30
Achnafalnich. Arg 1B 24
Achnagarron. High 1H 47
Achnaha. High 2F 29
Achnahanat. High 4C 54
Achnahannet. High 1C 40
Achnairn. High 2C 54
Achnamara. Arg 5E 23
Achnanellan. High 5B 38
Achnangoul. Arg 3H 23
Achnasheen. High 3C 46
Achnashellach. High 4B 46
Achosnich. High 2F 29
Achow. High 5F 59
Achranich. High 4A 30
Achreamie. High 2D 58
Achriabhach. High 2E 31
Achriesgill. High 3D 56
Achrimsdale. High 3G 55
Achscrabster. High 2D 58
Achtoty. High 2H 57
Achuvoldrach. High 3G 57
Achvaich. High 4E 55
Achvoan. High 3E 55
Ackergill. High 3G 59
Ackergillshore. High 3G 59
Adabroc. W Isl 1K 63
Addiewell. W Lot 2E 19
Addinston. Bord 3C 20
Advie. High 5E 49
Adziel. Abers 3E 51
Ae. Dum 5G 11
Affleck. Abers 1D 42
Affric Lodge. High 1C 38
Aglionby. Cumb 3H 7
Aiginis. W Isl 4J 63
Aikers. Orkn 5D 64
Aiketgate. Cumb 4H 7
Aikhead. Cumb 4F 7
Aikton. Cumb 3F 7
Aird. Arg 3C 23
Aird. Dum 2B 4
Aird. High 1G 45
Aird. W Isl 5H 61 (on Benbecula)
Aird. W Isl 4K 63 (on Isle of Lewis)
Aird a Mhachair. W Isl 6H 61
Aird a Mhulaidh. W Isl 3C 62
Aird Asaig. W Isl 4C 62
Aird Dhail. W Isl 1J 63
Airdens. High 4D 54
Airdeny. Arg 1G 23
Aird Mhidhinis. W Isl 4C 60
Aird Mhighe. W Isl 5C 62 (nr. Ceann a Bhaigh)
Aird Mhighe. W Isl 6B 62 (nr. Fionnsabhagh)
Aird Mhor. W Isl 4C 60 (on Barra)
Aird Mhor. W Isl 6J 61 (on South Uist)
Aird of Sleat. High 3E 37
Airdrie. N Lan 2C 18
Aird Shleibhe. W Isl 6C 62
Aird, The. High 3D 44
Aird Thunga. W Isl 4J 63
Aird Uig. W Isl 1B 62
Airidh a Bhruaich. W Isl 3D 62
Airies. Dum 2A 4
Airntully. Per 5F 33
Airor. High 3G 37
Airth. Falk 5A 26
Aisgernis. W Isl 2C 60
Aith. Shet 3K 67 (on Fetlar)
Aith. Shet 1C 66 (on Mainland)
Aithsetter. Shet 3D 66
Akeld. Nmbd 5G 21
Alcaig. High 3G 47
Aldclune. Per 2E 33
Aldochlay. Arg 4C 24
Aldoth. Cumb 4E 7
Alexandria. W Dun 5C 24
Alford. Abers 2A 42
Aline Lodge. W Isl 3C 62
Alladale Lodge. High 5B 54
Allanbank. N Lan 3D 18
Allanton. N Lan 3D 18
Allanton. Bord 3F 21
Allerby. Cumb 5D 6
Alligin Shuas. High 3H 45
Alloa. Clac 4H 25
Allonby. Cumb 4D 6
Alloway. S Ayr 2A 10
Alltgobhlach. N Ayr 4B 16
Alltnacaillich. High 4F 57
Allt na h-Airbhe. High 4G 53
Alltour. High 5D 38
Alltsigh. High 2F 39
Almondbank. Per 1B 26
Alness. High 2H 47
Alnessferry. High 2H 47
Altandhu. High 2E 53
Altanduin. High 1F 55
Altass. High 3B 54
Alterwall. High 2F 59
Altgaltraig. Arg 1D 16
Altnabreac. High 4D 58
Altnacealgach. High 2H 53
Altnafeadh. High 3F 31
Altnaharra. High 5G 57
Altonhill. E Ayr 5H 17
Altrua. High 4D 38
Alva. Clac 4H 25
Alves. Mor 2E 49
Alvie. High 3B 40
Alwinton. Nmbd 3H 13
Alyth. Per 4H 33
Amatnatua. High 4B 54
Am Baile. W Isl 3C 60
Amisfield. Dum 5H 11
Amulree. Per 5E 33
Anaheilt. High 2B 30
An Cnoc. W Isl 4J 63
An Cnoc Ard. W Isl 1K 63
An Coroghon. High 3B 36
Ancroft. Nmbd 4H 21
Ancrum. Bord 1F 13
Angerton. Cumb 3F 7
An Gleann Ur. W Isl 4J 63
Ankerville. High 1B 48
An Leth Meadhanach. W Isl 3C 60
Annan. Dum 2F 7
Annat. Arg 1H 23
Annat. High 3H 45
Annathill. N Lan 1C 18
Annbank. S Ayr 1B 10
Anston. S Lan 4F 19
Anstruther Easter. Fife 3G 27
Anstruther Wester. Fife 3G 27
Anthorn. Cumb 3E 7
An t-Ob. W Isl 6B 62
Anwoth. Dum 3G 5
Appin. Arg 4C 30
Applecross. High 4G 45
Applegarthtown. Dum 5A 12
Applethwaite. Cumb 5F 7
Appletreehall. Bord 2E 13
Arabella. High 1B 48
Arbeadie. Abers 4B 42
Arbirlot. Ang 4D 34
Arbroath. Ang 4D 34
Arbuthnott. Abers 1F 35
Arcan. High 3G 47
Archargary. High 3A 58
Archiestown. Mor 4F 49
Ardachu. High 3D 54
Ardalanish. Arg 2A 22
Ardaneaskan. High 5H 45
Ardarroch. High 5H 45
Ardbeg. Arg 5A 24 (nr. Dunoon)
Ardbeg. Arg 4F 15 (on Islay)
Ardbeg. Arg 2D 16 (on Isle of Bute)
Ardcharnich. High 5G 53
Ardchiavaig. Arg 2A 22
Ardchonnell. Arg 2G 23
Ardchrishnish. Arg 1B 22
Ardchronie. High 5D 54
Ardchullarie. Stir 2E 25
Ardchyle. Stir 1E 25
Ard-dhubh. High 4G 45
Ardechive. High 4C 38
Ardelve. High 1H 37
Arden. Arg 5C 24
Ardendrain. High 5G 47
Ardentinny. Arg 5A 24
Ardeonaig. Stir 5B 32
Ardersier. High 3A 48
Ardery. High 2A 30
Ardessie. High 5F 53
Ardfern. Arg 3F 23
Ardfernal. Arg 1G 15
Ardfin. Arg 2F 15
Ardgartan. Arg 3B 24
Ardgay. High 4C 54
Ardgour. High 2D 30
Ardheslaig. High 3G 45
Ardindrean. High 5G 53
Ardlamont House. Arg 2C 16
Ardler. Per 4H 33
Ardlui. Arg 2C 24
Ardlussa. Arg 5D 22
Ardmair. High 4G 53
Ardmay. Arg 3B 24
Ardminish. Arg 4H 15
Ardmolich. High 1A 30
Ardmore. High 3D 56 (nr. Kinlochbervie)
Ardmore. High 5E 55 (nr. Tain)
Ardnacross. Arg 4G 29
Ardnadam. Arg 5A 24
Ardnagrask. High 4G 47
Ardnamurach. High 4H 37
Ardnarff. High 5H 45
Ardnastang. High 2B 30
Ardoch. Per 5F 33
Ardochy House. High 3D 38
Ardpatrick. Arg 2A 16
Ardrishaig. Arg 5F 23
Ardroag. High 4B 44
Ardross. High 1H 47
Ardrossan. N Ayr 4F 17
Ardshealach. High 2H 29
Ardslignish. High 2G 29
Ardtalla. Arg 3F 15
Ardtalnaig. Per 5C 32
Ardtoe. High 1H 29
Arduaine. Arg 2E 23
Ardullie. High 2G 47
Ardvasar. High 3F 37
Ardvorlich. Per 1F 25
Ardwell. Dum 4C 4
Ardwell. Mor 5G 49
Arean. High 1H 29
Aridhglas. Arg 1A 22
Arinacrinachd. High 3G 45
Arinagour. Arg 3D 28
Arisaig. High 5F 37
Ariundle. High 2B 30
Arivegaig. High 2H 29
Armadale. High 2A 58
Armadale. W Lot 2E 19
Armathwaite. Cumb 4H 7
Arncroach. Fife 3G 27
Arnicle. Arg 5A 16
Arnisdale. High 2H 37
Arnish. High 4E 45
Arniston. Midl 2A 20
Arnol. W Isl 3H 63
Arnprior. Stir 4F 25
Aros Mains. Arg 4G 29
Arpafeelie. High 3H 47
Arrochar. Arg 3B 24
Arscaig. High 2C 54
Artafallie. High 4H 47
Arthrath. Abers 5E 51
Arthurstone. Per 4H 33
Ascog. Arg 2E 17
Ashfield. Stir 3G 25
Ashgill. S Lan 4C 18
Ashgrove. Mor 2F 49
Ashkirk. Bord 1D 12
Ashton. Inv 1F 17
Aspatria. Cumb 4E 7
Astle. High 4E 55
Athelstaneford. E Lot 1C 20
Attadale. High 5A 46
Aucharnie. Abers 4B 50
Auchattie. Abers 4B 42
Auchavan. Ang 2G 33
Auchbreck. Mor 1F 41
Auchenback. E Ren 3A 18
Auchenblae. Abers 1E 35
Auchenbrack. Dum 4E 11
Auchenbreck. Arg 5H 23
Auchencairn. Dum 3A 6 (nr. Dalbeattie)
Auchencairn. Dum 5G 11 (nr. Dumfries)
Auchencarroch. W Dun 5D 24
Auchencrow. Bord 2F 21
Auchendennan. W Dun 5C 24
Auchendinny. Midl 2H 19
Auchengray. S Lan 3E 19
Auchenhalrig. Mor 2G 49
Auchenheath. S Lan 4D 18
Auchenlochan. Arg 1C 16
Auchenmade. N Ayr 4G 17
Auchenmalg. Dum 3D 4
Auchentiber. N Ayr 4G 17
Auchenvennel. Arg 5B 24
Auchindrain. Arg 3H 23
Auchininna. Abers 4B 50
Auchinleck. Dum 1F 5
Auchinleck. E Ayr 1C 10
Auchinloch. N Lan 1B 18
Auchinstarry. N Lan 1C 18
Auchleven. Abers 1B 42
Auchlochan. S Lan 5D 18
Auchlunachan. High 5G 53
Auchmillan. E Ayr 1C 10
Auchmithie. Ang 4D 34
Auchmuirbridge. Per 3D 26
Auchmull. Ang 1C 34
Auchnacree. Ang 2B 34
Auchnafree. Per 5D 32
Auchnagallin. High 5D 48
Auchnagatt. Abers 4E 51
Aucholzie. Abers 4G 41
Auchreddie. Abers 4D 50
Auchterarder. Per 2A 26
Auchteraw. High 3E 39
Auchterderran. Fife 4D 26
Auchterhouse. Ang 5A 34
Auchtermuchty. Fife 2D 26
Auchterneed. High 3F 47
Auchtertool. Fife 4D 26
Auchtertyre. High 1H 37
Auchtubh. Stir 1E 25
Auckengill. High 2G 59
Auds. Abers 2B 50
Auldearn. High 3C 48
Auldgirth. Dum 5G 11
Auldhouse. S Lan 3B 18
Ault a' chruinn. High 1A 38
Aultbea. High 5D 52
Aultdearg. High 2D 46
Aultgrishan. High 5C 52
Aultguish Inn. High 1E 47
Aultibea. High 1H 55
Aultiphurst. High 2B 58
Aultivullin. High 2B 58
Aultmore. Mor 3H 49
Aultnamain Inn. High 5D 54
Avielochan. High 2C 40
Aviemore. High 2B 40 & 70
Avoch. High 3A 48
Avonbridge. Falk 1E 19
Ayr. S Ayr 1A 10 & 70
Ayres of Selivoe. Shet 2B 66
Ayton. Bord 2G 21
Aywick. Shet 4J 67

B

Bac. W Isl 3J 63
Backaland. Orkn 1E 64
Backaskaill. Orkn 2G 65
Backfolds. Abers 3F 51
Backhill. Abers 5C 50
Backhill of Clackriach. Abers 4E 51
Backies. High 3F 55
Backmuir of New Gilston. Fife 3F 27
Back of Keppoch. High 5F 37
Badachonacher. High 1H 47
Badachro. High 1G 45
Badanloch Lodge. High 5A 58
Badavanich. High 3C 46
Badcall. High 3D 56
Badcaul. High 4F 53
Baddidarach. High 1F 53
Baddoch. Abers 5E 41
Badenscallie. High 3F 53
Badenscoth. Abers 5C 50
Badentarbat. High 2F 53
Badicaul. High 1G 37
Badlipster. High 4E 59
Badluarach. High 4E 53
Badnaban. High 1F 53
Badnabay. High 4D 56
Badnagie. High 5E 59
Badnellan. High 3F 55
Badninish. High 4E 55
Badrallach. High 4F 53
Bàgh a Chàise. W Isl 3K 61
Bàgh a' Chaisteil. W Isl 5B 60
Baghasdal. W Isl 3C 60
Bagh Mor. W Isl 5J 61
Bagh Shiarabhagh. W Isl 4C 60
Baile. W Isl 2K 61
Baile Ailein. W Isl 2D 62
Baile an Truiseil. W Isl 2H 63
Baile Boidheach. Arg 1A 16
Baile Glas. W Isl 5J 61
Bailemeonach. Arg 4H 29
Baile Mhanaich. W Isl 5H 61
Baile Mhartainn. W Isl 3H 61
Baile MhicPhail. W Isl 3J 61
Baile Mor. Arg 3A 22
Baile Mor. W Isl 4H 61
Baile nan Cailleach. W Isl 5H 61
Baile Raghaill. W Isl 4H 61
Baileyhead. Cumb 5E 13
Bailiesward. Abers 5H 49
Bail' Iochdrach. W Isl 5J 61
Baillieston. Glas 2B 18
Bail' Uachdraich. W Isl 4J 61
Bail Ur Tholastaidh. W Isl 3K 63
Bainsford. Falk 5H 25
Bainshole. Abers 5B 50
Baintown. Fife 3E 27
Balachuirn. High 4E 45
Balbeg. High 5F 47 (nr. Cannich)
Balbeg. High 1F 39 (nr. Loch Ness)
Balbeggie. Per 1C 26
Balblair. High 4C 54 (nr. Bonar Bridge)
Balblair. High 2A 48 (nr. Invergordon)
Balblair. High 4G 47 (nr. Inverness)
Balcathie. Ang 5D 34
Balchladich. High 5B 56
Balchraggan. High 4G 47
Balchrick. High 3C 56
Balcurvie. Fife 3E 27
Baldinnie. Fife 2F 27
Baldwinholme. Cumb 3G 7
Balearn. Abers 3F 51
Balemartine. Arg 4A 28
Balephretrish. Arg 4B 28
Balephuil. Arg 4A 28
Balerno. Edin 2G 19
Balevullin. Arg 4A 28
Balfield. Ang 2C 34
Balfour. Orkn 3D 64
Balfron. Stir 5E 25
Balgaveny. Abers 4B 50
Balgonar. Fife 4B 26
Balgowan. High 4H 39
Balgown. High 2C 44
Balgrochan. E Dun 1B 18
Balgy. High 3H 45
Balhalgardy. Abers 1C 42
Baliasta. Shet 2K 67
Baligill. High 2B 58
Balintore. Ang 3H 33
Balintore. High 1B 48
Balintraid. High 1A 48
Balkeerie. Ang 4A 34
Ballachulish. High 3D 30
Ballantrae. S Ayr 5F 9
Ballater. Abers 4G 41
Ballencrieff. E Lot 1B 20
Ballencrieff Toll. W Lot 1E 19
Ballentoul. Per 2D 32
Balliemore. Arg 5H 23 (nr. Dunoon)
Balliemore. Arg 1F 23 (nr. Oban)
Ballieward. High 5D 48
Ballimore. Stir 2E 25
Ballingry. Fife 4C 26
Ballinluig. Per 3E 33
Ballintuim. Per 3G 33
Balliveolan. Arg 4B 30
Balloan. High 3C 54
Balloch. High 4A 48
Balloch. N Lan 1C 18
Balloch. Per 2H 25
Balloch. W Dun 5C 24
Ballochan. Abers 4A 42
Ballochgoy. Arg 2D 16
Ballochmyle. E Ayr 1C 10
Ballochroy. Arg 3A 16
Ballygown. Arg 4F 29
Ballygrant. Arg 2E 15
Ballymichael. N Ayr 5C 16
Balmacara. High 1H 37
Balmaclellan. Dum 1H 5
Balmacqueen. High 1D 44
Balmaha. Stir 4D 24
Balmalcolm. Fife 3E 27
Balmalloch. N Lan 1C 18
Balmeanach. High 5E 45
Balmedie. Abers 2E 43
Balmerino. Fife 1E 27
Balmore. E Dun 1B 18
Balmore. High 4B 44
Balmuir. Ang 5B 34
Balmullo. Fife 1F 27
Balmurrie. Dum 2D 4
Balnaboth. Ang 2A 34
Balnabruaich. High 1A 48
Balnabruich. High 1E 59
Balnacoil. High 2F 55
Balnacra. High 4A 46
Balnacroft. Abers 4F 41
Balnageith. Mor 3D 48
Balnaglaic. High 5F 47
Balnagrantach. High 5F 47
Balnaguard. Per 3E 33
Balnahard. Arg 4B 22
Balnain. High 5F 47
Balnakeil. High 2E 57
Balnaknock. High 2D 44
Balnamoon. Abers 3E 51
Balnamoon. Ang 2C 34
Balnapaling. High 2A 48
Balornock. Glas 2B 18
Balquhidder. Stir 1E 25
Baltasound. Shet 2K 67
Baltersan. Dum 2F 5
Balthangie. Abers 3D 50
Balvaird. High 3G 47
Balvaird. Per 2C 26
Balvenie. Mor 4G 49
Balvicar. Arg 2E 23
Balvraid. High 2H 37
Balvraid Lodge. High 5B 48
Banavie. High 1E 31
Banchory. Abers 4B 42
Banchory-Devenick. Abers 3E 43
Banff. Abers 2B 50
Bankend. Dum 2D 6
Bankfoot. Per 5F 33
Bankglen. E Ayr 2C 10
Bankhead. Aber 2D 42
Bankhead. Abers 3B 42
Bankhead. S Lan 4D 18
Banknock. Falk 1C 18
Bankshill. Dum 5A 12
Banniskirk. High 3E 59
Bannockburn. Stir 4H 25
Banton. N Lan 1C 18
Barabhas. W Isl 2H 63
Barabhas Iarach. W Isl 3H 63
Baramore. High 1H 29
Barassie. S Ayr 5G 17
Baravullin. Arg 4C 30
Barbaraville. High 1A 48
Barbhas Uarach. W Isl 2H 63
Barbieston. S Ayr 2B 10
Barcaldine. Arg 4C 30
Barclose. Cumb 2H 7
Bardister. Shet 5G 67
Bardnabeinne. High 4E 55
Bardowie. E Dun 1A 18
Bardrainney. Inv 1G 17
Barelees. Nmbd 5F 21
Bargeddie. N Lan 2C 18
Bargrennan. Dum 1E 5
Barharrow. Dum 3H 5
Barlanark. Glas 2B 18
Barmoor. Nmbd 5H 21
Barmulloch. Glas 2B 18
Barnbarroch. Dum 3B 6
Barnhead. Ang 3D 34
Barnhill. D'dee 5B 34
Barnhill. Mor 3E 49
Barnhill. Per 1C 26

Barnhills. Dum 1A 4
Barony, The. Orkn 2B 64
Barr. Dum 3E 11
Barr. S Ayr 4H 9
Barra Airport. W Isl 4C 60
Barrachan. Dum 4E 5
Barraglom. W Isl 1C 62
Barrahormid. Arg 5E 23
Barrapol. Arg 4A 28
Barravullin. Arg 3F 23
Barrhead. E Ren 3A 18
Barrhill. S Ayr 5H 9
Barrmill. N Ayr 3G 17
Barrock. High 1F 59
Barrowburn. Nmbd 2H 13
Barry. Ang 5C 34
Barthol Chapel. Abers 5D 50
Barton. Cumb 5H 7
Bassendean. Bord 4D 20
Bassenthwaite. Cumb 5F 7
Basta. Shet 3J 67
Bathgate. W Lot 2E 19
Bathville. W Lot 2E 19
Bauds of Cullen. Mor 2H 49
Baugh. Arg 4B 28
Beacrabhaicg. W Isl 5C 62
Beal. Nmbd 4H 21
Beaquoy. Orkn 2C 64
Bearsden. E Dun 1A 18
Beattock. Dum 3H 11
Beauly. High 4G 47
Beaumont. Cumb 3G 7
Beckfoot. Cumb 4D 6
Bedrule. Bord 2F 13
Beeswing. Dum 2B 6
Beinn Casgro. W Isl 5J 63
Beith. N Ayr 3G 17
Belfatton. Abers 3F 51
Belford. Nmbd 5H 21
Belhaven. E Lot 1D 20
Belhelvie. Abers 2E 43
Belhinnie. Abers 1H 41
Bellabeg. Abers 2G 41
Belladrum. High 4G 47
Bellamore. S Ayr 5H 9
Bellanoch. Arg 4F 23
Belleheiglash. Mor 5E 49
Belle Vue. Cumb 5E 7
Bellfield. S Lan 5D 18
Belliehill. Ang 2C 34
Bellingham. Nmbd 5H 13
Bellochantuy. Arg 5H 15
Bellsbank. E Ayr 3B 10
Bellshill. N Lan 3C 18
Bellshill. Nmbd 5H 21
Bellside. N Lan 3D 18
Bellspool. Bord 5G 19
Bellsquarry. W Lot 2F 19
Belmaduthy. High 3H 47
Belmont. Shet 2J 67
Belmont. S Ayr 2A 10
Belnacraig. Abers 2G 41
Belston. S Ayr 1A 10
Belts of Collonach. Abers 4B 42
Bemersyde. Bord 5C 20
Ben Alder Lodge. High 1A 32
Ben Armine Lodge. High 2E 55
Benbecula Airport. W Isl 5H 61
Benbuie. Dum 4E 11
Benderloch. Arg 5C 30
Bendronaig Lodge. High 5B 46
Benera. High 1H 37
Benholm. Abers 2F 35
Benmore Lodge. High 2A 54
Bennecarnigan. N Ayr 1E 9
Benston. Shet 1D 66
Benstonhall. Orkn 1E 64
Bent. Abers 1D 34
Benthoul. Aber 3D 42
Bentpath. Dum 4C 12
Bents. W Lot 2E 19
Benvie. D'dee 5A 34
Beoraidbeg. High 4F 37
Bernice. Arg 4A 24
Bernisdale. High 3D 44
Berriedale. High 1H 55
Berrier. Cumb 5H 7
Berrington. Nmbd 4H 21
Berrington Law. Nmbd 4G 21
Berryhillock. Mor 2A 50
Berryscaur. Dum 4A 12
Berwick-upon-Tweed.
Nmbd 3H 21
Betishill. N Lan 2C 18
Bettyhill. High 2A 58
Beul an Atha. Arg 2E 15
Bewaldeth. Cumb 5F 7
Bhalton. W Isl 1B 62
Bhatarsaigh. W Isl 5B 60
Bieldside. Aber 3D 42
Biggar. S Lan 5F 19
Biggings. Shet 1A 66
Bighouse. High 2B 58
Biglands. Cumb 3F 7
Big Sand. High 1G 45
Bigton. Shet 4C 66
Bilbster. High 3F 59
Bilston. Midl 2H 19
Bimbister. Orkn 3C 64
Bindal. High 5G 55
Binniehill. Falk 1D 18
Birchburn. N Ayr 1E 9
Birchview. Mor 5E 49
Birdston. E Dun 1B 18
Birgham. Bord 5E 21
Birichen. High 4E 55
Birkby. Cumb 5D 6
Birkenhills. Abers 4C 50
Birkenshaw. N Lan 2B 18
Birkhall. Abers 4G 41
Birkhill. Ang 5A 34
Birnam. Per 4F 33
Birsay. Orkn 2B 64
Birse. Abers 4A 42
Birsemore. Abers 4A 42
Birtley. Nmbd 5H 13
Bishopbriggs. E Dun 1B 18
Bishopmill. Mor 2F 49
Bishopton. Dum 4F 5
Bishopton. Ren 1H 17
Bixter. Shet 1C 66
Blackburn. Abers 2D 42
Blackburn. W Lot 2E 19
Black Clauchrie. S Ayr 5H 9
Black Corries. High 3F 31
Black Crofts. Arg 5C 30
Blackdog. Abers 2E 43
Blackdyke. Cumb 3E 7
Blackford. Cumb 2G 7
Blackford. Per 3H 25
Blackhall. Edin 1H 19
Blackhall. Ren 2H 17
Blackhill. Abers 4F 51
Blackhill. High 3C 44
Blackhills. Abers 2E 51
Blackhills. High 3C 48
Blacklunans. Per 2G 33
Black Mount. Arg 4F 31
Blackness. Falk 1F 19
Blackpool Gate. Cumb 5E 13
Blackridge. W Lot 2E 19
Blackrock. Arg 2E 15
Blackshaw. Dum 2D 6
Blacktop. Aber 3D 42
Blackwaterfoot. N Ayr 1D 8
Blackwood. Dum 5G 11
Blackwood. S Lan 4C 18
Bladnoch. Dum 3F 5
Blaich. High 1D 30
Blain. High 2H 29
Blair Atholl. Per 2D 32
Blair Drummond. Stir 4G 25
Blairgowrie. Per 4G 33
Blairhall. Fife 5B 26
Blairingone. Per 4A 26
Blairlogie. Stir 4H 25
Blairmore. Abers 5H 49
Blairmore. Arg 5A 24
Blairmore. High 3C 56
Blairquhanan. W Dun 5D 24
Blandy. High 3H 57
Blanefield. Stir 1A 18
Blantyre. S Lan 3B 18
Blarmachfoldach. High 2D 30
Blarnalearoch. High 4G 53
Blathaisbhal. W Isl 3J 61
Blebocraigs. Fife 2F 27
Blencogo. Cumb 4E 7
Blennerhasset. Cumb 4E 7
Blindburn. Nmbd 2H 13
Blindcrake. Cumb 5E 7
Blitterlees. Cumb 3E 7
Bloomfield. Bord 1E 13
Blyth. Bord 4G 19
Blyth Bank. Bord 4G 19
Blyth Bridge. Bord 4G 19
Boarhills. Fife 2G 27
Boath. High 1G 47
Boat of Garten. High 2C 40
Boddam. Abers 4G 51
Boddam. Shet 5C 66
Bogallan. High 3H 47
Bogbrae Croft. Abers 5F 51
Bogend. S Ayr 5G 17
Boghall. Midl 2H 19
Boghall. W Lot 2E 19
Boghead. S Lan 4C 18
Bogindollo. Ang 3B 34
Bogmoor. Mor 2G 49
Bogniebrae. Abers 4A 50
Bograxie. Abers 2C 42
Bogside. N Lan 3D 18
Bogton. Abers 3B 50
Bogue. Dum 5D 10
Bohenie. High 5D 38
Boirseam. W Isl 6B 62
Boleside. Bord 5B 20
Bolshan. Ang 3D 34
Boltachan. Per 3D 32
Bolton. E Lot 1C 20
Boltonfellend. Cumb 2H 7
Boltongate. Cumb 4F 7
Bolton Low Houses. Cumb 4F 7
Bolton New Houses. Cumb 4F 7
Bolton Wood Lane. Cumb 4F 7
Bonar Bridge. High 4D 54
Bonawe. Arg 5D 30
Bonchester Bridge. Bord 2E 13
Bo'ness. Falk 5A 26
Bonhill. W Dun 1G 17
Bonjedward. Bord 1F 13
Bonkle. N Lan 3D 18
Bonnington. Ang 5C 34
Bonnington. Edin 2G 19
Bonnybank. Fife 3E 27
Bonnybridge. Falk 5H 25
Bonnykelly. Abers 3D 50
Bonnyrigg. Midl 2A 20
Bonnyton. Ang 5A 34
Bonnytown. Fife 2G 27
Booth of Toft. Shet 5H 67
Boquhan. Stir 5E 25
Bordlands. Bord 4G 19
Boreland. Dum 4A 12
Borestone Brae. Stir 4H 25
Borgh. W Isl 4B 60
(on Barra)
Borgh. W Isl 5H 61
(on Benbecula)
Borgh. W Isl 2K 61
(on Berneray)
Borgh. W Isl 2J 63
(on Isle of Lewis)
Borghasdal. W Isl 6B 62
Borghastan. W Isl 3F 63
Borgie. High 3H 57
Borgue. Dum 4H 5
Borgue. High 5E 59
Borlum. High 1G 39
Bornais. W Isl 2C 60
Bornesketaig. High 1C 44
Borreraig. High 3A 44
Borrobol Lodge. High 1F 55
Borrodale. High 4A 44
Borrowston. High 4G 59
Borrowstonehill. Orkn 4D 64
Borrowstoun. Falk 5A 26
Borthwick. Midl 3A 20
Borve. High 4D 44
Bostadh. W Isl 3F 63
Bothel. Cumb 5E 7
Bothwell. S Lan 3B 18
Bottacks. High 2F 47
Bottomcraig. Fife 1E 27
Bousd. Arg 2D 28
Bousta. Shet 1B 66
Boustead Hill. Cumb 3F 7
Bowden. Bord 5C 20
Bower. Nmbd 5G 13
Bowermadden. High 2F 59
Bowershall. Fife 4B 26
Bowertower. High 2F 59
Bowhousebog. N Lan 3D 18
Bowling. W Dun 1H 17
Bowmore. Arg 3E 15
Bowness-on-Solway. Cumb 2F 7
Bow of Fife. Fife 2E 27
Bowriefauld. Ang 4C 34
Bowscale. Cumb 5G 7
Bowsden. Nmbd 4G 21
Bowside Lodge. High 2B 58
Boyndlie. Abers 2B 50
Braal Castle. High 2E 59
Brabster. High 2G 59
Bracadale. High 5C 44
Brackenlands. Cumb 4F 7
Brackenthwaite. Cumb 4F 7
Brackla. High 3B 48
Brackletter. High 5C 38
Brackloch. High 1G 53
Braco. Per 3H 25
Bracobrae. Mor 3A 50
Bracora. High 4G 37
Brae. High 5D 52
Brae. Shet 6G 67
Braeantra. High 1G 47
Braefield. High 5F 47
Braefindon. High 3H 47
Braegrum. Per 1B 26
Braehead. Ang 3D 34
Braehead. Dum 3F 5
Braehead. Mor 4F 49
Braehead. Orkn 3G 65
Braehead. S Lan 5D 18
(nr. Coalburn)
Braehead. S Lan 3E 19
(nr. Forth)
Braehoulland. Shet 5F 67
Braemar. Abers 4E 41
Braemore. High 5D 58
(nr. Dunbeath)
Braemore. High 1C 46
(nr. Ullapool)
Brae of Achnahaird. High 2F 53
Brae Roy Lodge. High 4E 39
Braeside. Abers 5E 51
Braeside. Inv 1F 17
Braes of Coul. Ang 3H 33
Braeswick. Orkn 4J 65
Braetongue. High 3G 57
Braeval. Stir 3E 25
Braevallich. Arg 3G 23
Braewick. Shet 1C 66
Bragar. W Isl 3G 63
Bragleenbeg. Arg 1G 23
Braidwood. S Lan 4D 18
Braigo. Arg 2D 14
Brampton. Cumb 2H 7
Branault. High 2G 29
Branchill. Mor 3D 48
Branderburgh. Mor 1F 49
Branthwaite. Cumb 5F 7
(nr. Caldbeck)
Branthwaite. Cumb 5D 6
(nr. Workington)
Branxholme. Bord 2D 12
Branxton. Nmbd 5F 21
Brathens. Abers 4B 42
Braulen Lodge. High 5D 46
Brawl. High 2B 58
Brawlbin. High 3D 58
Breacleit. W Isl 1C 62
Breakachy. High 4G 47
Breanais. W Isl 2A 62
Breascleit. W Isl 1D 62
Brechin. Ang 3D 34
Breibhig. W Isl 5B 60
(on Barra)
Breibhig. W Isl 4J 63
(on Isle of Lewis)
Breich. W Lot 2E 19
Breiwick. Shet 2D 66
Brenachie. High 1A 48
Brettabister. Shet 1D 66
Brewlands Bridge. Ang 2G 33
Brideswell. Abers 5A 50
Bridge End. Shet 3C 66
Bridgefoot. Ang 5A 34
Bridgefoot. Cumb 5D 6
Bridgend. Abers 5A 50
(nr. Huntly)
Bridgend. Abers 5F 51
(nr. Peterhead)
Bridgend. Ang 2C 34
(nr. Brechin)
Bridgend. Ang 4A 34
(nr. Kirriemuir)
Bridgend. Arg 4F 23
(nr. Lochgilphead)
Bridgend. Arg 2E 15
(on Islay)
Bridgend. Fife 2E 27
Bridgend. High 3E 47
Bridgend. Mor 5G 49
Bridgend. Per 1C 26
Bridgend. W Lot 1F 19
Bridgend of Lintrathen. Ang 3H 33
Bridgeness. Falk 5B 26
Bridge of Alford. Abers 2A 42
Bridge of Allan. Stir 4G 25
Bridge of Avon. Mor 5E 49
Bridge of Awe. Arg 1H 23
Bridge of Balgie. Per 4A 32
Bridge of Brown. High 1E 41
Bridge of Cally. Per 3G 33
Bridge of Canny. Abers 4B 42
Bridge of Dee. Dum 2A 6
Bridge of Don. Aber 2E 43
Bridge of Dun. Ang 3D 34
Bridge of Dye. Abers 5B 42
Bridge of Earn. Per 2C 26
Bridge of Ericht. Per 3A 32
Bridge of Feugh. Abers 4C 42
Bridge of Forss. High 2D 58
Bridge of Gairn. Abers 4G 41
Bridge of Gaur. Per 3A 32
Bridge of Muchalls. Abers 4D 42
Bridge of Oich. High 3E 39
Bridge of Orchy. Arg 5G 31
Bridge of Walls. Shet 1B 66
Bridge of Weir. Ren 2G 17
Bridister. Shet 1B 66
Brigham. Cumb 5D 6
Brightons. Falk 1E 19
Brig o'Turk. Stir 3E 25
Brims. Orkn 6B 64
Brindister. Shet 3D 66
Brinian. Orkn 2D 64
Brisco. Cumb 3H 7
Broadfield. Inv 1G 17
Broadford. High 1F 37
Broadhaven. High 3G 59
Broadley. Mor 2G 49
Broadrashes. Mor 3H 49
Broadsea. Abers 2E 51
Broadwath. Cumb 3H 7
Broallan. High 4F 47
Brochel. High 4E 45
Brocketsbrae. S Lan 5D 18
Brockhill. Bord 1C 12
Brockleymoor. Cumb 5H 7
Brodick. N Ayr 5D 16
Brodie. Mor 3C 48
Brodiesord. Abers 3A 50
Brogaig. High 2D 44
Bromfield. Cumb 4E 7
Brookfield. Ren 2H 17
Broom. Fife 3E 27
Broomend. Abers 2C 42
Broomfield. Abers 5E 51
Broomhill. High 1C 40
(nr. Grantown-on-Spey)
Broomhill. High 1A 48
(nr. Invergordon)
Broomhillbank. Dum 4A 12
Broomlands. Dum 3H 11
Broom of Moy. Mor 3D 48
Brora. High 3G 55
Broubster. High 2D 58
Brough. High 1F 59
Brough. Orkn 3C 64
(nr. Finstown)
Brough. Orkn 6D 64
(nr. St Margaret's Hope)
Brough. Shet 1D 66
(nr. Benston)
Brough. Shet 5H 67
(nr. Booth of Toft)
Brough. Shet 2E 66
(on Bressay)
Brough. Shet 6J 67
(on Whalsay)
Brough Lodge. Shet 3J 67
Broughton. Orkn 3G 65
Broughton. Bord 5G 19
Broughton Cross. Cumb 5D 6
Broughton Moor. Cumb 5D 6
Broughtown. Orkn 3J 65
Broughty Ferry. D'dee 5B 34
Browland. Shet 1B 66
Broxburn. E Lot 1D 20
Broxburn. W Lot 1F 19
Brù. W Isl 3H 63
Bruach Mairi. W Isl 4J 63
Bruairnis. W Isl 4C 60
Bruan. High 5G 59
Bruar Lodge. Per 1D 32
Brucehill. W Dun 1G 17
Brucklay. Abers 3E 51
Bruichladdich. Arg 2D 14
Brunery. High 1A 30
Brunton. Fife 1E 27
Brusta. W Isl 2K 61
Brydekirk. Dum 1E 7
Buaile nam Bodach. W Isl 4C 60
Bualintur. High 1D 36
Buccleuch. Bord 2C 12
Buchanan Smithy. Stir 5D 24
Buchanhaven. Abers 4G 51
Buchanty. Per 1A 26
Buchany. Stir 3G 25
Buchley. E Dun 1A 18
Buchlyvie. Stir 4E 25
Buckabank. Cumb 4G 7
Buckhaven. Fife 4E 27
Buckholm. Bord 5B 20
Buckie. Mor 2H 49
Buckpool. Mor 2H 49
Bucksburn. Aber 3D 42
Buckton. Nmbd 5H 21
Buldoo. High 2C 58
Bullgill. Cumb 5D 6
Bullwood. Arg 1E 17
Bulwark. Abers 4E 51
Bun Abhainn Eadarra. W Isl 4C 62
Bunacaimb. High 5F 37
Bun a' Mhuillinn. W Isl 3C 60
Bunarkaig. High 5C 38
Bunchrew. High 4H 47
Bundalloch. High 1H 37
Buness. Shet 2K 67
Bunessan. Arg 1A 22
Bunkegivie. High 2G 39
Bunloit. High 1G 39
Bunnahabhain. Arg 1F 15
Bunoich. High 3E 39
Bunree. High 2D 30
Bunroy. High 5D 38
Buntait. High 5E 47
Burg. Arg 4E 29
Burgh by Sands. Cumb 3G 7
Burghead. Mor 2E 49
Burgh Muir. Abers 2C 42
Burgie. Mor 3D 48
Burland. Shet 3C 66
Burness. Orkn 3J 65
Burnfoot. E Ayr 3B 10
Burnfoot. Per 3A 26
Burnfoot. Bord 2E 13
(nr. Hawick)
Burnfoot. Bord 2D 12
(nr. Roberton)
Burnhaven. Abers 4G 51
Burnhead. Dum 4F 11
Burnhervie. Abers 2C 42
Burnhouse. N Ayr 3G 17
Burnmouth. Bord 2G 21
Burn of Cambus. Stir 3G 25
Burnside. Ang 3C 34
Burnside. E Ayr 2C 10
Burnside. Per 3C 26
Burnside. Shet 5F 67
Burnside. S Lan 3B 18
Burnside. W Lot 1F 19
(nr. Broxburn)
Burnside. W Lot 1F 19
(nr. Winchburgh)
Burntisland. Fife 5D 26
Burnton. E Ayr 3B 10
Burnwynd. Edin 2G 19
Burrafirth. Shet 1K 67
Burragarth. Shet 2J 67
Burravoe. Shet 4G 67
(nr. North Roe)
Burravoe. Shet 6G 67
(on Mainland)
Burravoe. Shet 5J 67
(on Yell)
Burray Village. Orkn 5D 64
Burrelton. Per 5G 33
Burrigill. High 5F 59
Burroughston. Orkn 2E 64
Burthwaite. Cumb 4H 7
Burwick. Orkn 6D 64
Busby. E Ren 3A 18
Busby. Per 1B 26
Busta. Shet 6G 67
Butterstone. Per 4F 33
Butteryhaugh. Nmbd 4F 13
Byrness. Nmbd 3G 13

C

Cabharstadh. W Isl 3E 62
Cabrach. Arg 2F 15
Cabrach. Mor 1G 41
Cadder. E Dun 1B 18
Caddonfoot. Bord 5B 20
Cadham. Fife 3D 26
Cadzow. S Lan 3C 18
Caenn-na-Cleithe. W Isl 5C 62
Caerlaverock. Per 2H 25
Cairinis. W Isl 4J 61
Cairisiadar. W Isl 1C 62
Cairminis. W Isl 6B 62
Cairnbaan. Arg 4F 23
Cairnbulg. Abers 2F 51
Cairncross. Ang 1B 34
Cairndow. Arg 2A 24
Cairness. Abers 2F 51
Cairneyhill. Fife 5B 26
Cairngarroch. Dum 4B 4
Cairnhill. Abers 5B 50
Cairnie. Abers 4H 49
Cairnorrie. Abers 4D 50
Cairnryan. Dum 2B 4
Cairston. Orkn 3B 64
Calanais. W Isl 1D 62
Calbost. W Isl 6J 63
Caldback. Shet 2K 67
Caldbeck. Cumb 5G 7
Calderbank. N Lan 2C 18
Caldercruix. N Lan 2D 18
Calder Mains. High 3D 58
Caldermill. S Lan 4B 18
Calderwood. S Lan 3B 18
Calebrack. Cumb 5G 7
Calfsound. Orkn 1E 64
Calgary. Arg 3E 29
Califer. Mor 3D 48
California. Falk 1E 19
Callakille. High 3F 45
Callander. Stir 3F 25
Callendoun. Arg 5C 24
Calligarry. High 3F 37
Calthwaite. Cumb 4H 7
Calvine. Per 2D 32
Calvo. Cumb 3E 7
Camaghael. High 1E 31
Camas-luinie. High 1A 38
Camasnacroise. High 3B 30
Camastianavaig. High 5E 45
Camasunary. High 2E 37
Camault Muir. High 4G 47
Camb. Shet 3J 67
Cambus. Clac 4H 25
Cambusbarron. Stir 4G 25
Cambuskenneth. Stir 4H 25
Cambuslang. S Lan 2B 18
Cambusnethan. N Lan 3D 18
Cambus o'May. Abers 4H 41
Camelon. Falk 5H 25
Camerton. Cumb 5D 6
Camghouran. Per 3A 32
Cammachmore. Abers 4E 43
Camore. High 4E 55
Campbelton. N Ayr 3E 17
Campbeltown. Arg 1C 8
Campbeltown Airport. Arg 1B 8
Cample. Dum 4G 11
Campmuir. Per 5H 33
Camptoun. E Lot 1C 20
Camptown. Bord 2F 13
Camserney. Per 4D 32
Camster. High 4F 59
Camuscross. High 2F 37
Camusdarach. High 4F 37
Camusnagaul. High 1D 30
(nr. Fort William)
Camusnagaul. High 5F 53
(nr. Little Loch Broom)
Camusteel. High 4G 45
Camusterrach. High 4G 45
Camusvrachan. Per 4B 32
Candy Mill. S Lan 4F 19
Canisbay. High 1G 59
Cannich. High 5E 47
Canonbie. Dum 1G 7
Cantray. High 4A 48
Cantraybruich. High 4A 48
Cantraywood. High 4A 48
Cantsdam. Fife 4C 26
Caol. High 1E 31
Caolas. W Isl 5B 60
Caolas Liubharsaigh. W Isl 6J 61
Caolas Scalpaigh. W Isl 5D 62
Caolas Stocinis. W Isl 5C 62
Caoles. Arg 4B 28
Caol Ila. Arg 2F 15
Cappercleuch. Bord 1B 12
Capplegill. Dum 3A 12
Caputh. Per 5F 33
Carbost. High 5C 44
(nr. Loch Harport)
Carbost. High 4D 44
(nr. Portree)
Carcluie. S Ayr 2A 10
Cardenden. Fife 4D 26
Cardewless. Cumb 3G 7
Cardno. Abers 2E 51
Cardow. Mor 4E 49
Cardross. Arg 1G 17
Cardurnock. Cumb 3E 7
Careston. Ang 2C 34
Carfin. N Lan 3C 18
Carfrae. Bord 3C 20
Cargenbridge. Dum 1C 6
Cargill. Per 5G 33
Cargo. Cumb 3G 7
Carham. Nmbd 5E 21
Carie. Per 3B 32
(nr. Loch Rannah)
Carie. Per 5B 32
(nr. Loch Tay)
Carlabhagh. W Isl 3G 63
Carleton. Cumb 3H 7
(nr. Carlisle)
Carleton. Cumb 5H 7
(nr. Penrith)
Carlisle. Cumb 3H 7
Carloonan. Arg 2H 23
Carlops. Bord 3G 19
Carluke. S Lan 3D 18
Carmichael. S Lan 5E 19
Carmunnock. Glas 3B 18
Carmyle. Glas 2B 18
Carmyllie. Ang 4C 34
Carnach. High 1B 38
(nr. Lochcarron)
Carnach. High 4F 53
(nr. Ullapool)
Carnach. Mor 4D 48
Carnach. W Isl 5D 62
Carnachy. High 3A 58
Carnain. Arg 2E 15
Carnais. W Isl 1B 62
Carnan. Arg 4B 28
Carnan. W Isl 6H 61
Carnbee. Fife 3G 27
Carnbo. Per 3B 26
Carndu. High 1H 37
Carnell. S Ayr 5H 17
Carn-gorm. High 1A 38
Carnie. Abers 3D 42
Carnock. Fife 5B 26
Carnoustie. Ang 5C 34
Carntyne. Glas 2B 18
Carnwath. S Lan 4E 19
Carradale. Arg 5B 16
Carragraich. W Isl 5C 62
Carrbridge. High 1C 40
Carrick Castle. Arg 4A 24
Carrick Ho. Orkn 1E 64
Carriden. Falk 5B 26
Carrington. Midl 2A 20
Carron. Falk 5H 25
Carron. Mor 4F 49
Carronbridge. Dum 4F 11
Carronshore. Falk 5H 25
Carrutherstown. Dum 1E 7
Carrycoats Hall. Nmbd 5H 13
Carsaig. Arg 1C 22
Carscreugh. Dum 2D 4
Carsegowan. Dum 3F 5
Carse House. Arg 2A 16
Carseriggan. Dum 2E 5
Carsethorn. Dum 3C 6
Carskiey. Arg 3B 8
Carsluith. Dum 3F 5
Carsphairn. Dum 4C 10
Carstairs. S Lan 4E 19
Carstairs Junction. S Lan 4E 19
Carterhaugh. Ang 4B 34
Cartland. S Lan 4D 18
Carwath. Cumb 4G 7
Carwinley. Cumb 1H 7
Cash Feus. Fife 3D 26
Cashlie. Per 4H 31
Castlebay. W Isl 5B 60
Castlecary. N Lan 1C 18
Castlecraig. High 2B 48
Castle Douglas. Dum 2A 6
Castle Heaton. Nmbd 4G 21
Castlehill. Per 5H 33

Castlehill. *S Lan* 3D 18
Castlehill. *W Dun* 1G 17
Castle Kennedy. *Dum* 3C 4
Castle Lachlan. *Arg* 4H 23
Castlemilk. *Glas* 3B 18
Castle O'er. *Dum* 4B 12
Castleton. *Abers* 4E 41
Castleton. *Arg* 5F 23
Castleton. *Mor* 1E 41
Castleton. *Per* 2A 26
Castletown. *Cumb* 5H 7
Castletown. *High* 2E 59
Catacol. *N Ayr* 4C 16
Catcleugh. *Nmbd* 3G 13
Catfirth. *Shet* 1D 66
Cathcart. *Glas* 3A 18
Catlodge. *High* 4H 39
Catlowdy. *Cumb* 1H 7
Catrine. *E Ayr* 1C 10
Catterlen. *Cumb* 5H 7
Catterline. *Abers* 1F 35
Cauldhame. *Stir* 4F 25
Cauldmill. *Bord* 2E 13
Cauldwells. *Abers* 3C 50
Caulkerbush. *Dum* 3C 6
Caulside. *Dum* 5D 12
Causewayend. *S Lan* 5F 19
Causewayhead. *Stir* 4H 25
Cawdor. *High* 4B 48
Ceallan. *W Isl* 5J 61
Ceann a Bhaigh. *W Isl* 4H 61
(on North Uist)
Ceann a Bhaigh. *W Isl* 5D 62
(on Scalpay)
Ceann a Bhàigh. *W Isl* 6B 62
(on Harris)
Ceannacroc Lodge. *High* 2D 38
Ceann a Deas Loch Baghasdail. *W Isl* 3C 60
Ceann a Tuath Loch Baghasdail. *W Isl* 2C 60
Ceann Shiphoirt. *W Isl* 3D 62
Ceann Tarabhaigh. *W Isl* 3D 62
Cearsiadar. *W Isl* 2E 62
Ceathramh Meadhanach. *W Isl* 3H 61
Cellardyke. *Fife* 3G 27
Ceos. *W Isl* 2E 62
Ceres. *Fife* 2F 27
Cessford. *Bord* 1G 13
Challister. *Shet* 6J 67
Challoch. *Dum* 2E 5
Champany. *Falk* 1F 19
Chance Inn. *Fife* 2E 27
Chanlockfoot. *Dum* 3E 11
Channerwick. *Shet* 4D 66
Chapel. *Cumb* 5F 7
Chapel. *Fife* 4D 26
Chapelfield. *Abers* 2E 35
Chapelhall. *N Lan* 2C 18
Chapel Hill. *Abers* 5F 51
Chapelhill. *Per* 1D 26
(nr. Glencarse)
Chapelhill. *Per* 5F 33
(nr. Harrietfield)
Chapelknowe. *Dum* 1G 7
Chapel of Garioch. *Abers* 1C 42
Chapelton. *Ang* 4D 34
Chapelton. *High* 2C 40
(nr. Grantown-on-Spey)
Chapelton. *High* 3G 47
(nr. Inverness)
Chapelton. *S Lan* 4B 18
Chapeltown. *Mor* 1F 41
Charlesfield. *Dum* 2E 7
Charleston. *Ang* 4A 34
Charleston. *Ren* 2H 17
Charlestown. *Aber* 3E 43
Charlestown. *Abers* 2F 51
Charlestown. *Fife* 5B 26
Charlestown. *High* 1H 45
(nr. Gairloch)
Charlestown. *High* 4H 47
(nr. Inverness)
Charlestown of Aberlour. *Mor* 4F 49
Charlton. *Nmbd* 5H 13
Chatton. *Nmbd* 5H 21
Cherrybank. *Per* 1C 26
Chesterhope. *Nmbd* 5H 13
Chesters. *Bord* 2F 13
Cheswick. *Nmbd* 4H 21
Chillingham. *Nmbd* 5H 21
Chirmorie. *S Ayr* 1D 4
Chirnside. *Bord* 3F 21
Chirnsidebridge. *Bord* 3F 21
Chryston. *N Lan* 1B 18
Churchtown. *Cumb* 4G 7
Churnsike Lodge. *Nmbd* 5F 13
Cill Amhlaidh. *W Isl* 6H 61
Cill Donnain. *High* 1G 55
Cill Donnain. *W Isl* 2C 60
Cille Bhrighde. *W Isl* 3C 60
Cille Pheadair. *W Isl* 3C 60
Cirbhig. *W Isl* 3F 63
Circebost. *W Isl* 1C 62
Clabhach. *Arg* 3C 28
Clachaig. *Arg* 5A 24
Clachaig. *High* 3E 31
(nr. Kinlochleven)
Clachaig. *High* 2D 40
(nr. Nethy Bridge)
Clachamish. *High* 3C 44
Clachan. *Arg* 3A 16
(on Kintyre)
Clachan. *Arg* 4B 30
(on Lismore)
Clachan. *High* 2A 58
(nr. Bettyhill)
Clachan. *High* 2D 44
(nr. Staffin)
Clachan. *High* 1C 44
(nr. Uig)
Clachan. *High* 5E 45
(on Raasay)
Clachan Farm. *Arg* 2A 24
Clachan na Luib. *W Isl* 4J 61
Clachan of Campsie. *E Dun* 1B 18
Clachan of Glendaruel. *Arg* 5G 23
Clachan-Seil. *Arg* 2E 23
Clachan Shannda. *W Isl* 3J 61
Clachan Strachur. *Arg* 3H 23
Clachbreck. *Arg* 1A 16
Clachnaharry. *High* 4H 47
Clachtoll. *High* 1F 53
Clackmannan. *Clac* 4A 26
Clackmarras. *Mor* 3F 49
Cladach a Chaolais. *W Isl* 4H 61
Cladach Chairinis. *W Isl* 5J 61
Cladach Chirceboist. *W Isl* 4H 61
Cladach Iolaraigh. *W Isl* 4H 61
Cladich. *Arg* 1H 23
Claggan. *High* 1E 31
(nr. Fort William)
Claggan. *High* 4H 29
(nr. Lochaline)
Claigan. *High* 3B 44
Claonaig. *Arg* 3B 16
Clappers. *Bord* 3G 21
Clapphoull. *Shet* 4D 66
Clarebrand. *Dum* 2A 6
Clarencefield. *Dum* 2D 6
Clarilaw. *Bord* 2E 13
Clarkston. *E Ren* 3A 18
Clasheddy. *High* 2H 57
Clashindarroch. *Abers* 5H 49
Clashmore. *High* 5E 55
(nr. Dornoch)
Clashmore. *High* 5B 56
(nr. Stoer)
Clashnessie. *High* 5B 56
Clashnoir. *Mor* 1F 41
Clate. *Shet* 6J 67
Clathick. *Per* 1H 25
Clathy. *Per* 2A 26
Clatt. *Abers* 1A 42
Clayholes. *Ang* 5C 34
Clayock. *High* 3E 59
Cleadale. *High* 5D 36
Cleat. *Orkn* 3G 65
(nr. Braehead)
Cleat. *Orkn* 6D 64
(nr. St Margaret's Hope)
Cleekhimin. *N Lan* 3C 18
Cleigh. *Arg* 1F 23
Cleish. *Per* 4B 26
Cleland. *N Lan* 3D 18
Clennell. *Nmbd* 3H 13
Clephanton. *High* 3B 48
Clerkhill. *High* 2A 58
Clestrain. *Orkn* 4C 64
Cliaid. *W Isl* 4B 60
Cliasmol. *W Isl* 4B 62
Clibberswick. *Shet* 1K 67
Cliffburn. *Ang* 4E 35
Clifton. *Stir* 5G 31
Climpy. *S Lan* 3E 19
Clintmains. *Bord* 5D 20
Cliobh. *W Isl* 1B 62
Cliuthar. *W Isl* 5C 62
Clivocast. *Shet* 2K 67
Clochan. *Mor* 2H 49
Clochforbie. *Abers* 3D 50
Cloddymoss. *Mor* 2C 48
Clola. *Abers* 4F 51
Closeburn. *Dum* 4F 11
Clousta. *Shet* 1C 66
Clouston. *Orkn* 3B 64
Clova. *Abers* 1H 41
Clova. *Ang* 1A 34
Clovenfords. *Bord* 5B 20
Clovenstone. *Abers* 2C 42
Clovullin. *High* 2D 30
Cluanie Inn. *High* 2B 38
Cluanie Lodge. *High* 2B 38
Clunas. *High* 4B 48
Clune. *High* 1A 40
Clunes. *High* 5D 38
Clunie. *Per* 4G 33
Cluny. *Fife* 4D 26
Clydebank. *W Dun* 1A 18
Clynder. *Arg* 5B 24
Clynelish. *High* 3F 55
Clyth. *High* 5F 59
Cnip. *W Isl* 1B 62
Cnoc Amhlaigh. *W Isl* 4K 63
Coalburn. *S Lan* 5D 18
Coalford. *Abers* 4D 42
Coalhall. *E Ayr* 2B 10
Coalsnaughton. *Clac* 4A 26
Coaltown of Balgonie. *Fife* 4E 27
Coaltown of Wemyss. *Fife* 4E 27
Coatbridge. *N Lan* 2C 18
Coatdyke. *N Lan* 2C 18
Cock Bridge. *Abers* 3F 41
Cockburnspath. *Bord* 1E 21
Cockenzie and Port Seton. *E Lot* 1B 20
Cockermouth. *Cumb* 5E 7
Cocklaw. *Abers* 4F 51
Cockmuir. *Abers* 3E 51
Coignafearn Lodge. *High* 2H 39
Coig Peighinnean. *W Isl* 1K 63
Coig Peighinnean Bhuirgh. *W Isl* 2J 63
Coilleag. *W Isl* 3C 60
Coilliemore. *High* 1H 47
Coillore. *High* 5C 44
Coire an Fhuarain. *W Isl* 1D 62
Col. *W Isl* 3J 63
Colaboll. *High* 2C 54
Colbost. *High* 4B 44
Coldbackie. *High* 3H 57
Coldingham. *Bord* 2G 21
Coldrain. *Per* 3B 26
Coldstream. *Bord* 4F 21
Coldwells. *Abers* 5G 51
Coldwells Croft. *Abers* 1A 42
Cole. *Shet* 6G 67
Coleburn. *Mor* 3F 49
Colinsburgh. *Fife* 3F 27
Colinton. *Edin* 2H 19
Colintraive. *Arg* 1D 16
Collace. *Per* 5H 33
Collam. *W Isl* 5C 62
College of Roseisle. *Mor* 2E 49
Collessie. *Fife* 2D 26
Collieston. *Abers* 1F 43
Collin. *Dum* 1D 6
Colliston. *Ang* 4D 34
Collydean. *Fife* 3D 26
Colmonell. *S Ayr* 5G 9
Colpy. *Abers* 5B 50
Colstoun House. *E Lot* 1C 20
Coltfield. *Mor* 2E 49
Coltness. *N Lan* 3C 18
Col Uarach. *W Isl* 4J 63
Colvend. *Dum* 3B 6
Colvister. *Shet* 3J 67
Comers. *Abers* 3B 42
Comrie. *Fife* 5B 26
Comrie. *Per* 1G 25
Conaglen. *High* 2D 30
Conchra. *Arg* 5H 23
Conchra. *High* 1H 37
Condorrat. *N Lan* 1C 18
Conicaval. *Mor* 3C 48
Conisby. *Arg* 2D 14
Connel. *Arg* 5C 30
Connel Park. *E Ayr* 2D 10
Connista. *High* 1D 44
Conon Bridge. *High* 3G 47
Cononsyth. *Ang* 4C 34
Conordan. *High* 5E 45
Contin. *High* 3F 47
Contullich. *High* 1H 47
Cookney. *Abers* 4D 42
Copister. *Shet* 5H 67
Cordon. *N Ayr* 5D 16
Corgarff. *Abers* 3F 41
Corlae. *Dum* 4D 10
Cormiston. *S Lan* 5F 19
Cornaigbeg. *Arg* 4A 28
Cornaigmore. *Arg* 2D 28
(on Coll)
Cornaigmore. *Arg* 4A 28
(on Tiree)
Cornhill. *Abers* 3A 50
Cornhill. *High* 4C 54
Cornhill-on-Tweed. *Nmbd* 5F 21
Cornquoy. *Orkn* 4E 64
Corntown. *High* 3G 47
Corpach. *High* 1D 30
Corra. *Dum* 2B 6
Corran. *High* 2D 30
(nr. Arnisdale)
Corran. *High* 3H 37
(nr. Fort William)
Corribeg. *High* 1C 30
Corrie. *N Ayr* 4D 16
Corrie Common. *Dum* 5B 12
Corriecravie. *N Ayr* 1E 9
Corriekinloch. *High* 1A 54
Corriemoillie. *High* 2E 47
Corrievarkie Lodge. *Per* 1A 32
Corrievorrie. *High* 1A 40
Corrigall. *Orkn* 3C 64
Corrimony. *High* 5E 47
Corrour Shooting Lodge. *High* 2H 31
Corry. *High* 1F 37
Corrybrough. *High* 1B 40
Corrygills. *N Ayr* 5D 16
Corry of Ardnagrask. *High* 4G 47
Corsback. *High* 1F 59
(nr. Dunnet)
Corsback. *High* 3F 59
(nr. Halkirk)
Corse. *Abers* 4B 50
Corsehill. *Abers* 3E 51
Corse of Kinnoir. *Abers* 4A 50
Corsock. *Dum* 1A 6
Corstorphine. *Edin* 1H 19
Cortachy. *Ang* 3A 34
Corwar House. *S Ayr* 5H 9
Costa. *Orkn* 2C 64
Cotehill. *Cumb* 3H 7
Cothall. *Abers* 2D 42
Cott. *Orkn* 5J 65
Cottartown. *High* 5D 48
Cottown. *Abers* 4D 50
Coulags. *High* 4A 46
Coulin Lodge. *High* 3B 46
Coull. *Abers* 3A 42
Coulport. *Arg* 5B 24
Coulter. *S Lan* 5F 19
Coupar Angus. *Per* 4H 33
Coupland. *Nmbd* 5G 21
Cour. *Arg* 4B 16
Courance. *Dum* 4H 11
Courteachan. *High* 4F 37
Cousland. *Midl* 2A 20
Couston. *Arg* 1D 16
Cove. *Arg* 5B 24
Cove. *High* 4D 52
Cove. *Bord* 1E 21
Cove Bay. *Aber* 3E 43
Covesea. *Mor* 1E 49
Covington. *S Lan* 5E 19
Cowdenbeath. *Fife* 4C 26
Cowdenburn. *Bord* 3H 19
Cowdenend. *Fife* 4C 26
Cowfords. *Mor* 2G 49
Cowgate. *Cumb* 4D 6
Cowie. *Abers* 5D 42
Cowie. *Stir* 5H 25
Cowstrandburn. *Fife* 4B 26
Coylton. *S Ayr* 2B 10
Coylumbridge. *High* 2C 40
Coynach. *Abers* 3H 41
Coynachie. *Abers* 5H 49
Crackaig. *High* 2G 55
Cradhlastadh. *W Isl* 1B 62
Cragabus. *Arg* 4E 15
Craggan. *High* 1D 40
Cragganmore. *Mor* 5E 49
Cragganvallie. *High* 5G 47
Craggie. *High* 1F 55
Craggiemore. *High* 5A 48
Craibstone. *Aber* 2D 42
Craichie. *Ang* 4C 34
Craig. *Arg* 5D 30
Craig. *Dum* 1H 5
Craig. *High* 4B 46
(nr. Achnashellach)
Craig. *High* 2G 45
(nr. Lower Diabaig)
Craig. *High* 5H 45
(nr. Stromeferry)
Craiganour Lodge. *Per* 3B 32
Craigbrack. *Arg* 4A 24
Craigdallie. *Per* 1D 26
Craigdam. *Abers* 5D 50
Craigdarroch. *E Ayr* 3D 10
Craigdarroch. *High* 3F 47
Craigdhu. *High* 4F 47
Craigearn. *Abers* 2C 42
Craigellachie. *Mor* 4F 49
Craigend. *Per* 1C 26
Craigendoran. *Arg* 5C 24
Craigends. *Ren* 2H 17
Craigenputtock. *Dum* 5E 11
Craigens. *E Ayr* 2C 10
Craighall. *Edin* 1G 19
Craighead. *Fife* 2H 27
Craighouse. *Arg* 2G 15
Craigie. *Abers* 2E 43
Craigie. *D'dee* 5B 34
Craigie. *Per* 4G 33
(nr. Blairgowrie)
Craigie. *Per* 1C 26
(nr. Perth)
Craigie. *S Ayr* 5H 17
Craigielaw. *E Lot* 1B 20
Craiglemine. *Dum* 5F 5
Craiglockhart. *Edin* 1H 19
Craig Lodge. *Arg* 1D 16
Craigmalloch. *E Ayr* 4B 10
Craigmaud. *Abers* 3D 50
Craigmill. *Stir* 4H 25
Craigmillar. *Edin* 1H 19
Craigmore. *Arg* 2E 17
Craigmuie. *Dum* 5E 11
Craignair. *Dum* 2B 6
Craigneuk. *N Lan* 2C 18
(nr. Airdrie)
Craigneuk. *N Lan* 3C 18
(nr. Motherwell)
Craignure. *Arg* 5A 30
Craigo. *Abers* 2D 34
Craigrory. *High* 4H 47
Craigrothie. *Fife* 2E 27
Craigs. *Dum* 1F 7
Craigshill. *W Lot* 2F 19
Craigs, The. *High* 4B 54
Craigton. *Aber* 3D 42
Craigton. *Abers* 3C 42
Craigton. *Ang* 5C 34
(nr. Carnoustie)
Craigton. *Ang* 3A 34
(nr. Kirriemuir)
Craigton. *High* 4H 47
Craigtown. *High* 3B 58
Craigyloch. *Ang* 3H 33
Craik. *Bord* 3C 12
Crail. *Fife* 3H 27
Crailing. *Bord* 1F 13
Crailinghall. *Bord* 1F 13
Cramond. *Edin* 1G 19
Cramond Bridge. *Edin* 1G 19
Cranloch. *Mor* 3F 49
Crannich. *Arg* 4G 29
Crannoch. *Mor* 3H 49
Cranshaws. *Bord* 2D 20
Craobh Haven. *Arg* 3E 23
Craobhnaclag. *High* 4F 47
Crarae. *Arg* 4G 23
Crask. *High* 2A 58
Crask Inn. *High* 1C 54
Crask of Aigas. *High* 4F 47
Crathes. *Abers* 4C 42
Crathie. *Abers* 4F 41
Crathie. *High* 4G 39
Crawford. *S Lan* 1G 11
Crawforddyke. *S Lan* 3D 18
Crawfordjohn. *S Lan* 1F 11
Crawick. *Dum* 2E 11
Crawton. *Abers* 5D 42
Cray. *Per* 2G 33
Creagan. *Arg* 4C 30
Creag Aoil. *High* 1E 31
Creag Ghoraidh. *W Isl* 6H 61
Creaguaineach Lodge. *High* 2G 31
Creca. *Dum* 1F 7
Creebridge. *Dum* 2F 5
Creetown. *Dum* 3F 5
Creggans. *Arg* 3H 23
Creich. *Arg* 1A 22
Crepkill. *High* 4D 44
Crianlarich. *Stir* 1C 24
Crichton. *Midl* 2A 20
Criech. *Fife* 1E 27
Crieff. *Per* 1H 25
Crimond. *Abers* 3F 51
Crimonmogate. *Abers* 3F 51
Crinan. *Arg* 4E 23
Crocketford. *Dum* 1B 6
Croftamie. *Stir* 5D 24
Croftfoot. *Glas* 2A 18
Croftmill. *Per* 5D 32
Crofton. *Cumb* 3G 7
Crofts. *Dum* 1A 6
Crofts of Benachielt. *High* 5E 59
Crofts of Dipple. *Mor* 3G 49
Croggan. *Arg* 1E 23
Croich. *High* 4B 54
Croick. *High* 3B 58
Croig. *Arg* 3E 29
Cromarty. *High* 2A 48
Crombie. *Fife* 5B 26
Cromdale. *High* 1D 40
Cromor. *W Isl* 5J 63
Cromra. *High* 5G 39
Cronberry. *E Ayr* 1D 10
Crookdake. *Cumb* 4E 7
Crookedholm. *E Ayr* 5H 17
Crookham. *Nmbd* 5G 21
Crook of Devon. *Per* 3B 26
Crookston. *Ren* 2A 18
Cros. *W Isl* 1K 63
Crosbie. *N Ayr* 4F 17
Crosbost. *W Isl* 2E 62
Crosby. *Cumb* 5D 6
Crosby Villa. *Cumb* 5D 6
Crossaig. *Arg* 3B 16
Crossapol. *Arg* 4A 28
Crosscanonby. *Cumb* 5D 6
Crossford. *Fife* 5B 26
Crossford. *S Lan* 4D 18
Crossgate. *Orkn* 3D 64
Crossgatehall. *E Lot* 2A 20
Crossgates. *Fife* 5C 26
Crosshands. *E Ayr* 5H 17
Crosshill. *E Ayr* 1B 10
Crosshill. *Fife* 4C 26
Crosshill. *S Ayr* 3A 10
Crosshills. *High* 1H 47
Crosshouse. *E Ayr* 5G 17
Crossings. *Cumb* 1H 7
Crosskirk. *High* 2D 58
Crosslee. *Ren* 2H 17
Crossmichael. *Dum* 2A 6
Cross of Jackston. *Abers* 5C 50
Crossroads. *Abers* 3E 43
(nr. Aberdeen)
Crossroads. *Abers* 4C 42
(nr. Banchory)
Crossroads. *E Ayr* 5H 17
Crosston. *Ang* 3C 34
Crothair. *W Isl* 1C 62
Crovie. *Abers* 2D 50
Croy. *High* 4A 48
Croy. *N Lan* 1C 18
Crubenbeg. *High* 4H 39
Crubenmore Lodge. *High* 4H 39
Cruden Bay. *Abers* 5F 51
Crudie. *Abers* 3C 50
Crulabhig. *W Isl* 1C 62
Cuaich. *High* 5H 39
Cuaig. *High* 3G 45
Cuan. *Arg* 2E 23
Cuckron. *Shet* 1D 66
Cuidhir. *W Isl* 4B 60
Cuidhsiadar. *W Isl* 2K 63
Cuidhtinis. *W Isl* 6B 62
Culbo. *High* 2H 47
Culbokie. *High* 3H 47
Culburnie. *High* 4F 47
Culcabock. *High* 4H 47
Culcharry. *High* 3B 48
Culduie. *High* 4G 45
Culeave. *High* 4C 54
Culkein. *High* 5B 56
Culkein Drumbeg. *High* 5C 56
Cullen. *Mor* 2A 50
Cullicudden. *High* 2H 47
Cullipool. *Arg* 2E 23
Cullivoe. *Shet* 2J 67
Culloch. *Per* 2G 25
Culnacnoc. *High* 2E 45
Culnacraig. *High* 3F 53
Culrain. *High* 4C 54
Culross. *Fife* 5A 26
Culroy. *S Ayr* 2A 10
Culswick. *Shet* 2B 66
Cults. *Aber* 3D 42
Cults. *Abers* 5A 50
Cults. *Fife* 3E 27
Cultybraggan Camp. *Per* 1G 25
Culzie Lodge. *High* 1G 47
Cumbernauld. *N Lan* 1C 18
Cumbernauld Village. *N Lan* 1C 18
Cumdivock. *Cumb* 4G 7
Cuminestown. *Abers* 3D 50
Cumledge Mill. *Bord* 3E 21
Cumlewick. *Shet* 4D 66
Cummersdale. *Cumb* 3G 7
Cummertrees. *Dum* 2E 7
Cummingstown. *Mor* 2E 49
Cumnock. *E Ayr* 2C 10
Cumwhinton. *Cumb* 3H 7
Cumwhitton. *Cumb* 3H 7
Cunninghamhead. *N Ayr* 4G 17
Cunning Park. *S Ayr* 2A 10
Cunningsburgh. *Shet* 4D 66
Cunnister. *Shet* 3J 67
Cupar. *Fife* 2E 27
Cupar Muir. *Fife* 2E 27
Currie. *Edin* 2G 19
Cuthill. *E Lot* 1A 20
Cutts. *Shet* 3D 66
Cuttyhill. *Abers* 3F 51

D

Dacre. *Cumb* 5H 7
Dail. *Arg* 5D 30
Dail Beag. *W Isl* 3G 63
Dail bho Dheas. *W Isl* 1J 63
Dailly. *S Ayr* 3H 9
Dail Mor. *W Isl* 3G 63
Dairsie. *Fife* 2F 27
Dalabrog. *W Isl* 2C 60
Dalavich. *Arg* 2G 23
Dalbeattie. *Dum* 2B 6
Dalblair. *E Ayr* 2D 10
Dalchalm. *High* 3G 55
Dalcharn. *High* 3H 57
Dalchork. *High* 2C 54
Dalchreichart. *High* 2D 38
Dalchruin. *Per* 2G 25
Dalcross. *High* 4A 48
Dalelia. *High* 2A 30
Dale of Walls. *Shet* 1A 66
Dalgarven. *N Ayr* 4F 17
Dalgety Bay. *Fife* 5C 26
Dalginross. *Per* 1G 25
Dalguise. *Per* 4E 33
Dalhalvaig. *High* 3B 58
Dalintart. *Arg* 1F 23
Dalkeith. *Midl* 2A 20
Dallas. *Mor* 3E 49
Dalleagles. *E Ayr* 2C 10
Dalmally. *Arg* 1A 24
Dalmarnock. *Glas* 2B 18
Dalmellington. *E Ayr* 3B 10
Dalmeny. *Edin* 1G 19
Dalmigavie. *High* 2A 40
Dalmilling. *S Ayr* 1A 10
Dalmore. *High* 2H 47
(nr. Alness)
Dalmore. *High* 3E 55
(nr. Rogart)
Dalmuir. *W Dun* 1H 17
Dalmunach. *Mor* 4F 49
Dalnabreck. *High* 2A 30
Dalnacardoch Lodge. *Per* 1C 32
Dalnamein Lodge. *Per* 2C 32
Dalnaspidal Lodge. *Per* 1B 32
Dalnatrat. *High* 3C 30
Dalnavie. *High* 1H 47
Dalnawillan Lodge. *High* 4D 58
Dalness. *High* 3E 31
Dalnessie. *High* 2D 54
Dalqueich. *Per* 3B 26
Dalquhairn. *S Ayr* 4A 10
Dalreavoch. *High* 3E 55
Dalreoch. *Per* 2B 26
Dalry. *Edin* 1H 19
Dalry. *N Ayr* 4F 17
Dalrymple. *E Ayr* 2A 10
Dalserf. *S Lan* 3C 18
Dalsmirren. *Arg* 2B 8
Dalston. *Cumb* 3G 7
Dalswinton. *Dum* 5G 11
Dalton. *Dum* 1E 7
Dalton. *S Lan* 3B 18
Daltot. *Arg* 5E 23
Dalvey. *High* 5E 49
Dalwhinnie. *High* 5H 39
Damhead. *Mor* 3D 48
Danderhall. *Midl* 2A 20
Danestone. *Aber* 2E 43
Danshillock. *Abers* 3C 50
Dargill. *Per* 2H 25
Darnford. *Abers* 4C 42
Darnick. *Bord* 5C 20
Darra. *Abers* 4C 50
Dartfield. *Abers* 3F 51
Darvel. *E Ayr* 5A 18
Dava. *Mor* 5D 48
Davidson's Mains. *Edin* 1H 19
Davidston. *High* 2A 48
Davington. *Dum* 3B 12
Daviot. *Abers* 1C 42
Daviot. *High* 5A 48
Deadwater. *Nmbd* 4F 13
Dean. *Cumb* 5D 6
Deanburnhaugh. *Bord* 2C 12
Deanich Lodge. *High* 5A 54
Deans. *W Lot* 2F 19
Deanscales. *Cumb* 5D 6
Deanston. *Stir* 3G 25
Dearham. *Cumb* 5D 6
Dechmont. *W Lot* 1F 19
Deebank. *Abers* 4B 42
Deerhill. *Mor* 3H 49
Deerness. *Orkn* 4E 64
Delfour. *High* 3B 40
Delliefure. *High* 5D 48
Delny. *High* 1A 48
Denbeath. *Fife* 4E 27
Denhead. *Abers* 5E 51
(nr. Ellon)
Denhead. *Abers* 3E 51
(nr. Strichen)
Denhead. *Fife* 2F 27
Denholm. *Bord* 2E 13
Denny. *Falk* 5H 25
Dennyloanhead. *Falk* 5H 25
Den of Lindores. *Fife* 2D 26
Denside. *Abers* 4D 42
Den, The. *N Ayr* 3G 17
Derculich. *Per* 3D 32
Derryguaig. *Arg* 5F 29
Dervaig. *Arg* 3F 29
Detchant. *Nmbd* 5H 21
Deuchar. *Ang* 2B 34
Devonside. *Clac* 4A 26
Dewartown. *Midl* 2A 20
Digg. *High* 2D 44
Dillarburn. *S Lan* 4D 18
Dingleton. *Bord* 5C 20
Dingwall. *High* 3G 47
Dinnet. *Abers* 4H 41
Dippen. *Arg* 5A 16
Dippin. *N Ayr* 1F 9
Dipple. *S Ayr* 3H 9
Dirleton. *E Lot* 5G 27
Dishes. *Orkn* 5J 65
Divach. *High* 1F 39
Dixonfield. *High* 2E 59
Dochgarroch. *High* 4H 47
Doddington. *Nmbd* 5G 21
Doll. *High* 3F 55
Dollar. *Clac* 4A 26
Dolphingstone. *E Lot* 1A 20
Dolphinton. *S Lan* 4G 19
Doonfoot. *S Ayr* 2A 10
Doonholm. *S Ayr* 2A 10
Dorback Lodge. *High* 2D 40
Dores. *High* 5G 47
Dornie. *High* 1H 37
Dornoch. *High* 5E 55
Dornock. *Dum* 2F 7
Dorrery. *High* 3D 58
Dougarie. *N Ayr* 5B 16
Douglas. *S Lan* 5D 18
Douglastown. *Ang* 4B 34
Douglas Water. *S Lan* 5D 18
Dounby. *Orkn* 2B 64
Doune. *High* 3B 40
(nr. Kingussie)
Doune. *High* 3B 54
(nr. Lairg)

Doune. *Stir* 3G 25
Dounie. *High* 4C 54
(nr. Bonar Bridge)
Dounie. *High* 5D 54
(nr. Tain)
Dounreay. *High* 2C 58
Doura. *N Ayr* 4G 17
Dovenby. *Cumb* 5D 6
Dowally. *Per* 4F 33
Downfield. *D'dee* 5A 34
Downham. *Nmbd* 5F 21
Downies. *Abers* 4E 43
Draffan. *S Lan* 4C 18
Dreghorn. *N Ayr* 3F 17
Drem. *E Lot* 1C 20
Dreumasdal. *W Isl* 1C 60
Drimnin. *High* 3G 29
Drinisiadar. *W Isl* 5C 62
Droman. *High* 3C 56
Dron. *Per* 2C 26
Drongan. *E Ayr* 2B 10
Dronley. *Ang* 5A 34
Druim. *High* 3C 48
Druimarbin. *High* 1D 30
Druimindarroch. *High* 5F 37
Druim Saighdinis. *W Isl* 4J 61
Drum. *Per* 3B 26
Drumbeg. *High* 5C 56
Drumblade. *Abers* 4A 50
Drumbuie. *Dum* 5C 10
Drumbuie. *High* 5G 45
Drumburn. *Cumb* 3F 7
Drumburn. *Dum* 2C 6
Drumchapel. *Glas* 1A 18
Drumchardine. *High* 4G 47
Drumchork. *High* 5D 52
Drumclog. *S Lan* 5B 18
Drumeldrie. *Fife* 3F 27
Drumelzier. *Bord* 5G 19
Drumfearn. *High* 2F 37
Drumgask. *High* 4H 39
Drumgelloch. *N Lan* 2C 18
Drumgley. *Ang* 3B 34
Drumguish. *High* 4A 40
Drumin. *Mor* 5E 49
Drumlamford House. *S Ayr* 1D 4
Drumlasie. *Abers* 3B 42
Drumlemble. *Arg* 2E 8
Drumlithie. *Abers* 5C 42
Drummoddie. *Dum* 4E 5
Drummond. *High* 2H 47
Drummore. *Dum* 5C 4
Drummuir. *Mor* 4G 49
Drumnadrochit. *High* 5G 47
Drumnagorrach. *Mor* 3A 50
Drumoak. *Abers* 4C 42
Drumrunie. *High* 3G 53
Drumry. *W Dun* 1A 18
Drums. *Abers* 1E 43
Drumsleet. *Dum* 1C 6
Drumsmittal. *High* 4H 47
Drums of Park. *Abers* 3A 50
Drumsturdy. *Ang* 5B 34
Drumtochty Castle. *Abers* 5B 42
Drumuie. *High* 4D 44
Drumuillie. *High* 1C 40
Drumvaich. *Stir* 3F 25
Drumwhindle. *Abers* 5E 51
Drunkendub. *Ang* 4D 34
Drybridge. *Mor* 2H 49
Drybridge. *N Ayr* 5G 17
Dryburgh. *Bord* 5C 20
Drymen. *Stir* 5D 24
Drymuir. *Abers* 4E 51
Drynachan Lodge. *High* 5B 48
Drynie Park. *High* 3G 47
Drynoch. *High* 5D 44
Dubford. *Abers* 2C 50
Dubiton. *Abers* 3B 50
Dubton. *Ang* 3C 34
Duchally. *High* 2A 54
Duddingston. *Edin* 1H 19
Duddo. *Nmbd* 4G 21
Dufftown. *Mor* 4G 49
Duffus. *Mor* 2E 49
Duirinish. *High* 5G 45
Duisdalemore. *High* 2F 37
Duisky. *High* 1D 30
Dull. *Per* 4D 32
Dullatur. *N Lan* 1C 18
Dulnain Bridge. *High* 1C 40
Dumbarton. *W Dun* 1H 17
Dumfin. *Arg* 5C 24
Dumfries. *Dum* . . . .1C 6 & 72
Dumgoyne. *Stir* 5F 25
Dun. *Ang* 2D 34
Dunagoil. *Arg* 3D 16
Dunalastair. *Per* 3C 32
Dunan. *High* 1E 37
Dunbar. *E Lot* 1D 20
Dunbeath. *High* 5E 59
Dunbeg. *Arg* 5D 30
Dunblane. *Stir* 3G 25
Dunbog. *Fife* 2D 26
Duncanston. *Abers* 1A 42
Duncanston. *High* 3G 47
Dun Charlabhaigh. *W Isl* 3F 63
Duncow. *Dum* 5G 11
Duncrievie. *Per* 3C 26
Dundee. *D'dee* . . . .5B 34 & 72
Dundee Airport. *D'dee* 1E 27
Dundonald. *S Ayr* 5G 17
Dundonnell. *High* 5F 53
Dundraw. *Cumb* 4F 7
Dundreggan. *High* 2E 39
Dundrennan. *Dum* 4A 6
Dunecht. *Abers* 3C 42
Dunfermline. *Fife* . . . .5B 26 & 73
Dunino. *Fife* 2G 27
Dunipace. *Falk* 5H 25
Dunira. *Per* 1G 25
Dunkeld. *Per* 4F 33
Dunlappie. *Ang* 2C 34

Dunlichity Lodge. *High* 5H 47
Dunlop. *E Ayr* 4H 17
Dunmaglass Lodge. *High* 1G 39
Dunmore. *Arg* 2A 16
Dunmore. *Falk* 5H 25
Dunmore. *High* 4G 47
Dunnet. *High* 1F 59
Dunnichen. *Ang* 4C 34
Dunning. *Per* 2B 26
Dunoon. *Arg* 1E 17
Dunphail. *Mor* 4D 48
Dunragit. *Arg* 3C 4
Dunrostan. *Arg* 1F 15
Duns. *Bord* 3E 21
Dunscore. *Dum* 5F 11
Dunshalt. *Fife* 2D 26
Dunshillock. *Abers* 4E 51
Dunsyre. *S Lan* 4E 19
Duntocher. *W Dun* 1H 17
Duntulm. *High* 1D 44
Dunure. *S Ayr* 2H 9
Dunvegan. *High* 4B 44
Durdar. *Cumb* 4H 7
Durisdeer. *Dum* 3F 11
Durisdeermill. *Dum* 3F 11
Durnamuck. *High* 4F 53
Durness. *High* 2F 57
Durno. *Abers* 1C 42
Duror. *High* 3C 30
Durran. *Arg* 3G 23
Durran. *High* 2E 59
Dury. *Shet* 1D 66
Duthil. *High* 1C 40
Dyce. *Aber* 2D 42
Dyke. *Mor* 3C 48
Dykehead. *Ang* 2A 34
Dykehead. *N Lan* 2D 18
Dykehead. *Stir* 4E 25
Dykend. *Ang* 3H 33
Dykesfield. *Cumb* 3G 7
Dysart. *Fife* 4E 27

E

Eadar Dha Fhadhail. *W Isl* 1B 62
Eaglesfield. *Cumb* 5D 6
Eaglesfield. *Dum* 1F 7
Eaglesham. *E Ren* 3A 18
Eallabus. *Arg* 2E 15
Eamont Bridge. *Cumb* 5H 7
Earle. *Nmbd* 5G 21
Earlish. *High* 2C 44
Earlsferry. *Fife* 3F 27
Earlsford. *Abers* 5E 51
Earlston. *E Ayr* 5H 17
Earlston. *Bord* 5C 20
Earlstoun. *Dum* 5D 10
Earlyvale. *Bord* 3H 19
Earsairidh. *W Isl* 5C 60
Easdale. *Arg* 2E 23
Easington. *Nmbd* 5H 21
Eassie. *Ang* 4A 34
Eassie and Nevay. *Ang* 4A 34
East Barns. *E Lot* 1E 21
East Bennan. *N Ayr* 1E 9
East Burrafirth. *Shet* 1C 66
East Calder. *W Lot* 2F 19
East Clyne. *High* 3F 55
East Clyth. *High* 5F 59
East Croachy. *High* 1H 39
Easter Ardross. *High* 1H 47
Easter Balgedie. *Per* 3C 26
Easter Balmoral. *Abers* 4F 41
Easter Brae. *High* 2H 47
Easter Buckieburn. *Stir* 5G 25
Easter Bush. *Midl* 2H 19
Easter Fearn. *High* 5D 54
Easter Galcantray. *High* 4B 48
Easterhouse. *Glas* 2B 18
Easter Howgate. *Midl* 2H 19
Easter Kinkell. *High* 3G 47
Easter Lednathie. *Ang* 2A 34
Easter Ogil. *Ang* 2B 34
Easter Ord. *Abers* 3D 42
Easter Quarff. *Shet* 3D 66
Easter Rhynd. *Per* 2C 26
Easter Skeld. *Shet* 2C 66
Easter Suddie. *High* 3H 47
Easter Tulloch. *Abers* 1E 35
Eastfield. *N Lan* 2D 18
(nr. Caldercruix)
Eastfield. *N Lan* 2D 18
(nr. Harthill)
Eastfield. *S Lan* 2B 18
East Fortune. *E Lot* 1C 20
East Haven. *Ang* 5C 34
East Helmsdale. *High* 2H 55
East Horton. *Nmbd* 5H 21
Easthouses. *Midl* 2A 20
East Kilbride. *S Lan* 3B 18
East Kyloe. *Nmbd* 5H 21
East Langwell. *High* 3E 55
East Learmouth. *Nmbd* 5F 21
East Linton. *E Lot* 1C 20
East Mains. *Abers* 4B 42
East Mey. *High* 1G 59
Easton. *Cumb* 3F 7
(nr. Burgh by Sands)
Easton. *Cumb* 1H 7
(nr. Longtown)
East Ord. *Nmbd* 3G 21
East Pitcorthie. *Fife* 3G 27
East Rhidorroch Lodge. *High* 4H 53
Eastriggs. *Dum* 2F 7
East Saltoun. *E Lot* 2B 20
Eastshore. *Shet* 5C 66
East Wemyss. *Fife* 4E 27
East Whitburn. *W Lot* 2E 19
East Woodburn. *Nmbd* 5H 13
Ecclefechan. *Dum* 1E 7
Eccles. *Bord* 4E 21
Ecclesmachan. *W Lot* 1F 19
Echt. *Abers* 3C 42

Eckford. *Bord* 1G 13
Eday Airport. *Orkn* 1E 64
Edderside. *Cumb* 4E 7
Edderton. *High* 5E 55
Eddlewood. *S Lan* 3C 18
Edendonich. *Arg* 1A 24
Edentaggart. *Arg* 4C 24
Edgehead. *Midl* 2A 20
Edinbane. *High* 3C 44
Edinburgh. *Edin* . . . .1H 19 & 74-75
Edinburgh Airport. *Edin* 1G 19
Edmonstone. *Orkn* 1E 64
Ednam. *Bord* 5E 21
Edrom. *Bord* 3F 21
Edzell. *Ang* 2C 34
Effirth. *Shet* 1C 66
Efstigarth. *Shet* 1E 66
Eight Mile Burn. *Midl* 3G 19
Eignaig. *High* 4A 30
Eilanreach. *High* 2G 37
Eildon. *Bord* 5C 20
Eileanach Lodge. *High* 2G 47
Eilean Fhlodaigh. *W Isl* 5J 61
Eilean Iarmain. *High* 2G 37
Einacleit. *W Isl* 2C 62
Eisgein. *W Isl* 3E 62
Elcho. *Per* 1C 26
Elderslie. *Ren* 2H 17
Eldrick. *S Ayr* 3B 8
Elford. *Nmbd* 5G 21
Elgin. *Mor* 2F 49
Elgol. *High* 3D 44
Elie. *Fife* 3F 27
Elishaw. *Nmbd* 4H 13
Elizafield. *Dum* 1D 6
Ellan. *High* 1B 40
Ellanbeich. *Arg* 2E 23
Ellary. *Arg* 1A 16
Ellemford. *Bord* 2E 21
Ellenborough. *Cumb* 5D 6
Elleric. *Arg* 1G 31
Elliot. *Ang* 5D 34
Ellishadder. *High* 2E 45
Ellon. *Abers* 5E 51
Ellonby. *Cumb* 5H 7
Elphin. *High* 1B 54
Elphinstone. *E Lot* 1A 20
Elrick. *Abers* 3D 42
Elrick. *Mor* 1H 41
Elrig. *Dum* 4E 5
Elsrickle. *S Lan* 4F 19
Elvanfoot. *S Lan* 2G 11
Elvingston. *E Lot* 1B 20
Elwick. *Nmbd* 5H 21
Embleton. *Cumb* 5E 7
Embo. *High* 4F 55
Embo Street. *High* 4F 55
Enoch. *Dum* 3F 11
Enochdhu. *Per* 2F 33
Ensay. *Arg* 4E 29
Eolaigearraidh. *W Isl* 4C 60
Eorabus. *Arg* 1A 22
Eoropaidh. *W Isl* 1K 63
Erbusaig. *High* 1G 37
Erchless Castle. *High* 4F 47
Eredine. *Arg* 3G 23
Eriboll. *High* 3F 57
Ericstane. *Dum* 2H 11
Erines. *Arg* 1B 16
Errogie. *High* 1G 39
Errol. *Per* 1D 26
Errol Station. *Per* 1D 26
Erskine. *Ren* 1H 17
Erskine Bridge. *Ren* 1H 17
Ervie. *High* 2B 4
Eskadale. *High* 5F 47
Eskbank. *Midl* 2A 20
Eskdalemuir. *Dum* 4B 12
Esknish. *Arg* 2E 15
Essich. *High* 5H 47
Eswick. *Shet* 1D 66
Etal. *Nmbd* 5G 21
Etteridge. *High* 4H 39
Etterby. *Cumb* 2B 12
Ethie Haven. *Ang* 4D 34
Ettrickbridge. *Bord* 1C 12
Evanton. *High* 2H 47
Evelix. *High* 4E 55
Everbay. *Orkn* 5J 65
Evertown. *Dum* 1G 7
Ewes. *Dum* 4C 12
Exnaboe. *Shet* 5C 66
Eyemouth. *Bord* 2G 21
Eynort. *High* 1C 36
Eyre. *High* 3D 44
(on Isle of Skye)
Eyre. *High* 5E 45
(on Raasay)

F

Faichem. *High* 3D 38
Faifley. *W Dun* 1A 18
Fail. *S Ayr* 1B 10
Failford. *S Ayr* 1B 10
Fair Hill. *Cumb* 5H 7
Fairhill. *S Lan* 3C 18
Fair Isle Airport. *Shet* 1J 65
Fairlie. *N Ayr* 3F 17
Fairmilehead. *Edin* 2H 19
Fala. *Midl* 2B 20
Fala Dam. *Midl* 2B 20
Falkirk. *Falk* . . . .1D 18 & 81
Falkland. *Fife* 3D 26
Fallin. *Stir* 4H 25
Fanagmore. *High* 4C 56
Fanellan. *High* 4F 47
Fankerton. *Falk* 5G 25
Fanmore. *Arg* 4F 29
Fannich Lodge. *High* 2D 46
Fans. *Bord* 4D 20
Farley. *High* 4F 47
Farmtown. *Mor* 3A 50
Farnell. *Ang* 3D 34

Farr. *High* 2A 58
(nr. Bettyhill)
Farr. *High* 4A 48
(nr. Inverness)
Farr. *High* 3B 40
(nr. Kingussie)
Farraline. *High* 1G 39
Fasag. *High* 3H 45
Fascadale. *High* 1G 29
Fasnacloich. *Arg* 4D 30
Fassfern. *High* 1D 30
Fauldhouse. *W Lot* 2E 19
Feabuie. *High* 4A 48
Feagour. *High* 4G 39
Fearn. *High* 1B 48
Fearnan. *Per* 4C 32
Fearnbeg. *High* 3G 45
Fearnmore. *High* 2G 45
Felkington. *Nmbd* 4G 21
Fell Side. *Cumb* 5G 7
Fenham. *Nmbd* 4H 21
Fenton. *Cumb* 3H 7
Fenton. *Nmbd* 5G 21
Fenton Barns. *E Lot* 5G 27
Fenwick. *E Ayr* 4H 17
Fenwick. *Nmbd* 4H 21
Feochaig. *Arg* 2C 8
Feolin Ferry. *Arg* 2F 15
Feorlan. *Arg* 3B 8
Feriniquarrie. *High* 3A 44
Fern. *Ang* 2B 34
Ferness. *High* 4C 48
Fernieflatt. *Abers* 1F 35
Ferniegair. *S Lan* 3C 18
Fernilea. *High* 5C 44
Ferrindonald. *High* 3F 37
Ferryden. *Ang* 3E 35
Ferryhill. *Abers* 3E 43
Ferryton. *High* 2H 47
Fersit. *High* 1G 31
Feshiebridge. *High* 3B 40
Fetterangus. *Abers* 3E 51
Fettercairn. *Abers* 1D 34
Fiag Lodge. *High* 1B 54
Fieldhead. *Cumb* 5H 7
Fife Keith. *Mor* 3H 49
Finavon. *Ang* 3B 34
Fincharn. *Arg* 3G 23
Findhorn. *Mor* 2D 48
Findhorn Bridge. *High* 1B 40
Findochty. *Mor* 2H 49
Findo Gask. *Per* 1B 26
Findon. *Abers* 4E 43
Findon Mains. *High* 2H 47
Fingland. *Cumb* 3F 7
Fingland. *Dum* 2E 11
Finiskaig. *High* 4H 37
Finnart. *Per* 3A 32
Finnygaud. *Abers* 3B 50
Finstown. *Orkn* 3C 64
Fintry. *Abers* 3C 50
Fintry. *D'dee* 5B 34
Fintry. *Stir* 5F 25
Finzean. *Abers* 4B 42
Fionnphort. *Arg* 1A 22
Fionnsabhagh. *W Isl* 6B 62
First Coast. *High* 4E 53
Firth. *Shet* 5H 67
Fishcross. *Clac* 4A 26
Fisherford. *Abers* 5B 50
Fisherrow. *E Lot* 1A 20
Fisherton. *High* 3A 48
Fisherton. *S Ayr* 2H 9
Fishnish. *Arg* 4A 30
Fishwick. *Bord* 3G 21
Fiskavaig. *High* 5C 44
Fitch. *Shet* 2C 66
Fiunary. *High* 4H 29
Fladda. *Shet* 4G 67
Fladdabister. *Shet* 3D 66
Flashader. *High* 3C 44
Flatt, The. *Cumb* 5E 13
Fleck. *Shet* 5C 66
Fleisirin. *W Isl* 4K 63
Flemington. *S Lan* 2B 18
(nr. Glasgow)
Flemington. *S Lan* 4C 18
(nr. Strathaven)
Fleoideabhagh. *W Isl* 6B 62
Fletchertown. *Cumb* 4F 7
Fleuchary. *High* 4E 55
Flimby. *Cumb* 5D 6
Flodden. *Nmbd* 5G 21
Flodigarry. *High* 1D 44
Flushing. *Abers* 4F 51
Fochabers. *Mor* 3G 49
Fodderty. *High* 3G 47
Foffarty. *Ang* 4B 34
Fogo. *Bord* 4E 21
Fogorig. *Bord* 4E 21
Foindle. *High* 4C 56
Folda. *Ang* 2G 33
Folla Rule. *Abers* 5C 50
Foodieash. *Fife* 2E 27
Footdee. *Aber* 3E 43
Forbestown. *Abers* 2G 41
Ford. *Arg* 3F 23
Ford. *Nmbd* 5G 21
Fordell. *Fife* 5C 26
Fordie. *Per* 1G 25
Fordoun. *Abers* 1E 35
Fordyce. *Abers* 2A 50
Foresterseat. *Mor* 3F 49
Forest Lodge. *Per* 1E 33
Forest Mill. *Clac* 4A 26
Forfar. *Ang* 3B 34
Forgandenny. *Per* 2B 26
Forgewood. *N Lan* 3G 49
Forgie. *Mor* 3G 49
Forgue. *Abers* 4B 50
Forneth. *Per* 4F 33
Forres. *Mor* 3D 48
Forrestfield. *N Lan* 2D 18
Forrest Lodge. *Dum* 5C 10
Forse. *High* 5F 59

Forsinard. *High* 4B 58
Forss. *High* 2D 58
Fort Augustus. *High* 3E 39
Forteviot. *Per* 2B 26
Forth. *S Lan* 3E 19
Forth Road Bridge. *Fife* 1G 19
Fortingall. *Per* 4C 32
Fortrie. *Abers* 4B 50
Fortrose. *High* 3A 48
Fort William. *High* . . . .1E 31 & 81
Foss. *Per* 3C 32
Fothergill. *Cumb* 5D 6
Foubister. *Orkn* 4E 64
Foula Airport. *Shet* 5A 66
Foulbridge. *Cumb* 4H 7
Foulden. *Bord* 3G 21
Fountainhall. *Bord* 4B 20
Foveran. *Abers* 1E 43
Fowlershill. *Abers* 2E 43
Fowlis. *Ang* 5A 34
Fowlis Wester. *Per* 1A 26
Foyers. *High* 1F 39
Foynesfield. *High* 3B 48
Fraserburgh. *Abers* 2E 51
Freester. *Shet* 1D 66
French. *Stir* 3D 24
Fresgoe. *High* 2C 58
Freswick. *High* 2G 59
Freuchie. *Fife* 3D 26
Friockheim. *Ang* 4C 34
Frobost. *W Isl* 2C 60
Frotoft. *Orkn* 2D 64
Fullwood. *E Ayr* 3H 17
Funzie. *Shet* 3K 67
Furnace. *Arg* 3H 23
Fyvie. *Abers* 5C 50

G

Gabhsann bho Dheas. *W Isl* 2J 63
Gabhsann bho Thuath. *W Isl* 2J 63
Gabroc Hill. *E Ayr* 3H 17
Gadgirth. *S Ayr* 1B 10
Gaick Lodge. *High* 5A 40
Gairletter. *Arg* 5A 24
Gairloch. *Abers* 3C 42
Gairlochy. *High* 5C 30
Gairney Bank. *Per* 4C 26
Gairnshiel Lodge. *Abers* 3F 41
Gaitsgill. *Cumb* 4G 7
Galashiels. *Bord* 5B 20
Gallatown. *Fife* 4D 26
Gallin. *Per* 4A 32
Gallowfauld. *Ang* 4B 34
Gallowhill. *E Dun* 1B 18
Gallowhill. *Per* 5G 33
Gallowhill. *Ren* 2H 17
Gallowhills. *Abers* 3F 51
Galltair. *High* 1H 37
Galmisdale. *High* 5D 36
Galston. *E Ayr* 5H 17
Galtrigill. *High* 3A 44
Gamelsby. *Cumb* 3F 7
Ganavan. *Arg* 5B 30
Gannochy. *Ang* 1C 34
Gannochy. *Per* 1C 26
Gansclet. *High* 4G 59
Garafad. *High* 2D 44
Gardenstown. *Abers* 2D 50
Garderhouse. *Shet* 2C 66
Gardie. *High* 1A 66
(on Papa Stour)
Gardie. *Shet* 1K 67
(on Unst)
Gardie Ho. *Shet* 2D 66
Garelochhead. *Arg* 4B 24
Gargunnock. *Stir* 4G 25
Garleffin. *S Ayr* 5F 9
Garlieston. *Dum* 4F 5
Garlogie. *Abers* 3C 42
Garmond. *Abers* 3D 50
Garmony. *Arg* 4H 29
Garmouth. *Mor* 2G 49
Garnkirk. *N Lan* 2B 18
Garrabost. *W Isl* 4K 63
Garrallan. *E Ayr* 2C 10
Garrogie Lodge. *High* 2G 39
Garros. *High* 2D 44
Garrow. *Per* 4D 32
Gartcosh. *N Lan* 2B 18
Garth. *Shet* 1B 66
(nr. Sandness)
Garth. *Shet* 1D 66
(nr. Skellister)
Garthamlock. *Glas* 2B 18
Gartly. *Abers* 5A 50
Gartmore. *Stir* 4E 25
Gartness. *N Lan* 2C 18
Gartness. *Stir* 5E 25
Gartocharn. *W Dun* 5D 24
Gartsherrie. *N Lan* 2C 18
Gartymore. *High* 2H 55
Garvald. *E Lot* 1C 20
Garvamore. *High* 4G 39
Garvard. *Arg* 4A 22
Garvault. *High* 5A 58
Garve. *High* 2E 47
Garvock. *Abers* 1E 35
Garvock. *Inv* 1F 17
Gaskan. *High* 1B 30
Gatehead. *E Ayr* 5G 17
Gatehouse of Fleet. *Dum* 3H 5
Gatelawbridge. *Dum* 4G 11
Gateside. *Ang* 4B 34
(nr. Forfar)
Gateside. *Ang* 3C 34
(nr. Kirriemuir)
Gateside. *Fife* 3C 26
Gateside. *N Ayr* 3G 17
Gattonside. *Bord* 5C 20

Gauldry. *Fife* 1E 27
Gavinton. *Bord* 3E 21
Gayfield. *Orkn* 2G 65
Geanies. *High* 1B 48
Gearraidh Bhailteas. *W Isl* 2C 60
Gearraidh ma Monadh. *W Isl* 3C 60
Gearraidh Bhaird. *W Isl* 3E 62
Gearraidh na h-Aibhne. *W Isl* 1D 62
Geary. *High* 2B 44
Geddes. *High* 3B 48
Gedintailor. *High* 5E 45
Geilston. *Arg* 1G 17
Geirinis. *W Isl* 6H 61
Geise. *High* 2E 59
Geisiadar. *W Isl* 1C 62
Gelder Shiel. *Abers* 5F 41
Gellyburn. *Per* 5F 33
Gelston. *Dum* 3A 6
Geocrab. *W Isl* 5C 62
Georgetown. *Ren* 2H 17
Georth. *Orkn* 2C 64
Gerston. *High* 3E 59
Giffnock. *E Ren* 3A 18
Gifford. *E Lot* 2C 20
Giffordtown. *Fife* 2D 26
Gilchriston. *E Lot* 2B 20
Gilcrux. *Cumb* 5E 7
Gillen. *High* 3B 44
Gills. *High* 1G 59
Gillock. *High* 3F 59
Gilmanscleuch. *Bord* 1C 12
Gilmerton. *Edin* 2H 19
Gilmerton. *Per* 1H 25
Gilston. *Midl* 3B 20
Giosla. *W Isl* 2C 62
Girdle Toll. *N Ayr* 4G 17
Girlsta. *Shet* 1D 66
Girthon. *Dum* 3H 5
Girvan. *S Ayr* 4G 9
Gladsmuir. *E Lot* 1B 20
Glaichbea. *High* 5G 47
Glame. *High* 4E 45
Glamis. *Ang* 4A 34
Glamisdale. *High* 5D 36
Glas Aird. *Arg* 4A 22
Glas-allt Shiel. *Abers* 5F 41
Glaschoil. *Mor* 5D 48
Glasgow. *Glas* . . . .2A 18 & 78-79
Glasgow Airport. *Ren* 2H 17
Glasgow Prestwick
International Airport.
S Ayr 1A 10
Glashvin. *High* 2D 44
Glasnakille. *High* 2E 37
Glasnarcardoch. *High* 4F 37
Glassburn. *High* 5E 47
Glasserton. *Dum* 5F 5
Glassford. *S Lan* 4C 18
Glassgreen. *Mor* 2F 49
Glasson. *Cumb* 2F 7
Glasterlaw. *Ang* 3C 34
Gleann Dail bho Dheas.
W Isl 3C 60
Gleann Tholastaidh. *W Isl* 3K 63
Glecknabae. *Arg* 2D 16
Glen. *Dum* 3G 5
Glenancross. *High* 4F 37
Glenbarr. *Arg* 5H 15
Glenbeg. *High* 2G 29
Glen Bernisdale. *High* 4D 44
Glenbervie. *Abers* 5C 42
Glenboig. *N Lan* 2C 18
Glenborrodale. *High* 2H 29
Glenbranter. *Arg* 4A 24
Glenbreck. *Bord* 1H 11
Glenbrein Lodge. *High* 2F 39
Glenbrittle. *High* 1D 36
Glenbuchat Lodge. *Abers* 2G 41
Glenbuck. *E Ayr* 1E 11
Glencalvie Lodge. *High* 5B 54
Glencaple. *Dum* 2C 6
Glencarron Lodge. *High* 3B 46
Glencarse. *Per* 1C 26
Glencassley Castle. *High* 3B 54
Glencat. *Abers* 4A 42
Glencoe. *High* 3E 31
Glen Cottage. *High* 5F 37
Glencraig. *Fife* 4C 26
Glendale. *High* 4A 44
Glendevon. *Per* 3A 26
Glendoebeg. *High* 3F 39
Glendoick. *Per* 1D 26
Glendoune. *S Ayr* 4G 9
Glenduckie. *Fife* 2D 26
Gleneagles. *Per* 3A 26
Glenegedale. *Arg* 3B 15
Glenegedale Lots. *Arg* 3E 15
Glenelg. *High* 2H 37
Glenernie. *Mor* 4D 48
Glenesslin. *High* 5F 11
Glenfarg. *Per* 2C 26
Glenfarquhar Lodge. *Abers* 5C 42
Glenferness Mains. *High* 4C 48
Glenfeshie Lodge. *High* 5B 40
Glenfiddich Lodge. *Mor* 5G 49
Glenfinnan. *High* 5H 37
Glenfintaig Lodge. *High* 5D 38
Glenfoot. *Per* 2C 26
Glenfyne Lodge. *Arg* 2B 24
Glengap. *Dum* 3H 5
Glengarnock. *N Ayr* 3G 17
Glengolly. *High* 2E 59
Glengorm Castle. *Arg* 3F 29
Glengrasco. *High* 4D 44
Glenhead Farm. *Ang* 2H 33
Glenholm. *Bord* 5D 19
Glen House. *Bord* 5H 19
Glenhurich. *High* 2B 30
Glenkerry. *Bord* 2B 12
Glenkiln. *Dum* 1B 6
Glenkindie. *Abers* 2A 42
Glenkinglass Lodge. *Arg* 5E 31
Glenkirk. *Bord* 1H 11

Glenlean. Arg 5H 23
Glenlee. Dum 5D 10
Glenleraig. High 5C 56
Glenlichorn. Per 2G 25
Glenlivet. Mor 1E 41
Glenlochar. Dum 2A 6
Glenlochsie Lodge. Per 1F 33
Glenluce. Dum 3C 4
Glenmarskie. High 3E 47
Glenmassan. Arg 5A 24
Glenmavis. N Lan 2C 18
Glenmazeran Lodge. High 1A 40
Glenmidge. Dum 5F 11
Glenmore. High 2G 29
(nr. Glenborrodale)
Glenmore. High 3C 40
(nr. Kingussie)
Glenmore. High 4D 44
(on Isle of Skye)
Glenmoy. Ang 2B 34
Glennoe. Arg 5D 30
Glen of Coachford. Abers 4H 49
Glenogil. Ang 2B 34
Glenprosen Village. Ang 2A 34
Glenree. N Ayr 1E 9
Glenrosa. N Ayr 5D 16
Glenrothes. Fife 3D 26
Glensanda. High 4B 30
Glensaugh. Abers 1D 34
Glenshero Lodge. High 4G 39
Glensluain. Arg 4H 23
Glenstockadale. Dum 2B 4
Glenstriven. Arg 1D 16
Glen Tanar House. Abers 4H 41
Glenton. Abers 1B 42
Glentress. Bord 5H 19
Glentromie Lodge. High 4A 40
Glentrool Lodge. Dum 5B 10
Glentrool Village. Dum 1E 5
Glentruim House. High 4H 39
Glenuig. High 1H 29
Glen Village. Falk 1D 18
Glenwhilly. Dum 1C 4
Glenzierfoot. Dum 1G 7
Glespin. S Lan 1F 11
Gletness. Shet 1D 66
Glib Cheois. W Isl 2E 62
Gloup. Shet 2J 67
Glutt Lodge. High 5C 58
Gobernuisgach Lodge. High 4F 57
Gobernuisgeach. High 5C 58
Gobhaig. W Isl 4B 62
Gogar. Edin 1G 19
Gollanfield. High 3B 48
Golspie. High 4F 55
Gometra House. Arg 4E 29
Gonfirth. Shet 6G 67
Gord. Shet 4D 66
Gordon. Bord 4D 20
Gordonbush. High 3F 55
Gordonstown. Abers 3A 50
(nr. Cornhill)
Gordonstown. Abers 5C 50
(nr. Fyvie)
Gorebridge. Midl 2A 20
Gorgie. Edin 1H 19
Gorseness. Orkn 3D 64
Gorstan. High 2E 47
Gortantaoid. Arg 1E 15
Gorteneorn. High 2H 29
Gortenfern. High 2H 29
Gossabrough. Shet 4J 67
Goswick. Nmbd 4H 21
Gott. Arg 4B 28
Gott. Shet 2D 66
Gourdon. Abers 1F 35
Gourock. Inv 1F 17
Govan. Glas 2A 18
Govanhill. Glas 2A 18
Gowanhill. Abers 2F 51
Gowkhall. Fife 5B 26
Grabhair. W Isl 3E 62
Gramasdail. W Isl 5J 61
Grandtully. Per 3E 33
Grange. E Ayr 5H 17
Grange. Per 1D 26
Grange Crossroads. Mor 3H 49
Grangemouth. Falk 5A 26
Grange of Lindores. Fife 2D 26
Grangepans. Falk 5B 26
Granish. High 2B 40
Grantlodge. Abers 2C 42
Granton. Edin 1H 19
Grantown-on-Spey. High 1D 40
Grantshouse. Bord 2F 21
Grassgarth. Cumb 4G 7
Graven. Shet 5H 67
Grealin. High 2E 45
Great Blencow. Cumb 5H 7
Great Broughton. Cumb 5D 6
Great Clifton. Cumb 5D 6
Great Corby. Cumb 3H 7
Great Orton. Cumb 3G 7
Greenbank. Shet 2J 67
Greenburn. W Lot 2E 19
Greendykes. Nmbd 5H 21
Greenfield. Arg 4B 24
Greenfoot. N Lan 2C 18
Greengairs. N Lan 1C 18
Greengill. Cumb 5E 7
Greenhaugh. Nmbd 5G 13
Greenhill. Dum 1E 7
Greenhill. Falk 1D 18
Greenhills. N Ayr 3G 17
Greenholm. E Ayr 5A 18
Greenigo. Orkn 4D 64
Greenland. High 2F 59
Greenland Mains. High 2F 59
Greenlaw. Bord 4E 21
Greenlea. Dum 1D 6
Greenloaning. Per 3H 25
Greenmow. Shet 4D 66
Greenock. Inv 1F 17
Greenock Mains. E Ayr 1D 10
Greenrow. Cumb 3E 7
Greens. Abers 4D 50
Greenwall. Orkn 4E 64
Grein. W Isl 4B 60
Greinetobht. W Isl 3J 61
Gremista. Shet 2D 66
Greosabhagh. W Isl 5C 62
Greshornish. High 3C 44
Gretna. Dum 2G 7
Gretna Green. Dum 2G 7
Greysouthen. Cumb 5D 6
Greystoke. Cumb 5H 7
Greystoke Gill. Cumb 5H 7
Greystone. Ang 4C 34
Griais. W Isl 3J 63
Grianan. W Isl 4J 63
Gribun. Arg 5F 29
Grimbister. Orkn 3C 64
Grimeston. Orkn 3C 64
Griminis. W Isl 5H 61
(on Benbecula)
Griminis. W Isl 3H 61
(on North Uist)
Grimister. Shet 3H 67
Grimness. Orkn 5D 64
Grindiscol. Shet 3D 66
Grindon. Nmbd 4G 21
Grinsdale. Cumb 3G 7
Griomsidar. W Isl 5J 63
Grishipoll. Arg 3C 28
Gritley. Orkn 4E 64
Grobister. Orkn 5J 65
Grobsness. Shet 6G 67
Grogport. Arg 4B 16
Groigearraidh. W Isl 6H 61
Grove, The. Dum 1C 6
Grudie. High 2E 47
Gruids. High 3C 54
Gruinard House. High 4E 53
Gruinart. Arg 2D 14
Grulinbeg. Arg 2D 14
Gruline. Arg 4G 29
Grummore. High 5H 57
Gruting. Shet 2B 66
Grutness. Shet 6D 66
Gualachulain. High 4E 31
Gualin House. High 3E 57
Guardbridge. Fife 2F 27
Guay. Per 4F 33
Guildtown. Per 5G 33
Gulberwick. Shet 3D 66
Gullane. E Lot 5F 27
Gunnerton. Nmbd 5H 13
Gunnista. Shet 2D 66
Gunsgreenhill. Bord 2G 21
Gutcher. Shet 3J 67
Guthrie. Ang 3C 34

H

Haa of Houlland. Shet 2J 67
Hackland. Orkn 2C 64
Hackness. Orkn 5C 64
Haclait. W Isl 6J 61
Hadden. Bord 5E 21
Haddington. E Lot 1C 20
Haddo. Abers 5D 50
Haggbeck. Cumb 1H 7
Haggersta. Shet 2C 66
Haggerston. Nmbd 4H 21
Haggrister. Shet 5G 67
Halbeath. Fife 5C 26
Halcro. High 2F 59
Halistra. High 3B 44
Halket. E Ayr 3H 17
Halkirk. High 3E 59
Hall. E Ren 3H 17
Halliburton. Bord 4D 20
Hallin. High 3B 44
Hallyne. Bord 4G 19
Haltcliff Bridge. Cumb 5G 7
Ham. High 1F 59
Ham. Shet 5A 66
Hamilton. S Lan 3C 18 & 82
Hamister. Shet 6J 67
Hamnavoe. Shet 4F 67
(nr. Braehoulland)
Hamnavoe. Shet 3C 66
(nr. Burland)
Hamnavoe. Shet 5H 67
(nr. Lunna)
Hamnavoe. Shet 4H 67
(on Yell)
Happas. Ang 4B 34
Happendon. S Lan 5D 18
Hardgate. Abers 3C 42
Hardgate. Dum 2B 6
Harelaw. Dum 1H 7
Hareshaw. N Lan 2D 18
Harker. Cumb 2G 7
Harkland. Shet 4H 67
Harlosh. High 4B 44
Haroldswick. Shet 1K 67
Harpsdale. High 3E 59
Harraby. Cumb 3H 7
Harrapool. High 1F 37
Harrietfield. Per 1A 26
Harrington. Cumb 5C 6
Harriston. Cumb 5E 7
Harthill. N Lan 2E 19
Hartmount. High 1A 48
Hartwood. N Lan 3D 18
Hassendean. Bord 1E 13
Haster. High 3G 59
Hastigrow. High 2F 59
Hatton. Abers 5F 51
Hattoncrook. Abers 1E 43
Hatton of Fintray. Abers 2D 42
Haugh. E Ayr 1B 10
Haugh Head. Nmbd 5H 21
Haugh of Ballechin. Per 3E 33
Haugh of Glass. Mor 5H 49
Haugh of Urr. Dum 2B 6
Haunn. Arg 4E 29
Haunn. W Isl 3C 60
Hawick. Bord 2E 13
Hawksdale. Cumb 4G 7
Hayhill. E Ayr 2B 10
Hayshead. Ang 4D 34
Hayston. Aber 3E 43
Hayton. Cumb 4E 7
(nr. Aspatria)
Hayton. Cumb 3H 7
(nr. Brampton)
Haywood. S Lan 3E 19
Hazelbank. S Lan 4D 18
Hazelton Walls. Fife 1E 27
Head of Muir. Falk 5H 25
Heads Nook. Cumb 3H 7
Heanish. Arg 4B 28
Heaste. High 2F 37
Heatherfield. High 4D 44
Heathfield. Cumb 4E 7
Heathfield. Ren 2G 17
Heathhall. Dum 1C 6
Heck. Dum 5H 11
Heddle. Orkn 3C 64
Heglibister. Shet 1C 66
Heights of Brae. High 2G 47
Heights of Fodderty. High 2G 47
Heights of Kinlochewe. High 2B 46
Heiton. Bord 5E 21
Helensburgh. Arg 5B 24
Hellister. Shet 2C 66
Helmsdale. High 2H 55
Hempriggs. High 4G 59
Heogan. Shet 2D 66
Heribusta. High 1D 44
Heriot. Bord 3B 20
Hermiston. Edin 1G 19
Hermitage. Bord 4E 13
Heronsford. S Ayr 5G 9
Herra. Shet 3K 67
Herston. Orkn 5D 64
Hesket Newmarket. Cumb 5G 7
Hesleyside. Nmbd 5H 13
Hessilhead. N Ayr 3G 17
Hestaford. Shet 1B 66
Hestinsetter. Shet 2B 66
Hestwall. Orkn 3B 64
Hethersgill. Cumb 2H 7
Hetherside. Cumb 2H 7
Hethpool. Nmbd 1H 13
Hetton Steads. Nmbd 5H 21
Heugh-head. Abers 2G 41
Heylipol. Arg 4A 28
High Auldgirth. Dum 5G 11
High Banton. N Lan 5G 25
High Blantyre. S Lan 3B 18
High Bonnybridge. Falk 1D 18
Highbridge. Cumb 4G 7
Highbridge. High 5C 38
High Crosby. Cumb 3H 7
High Dougarie. N Ayr 5B 16
Highfield. N Ayr 3G 17
Highgate. N Ayr 3G 17
Highgreen Manor. Nmbd 4H 13
High Harrington. Cumb 5D 6
High Hesket. Cumb 4H 7
High Ireby. Cumb 5F 7
High Keil. Arg 3B 8
Highlaws. Cumb 4E 7
High Longthwaite. Cumb 4F 7
High Lorton. Cumb 5E 7
Highmoor. Cumb 4F 7
High Row. Cumb 5G 7
High Scales. Cumb 4E 7
High Side. Cumb 5F 7
Hightae. Dum 1D 6
High Valleyfield. Fife 5B 26
Hillbrae. Abers 4B 50
(nr. Aberchirder)
Hillbrae. Abers 1C 42
(nr. Inverurie)
Hillbrae. Abers 5D 50
(nr. Methlick)
Hillend. Fife 5C 26
(nr. Inverkeithing)
Hill End. Fife 4B 26
(nr. Saline)
Hillend. N Lan 2D 18
Hillhead. Abers 5A 50
Hillhead. S Ayr 2B 10
Hillhead of Auchentumb.
Abers 3E 51
Hilliclay. High 2E 59
Hillington. Ren 2A 18
Hill of Beath. Fife 4C 26
Hill of Fearn. High 1B 48
Hill of Fiddes. Abers 1E 43
Hill of Keillor. Ang 4H 33
Hill of Overbrae. Abers 2D 50
Hillside. Abers 4E 43
Hillside. Ang 2E 35
Hillside. Orkn 2C 64
Hillside. Shet 6H 67
Hillside of Prieston. Ang 5A 34
Hillswick. Shet 5F 67
Hillwell. Shet 5C 66
Hillyland. Per 1B 26
Hilton. High 5E 55
Hilton of Cadboll. High 1B 48
Hirn. Abers 3C 42
Hirst. N Lan 2D 18
Hobbister. Orkn 4C 64
Hobkirk. Bord 2E 13
Hoddomcross. Dum 1E 7
Hogaland. Shet 5G 67
Hogha Gearraidh. W Isl 3H 61
Holburn. Nmbd 5H 21
Holland. Orkn 2G 65
(on Papa Westray)
Holland. Orkn 5J 65
(on Stronsay)
Hollandstoun. Orkn 2K 65
Hollows. Dum 1G 7
Hollybush. E Ayr 2A 10
Holmend. Dum 3H 11
Holme St Cuthbert. Cumb 4E 7
Holmhead. E Ayr 1C 10
Holmisdale. High 4A 44
Holm of Drumlanrig. Dum 4F 11
Holmsgarth. Shet 2D 66
Holmwrangle. Cumb 4H 7
Holy Island. Nmbd 4H 21
Holytown. N Lan 2C 18
Holywood. Dum 5G 11
Hoove. Shet 2C 66
Hope. High 2F 57
Hopeman. Mor 2E 49
Horgabost. W Isl 5B 62
Horncliffe. Nmbd 4G 21
Horndean. Bord 4F 21
Hornsby. Cumb 3H 7
Hornsbygate. Cumb 3H 7
Horsbrugh Ford. Bord 5H 19
Horsley. Nmbd 4H 13
Horsleyhill. Bord 2E 13
Hosh. Per 1H 25
Hosta. W Isl 3H 61
Hoswick. Shet 4D 66
Houbie. Shet 3K 67
Hough. Arg 4A 28
Houghton. Cumb 3H 7
Houlland. Shet 1C 66
(on Mainland)
Houlland. Shet 5J 67
(on Yell)
Houndslow. Bord 4D 20
Houndwood. Bord 2F 21
Housabister. Shet 1D 66
Housay. Shet 5K 67
Househill. High 3B 48
Housetter. Shet 4G 67
Houss. Shet 3C 66
Houston. Ren 2H 17
Housty. High 5E 59
Houton. Orkn 4C 64
How. Cumb 3H 7
Howe. High 2G 59
Howe of Teuchar. Abers 4C 50
Howes. Dum 2E 7
Howgate. Midl 3H 19
Hownam. Bord 2G 13
Howtel. Nmbd 5F 21
Howwood. Ren 2G 17
Hughton. High 4F 47
Huisinis. W Isl 3A 62
Humbie. E Lot 2B 20
Humbleton. Nmbd 5G 21
Hume. Bord 4E 21
Huna. High 1G 59
Hungladder. High 1C 44
Hunspow. High 1F 59
Hunterfield. Midl 2A 20
Hunter's Quay. Arg 1E 17
Hunthill Lodge. Ang 1B 34
Huntington. E Lot 1B 20
Huntingtower. Per 1B 26
Huntly. Abers 4A 50
Huntlywood. Bord 4D 20
Hurlet. Glas 2A 18
Hurlford. E Ayr 5H 17
Hurliness. Orkn 6B 64
Hutton. Cumb 5H 7
Hutton. Bord 3G 21
Hutton End. Cumb 5H 7
Hutton Roof. Cumb 5G 7
Huxter. Shet 1A 66
(on Mainland)
Huxter. Shet 6J 67
(on Whalsay)
Hyndford Bridge. S Lan 4E 19
Hynish. Arg 5A 28
Hythie. Abers 3F 51

I

Ianstown. Mor 2H 49
Iarsiadar. W Isl 1C 62
Ibrox. Glas 2A 18
Ichrachan. Arg 5D 30
Idrigill. High 2C 44
Imachar. N Ayr 4B 16
Inchbae Lodge. High 2F 47
Inchbare. Ang 2D 34
Inchberry. Mor 3G 49
Inchbraoch. Ang 3E 35
Incheril. High 2B 46
Inchinnan. Ren 2H 17
Inchlaggan. High 3C 38
Inchmichael. Per 1D 26
Inchnadamph. High 1H 53
Inchree. High 2D 30
Inchture. Per 1D 26
Inchyra. Per 1C 26
Inkstack. High 1F 59
Innellan. Arg 2E 17
Innerleith. Fife 2D 26
Innerleithen. Bord 5A 20
Innerleven. Fife 3E 27
Innermessan. Dum 2B 4
Innerwick. E Lot 1E 21
Innerwick. Per 4A 32
Insch. Abers 1B 42
Insh. High 3B 40
Inshegra. High 3D 56
Inshore. High 1E 57
Inver. Abers 4F 41
Inver. High 5F 55
Inver. Per 4F 33
Inverailort. High 5G 37
Inveralligin. High 3H 45
Inverallochy. Abers 2F 51
Inveramsay. Abers 1C 42
Inveran. High 4C 54
Inveraray. Arg 3H 23
Inverarish. High 5E 45
Inverarity. Ang 4B 34
Inverarnan. Arg 2C 24
Inverarnie. High 5H 47
Inverbeg. Arg 4C 24
Inverbervie. Abers 1F 35
Inverboyndie. Abers 2B 50
Invercassley. High 3B 54
Invercharnan. High 4E 31
Inverchoran. High 3D 46
Invercreran. Arg 4D 30
Inverdruie. High 2C 40
Inverebrie. Abers 5E 51
Invereck. Arg 5A 24
Inveresk. E Lot 1A 20
Inveresragan. Arg 5C 30
Inverey. Abers 5D 40
Inverfarigaig. High 1G 39
Invergarry. High 3E 39
Invergeldie. Per 1G 25
Invergordon. High 2A 48
Invergowrie. Per 5A 34
Inverguseran. High 3G 37
Inverharroch. Mor 5G 49
Inverie. High 3G 37
Inverinan. Arg 2G 23
Inverinate. High 1B 38
Inverkeilor. Ang 4D 34
Inverkeithing. Fife 5C 26
Inverkeithny. Abers 4B 50
Inverkip. Inv 1F 17
Inverkirkaig. High 2E 53
Inverlael. High 5G 53
Inverliever Lodge. Arg 3F 23
Inverliver. Arg 5D 30
Inverloch. High 1E 31
Inverlochlarig. Stir 2E 25
Inverlussa. Arg 5D 22
Inver Mallie. High 5C 38
Invermarkie. Abers 5H 49
Invermoriston. High 2F 39
Invernaver. High 2A 58
Inverneil House. Arg 5F 23
Inverness. High 4H 47 & 82
Inverness Airport. High 3A 48
Invernettie. Abers 4G 51
Inverpolly Lodge. High 2F 53
Inverquhomery. Abers 4F 51
Inverroy. High 5D 38
Inversanda. High 3C 30
Invershiel. High 2A 38
Invershin. High 4C 54
Invershore. High 5F 59
Inversnaid. Stir 3C 24
Inverugie. Abers 4G 51
Inveruglas. Arg 3C 24
Inverurie. Abers 1C 42
Invervar. Per 4B 32
Inverythan. Abers 4C 50
Iochdar. W Isl 6H 61
Ireby. Cumb 5F 7
Ireland. Shet 4C 66
Irthington. Cumb 2H 7
Irvine. N Ayr 5G 17
Irvine Mains. N Ayr 5G 17
Isauld. High 2C 58
Isbister. Orkn 3C 64
Isbister. Shet 3G 67
(on Mainland)
Isbister. Shet 6J 67
(on Whalsay)
Islay Airport. Arg 3E 15
Isle of Whithorn. Dum 5F 5
Isleornsay. High 2G 37
Islesburgh. Shet 6G 67
Islesteps. Dum 1C 6
Islibhig. W Isl 2A 62
Itlaw. Abers 3B 50
Ivegill. Cumb 4H 7
Iverchaolain. Arg 1D 16

J

Jackton. S Lan 3A 18
Jamestown. Dum 4C 12
Jamestown. Fife 5C 26
Jamestown. High 3F 47
Jamestown. W Dun 5C 24
Janetstown. High 2D 58
(nr. Thurso)
Janetstown. High 3G 59
(nr. Wick)
Jedburgh. Bord 1F 13
Jemimaville. High 2A 48
Jenkins Park. High 3E 39
Johnby. Cumb 5H 7
John o' Groats. High 1G 59
Johnshaven. Abers 2E 35
Johnstone. Ren 2H 17
Johnstonebridge. Dum 4H 11
Joppa. Edin 1A 20
Joppa. S Ayr 2B 10
Juniper Green. Edin 2G 19

K

Kaimend. S Lan 4E 19
Kaimes. Edin 2H 19
Kaimrig End. Bord 4F 19
Kames. Arg 1C 16
Kames. E Ayr 1D 10
Kearvaig. High 1D 56
Kedlock Feus. Fife 2E 27
Keig. Abers 2B 42
Keilarsbrae. Clac 4H 25
Keillmore. Arg 5D 22
Keillor. Per 4H 33
Keillour. Per 1A 26
Keills. Arg 2F 15
Keiloch. Abers 4E 41
Keils. Arg 2G 15
Keir Mill. Dum 4F 11
Keiss. High 2G 59
Keith. Mor 3H 49
Keith Inch. Abers 4G 51
Kellan. Arg 4G 29
Kellas. Ang 5B 34
Kellas. Mor 3E 49
Kelloholm. Dum 2E 11
Kelsick. Cumb 3E 7
Kelso. Bord 5E 21
Keltneyburn. Per 4C 32
Kelton. Dum 1C 6
Kelton Hill. Dum 3A 6
Kelty. Fife 4C 26
Kelvinside. Glas 2A 18
Kemback. Fife 2F 27
Kemnay. Abers 2C 42
Kengharair. Arg 4F 29
Kenknock. Stir 5H 31
Kenmore. High 3G 45
Kenmore. Per 4C 32
Kennacraig. Arg 2B 16
Kennet. Clac 4A 26
Kennethmont. Abers 1A 42
Kennoway. Fife 3E 27
Kenovay. Arg 4A 28
Kensaleyre. High 3D 44
Kentallen. High 3D 30
Kentra. High 2H 29
Keoldale. High 2E 57
Keppoch. High 1A 38
Kerrow. High 5E 47
Kerrycroy. Arg 2E 17
Kerse. Ren 3G 17
Kershopefoot. Cumb 5D 12
Kettins. Per 5H 33
Kettlebridge. Fife 3E 27
Kettleholm. Dum 1E 7
Kettletoft. Orkn 4J 65
Keyhead. Abers 3F 51
Kiel Crofts. Arg 5C 30
Kielder. Nmbd 4F 13
Kilbagie. Fife 4A 26
Kilbarchan. Ren 2H 17
Kilbeg. High 3F 37
Kilberry. Arg 2A 16
Kilbirnie. N Ayr 3G 17
Kilbride. Arg 1F 23
Kilbride. High 1E 37
Kilbucho Place. Bord 5F 19
Kilchattan. Arg 4A 22
(on Colonsay)
Kilchattan. Arg 3E 17
(on Isle of Bute)
Kilchattan Bay. Arg 3D 16
Kilchenzie. Arg 1B 8
Kilcheran. Arg 5B 30
Kilchiaran. Arg 2D 14
Kilchoan. High 4G 37
(nr. Inverie)
Kilchoan. High 2F 29
(nr. Tobermory)
Kilchoman. Arg 2D 14
Kilchrenan. Arg 1H 23
Kilconquhar. Fife 3F 27
Kilcoy. High 3G 47
Kilcreggan. Arg 5B 24
Kildary. High 1A 48
Kildermorie Lodge. High 1G 47
Kildonan. Dum 3B 4
Kildonan. High 1G 55
(nr. Helmsdale)
Kildonan. High 3C 44
(on Isle of Skye)
Kildonan. N Ayr 1F 9
Kildonnan. High 5D 36
Kildrummy. Abers 2H 41
Kilfillan. Dum 3D 4
Kilfinan. Arg 1C 16
Kilfinnan. High 4D 38
Kilgour. Fife 3D 26
Kilgrammie. S Ayr 3H 9
Kilham. Nmbd 5F 21
Kilkenneth. Arg 4A 28
Killandrist. Arg 4B 30
Killean. Arg 4H 15
Killearn. Stir 5E 25
Killellan. Arg 2B 8
Killen. High 3H 47
Killichonan. Per 3A 32
Killiechronan. Arg 4G 29
Killiecrankie. Per 2E 33
Killilan. High 5A 46
Killimster. High 3G 59
Killin. Stir 5A 32
Killin Lodge. High 3G 39
Killinochonoch. Arg 4F 23
Killochyett. Bord 4B 20
Killundine. High 4G 29
Kilmacolm. Inv 1G 17
Kilmahog. Stir 3F 25
Kilmahumaig. Arg 4E 23
Kilmalieu. High 3B 30
Kilmaluag. High 1D 44
Kilmany. Fife 1E 27
Kilmarie. High 2E 37
Kilmarnock. E Ayr 5H 17 & 83
Kilmaron. Fife 2E 27
Kilmartin. Arg 4F 23
Kilmaurs. E Ayr 4H 17
Kilmelford. Arg 2F 23
Kilmeny. Arg 2E 15
Kilmichael Glassary. Arg 4F 23
Kilmichael of Inverlussa.
Arg 5E 23
Kilmoluag. Arg 4A 28
Kilmorack. High 4F 47
Kilmore. Arg 1F 23
Kilmore. High 3F 37
Kilmory. Arg 2A 16
Kilmory. High 1G 29
(nr. Kilchoan)
Kilmory. High 3C 36
(on Rùm)
Kilmory. N Ayr 1E 9
Kilmory Lodge. Arg 3E 23
Kilmote. High 2G 55
Kilmuir. High 4B 44
(nr. Dunvegan)
Kilmuir. High 1A 48
(nr. Invergordon)
Kilmuir. High 4H 47
(nr. Inverness)
Kilmuir. High 1C 44
(nr. Uig)
Kilmun. Arg 5A 24
Kilnave. Arg 1D 14
Kilncadzow. S Lan 4D 18
Kilnhill. Cumb 5F 7
Kilninian. Arg 4E 29

Kilninver. Arg 1F 23
Kiloran. Arg 4A 22
Kilpatrick. N Ayr 1E 9
Kilrenny. Fife 3G 27
Kilspindie. Per 1D 26
Kilsyth. N Lan 1C 18
Kiltarlity. High 4G 47
Kilvaxter. High 2C 44
Kilwinning. N Ayr 4F 17
Kimmerston. Nmbd 5G 21
Kinbeachie. High 2H 47
Kinbrace. High 5B 58
Kinbuck. Stir 3G 25
Kincaple. Fife 2F 27
Kincardine. Fife 5A 26
Kincardine. High 5D 54
Kincardine Bridge. Fife 5A 26
Kincardine O'Neil. Abers 4A 42
Kinchrackine. Arg 1A 24
Kincorth. Aber 3E 43
Kincraig. High 3B 40
Kincraigie. Per 4E 33
Kindallachan. Per 3E 33
Kinfauns. Per 1C 26
Kingairloch. High 3B 30
Kingarth. Arg 3D 16
Kingholm Quay. Dum 1C 6
Kinghorn. Fife 5D 26
Kingie. High 3C 38
Kinglassie. Fife 4D 26
Kingledores. Bord 1A 12
Kingodie. Per 1E 27
King o' Muirs. Clac 4H 25
Kingsbarns. Fife 2G 27
Kingsburgh. High 3C 44
Kingscavil. W Lot 1F 19
Kingscross. N Ayr 1F 9
Kingseat. Fife 4C 26
Kingsford. E Ayr 4H 17
Kingshouse. High 3F 31
Kingshouse. Stir 1E 25
Kingskettle. Fife 3E 27
Kingsmuir. Ang 4B 34
Kingsmuir. Fife 3G 27
Kings Muir. Bord 5H 19
Kingsteps. High 3C 48
Kingston. E Lot 5G 27
Kingston. Mor 2G 49
Kingswells. Aber 3D 42
Kingswood. Per 5F 33
Kingussie. High 3A 40
Kinharrachie. Abers 5E 51
Kinhrive. High 1A 48
Kinkell Bridge. Per 2A 26
Kinknockie. Abers 4F 51
Kinkry Hill. Cumb 1H 7
Kinloch. High 5E 57
(nr. Loch More)
Kinloch. High 3H 29
(nr. Lochaline)
Kinloch. High 4D 36
(on Rùm)
Kinloch. Per 4G 33
Kinlochard. Stir 3D 24
Kinlochbervie. High 3D 56
Kinlocheil. High 1C 30
Kinlochewe. High 2B 46
Kinloch Hourn. High 3A 38
Kinloch Laggan. High 5G 39
Kinlochleven. High 2E 31
Kinloch Lodge. High 3G 57
Kinlochmoidart. High 1A 30
Kinlochmore. High 2E 31
Kinloch Rannoch. Per 3B 32
Kinlochspelve. Arg 1D 22
Kinloid. High 5F 37
Kinloss. Mor 2D 48
Kinmuck. Abers 2D 42
Kinnadie. Abers 4E 51
Kinnaird. Per 1D 26
Kinneff. Abers 1F 35
Kinnelhead. Dum 3H 11
Kinnell. Ang 3D 34
Kinnernie. Abers 2C 42
Kinnesswood. Per 3C 26
Kinnordy. Ang 3A 34
Kinross. Per 3C 26
Kinrossie. Per 5G 33
Kintessack. Mor 2D 48
Kintillo. Per 2C 26
Kintore. Abers 2C 42
Kintour. Arg 3F 15
Kintra. Arg 1A 22
Kintraw. Arg 3F 23
Kinveachy. High 2C 40
Kippen. Stir 4F 25
Kippford. Dum 3B 6
Kirbister. Orkn 4C 64
(nr. Hobbister)
Kirbister. Orkn 3B 64
(nr. Quholm)
Kirbuster. Orkn 5J 65
Kirk. High 3F 59
Kirkabister. Shet 3D 66
(on Bressay)
Kirkabister. Shet 1D 66
(on Mainland)
Kirkandrews. Dum 4H 5
Kirkandrews-on-Eden. Cumb 3G 7
Kirkapol. Arg 4B 28
Kirkbampton. Cumb 3G 7
Kirkbean. Dum 3C 6
Kirkbride. Cumb 3F 7
Kirkbuddo. Ang 4C 34
Kirkcaldy. Fife 4D 26 & 83
Kirkcolm. Dum 2B 4
Kirkconnel. Dum 2E 11
Kirkconnell. Dum 2C 6
Kirkcowan. Dum 2E 5
Kirkcudbright. Dum 3H 5
Kirkfieldbank. S Lan 4D 18
Kirkforthar Feus. Fife 3D 26
Kirkgunzeon. Dum 2B 6
Kirkhill. Ang 2D 34
Kirkhill. High 4G 47
Kirkhope. S Lan 3G 11
Kirkhouse. Bord 5A 20
Kirkibost. High 2E 37
Kirkinch. Ang 4A 34
Kirkinner. Dum 3F 5
Kirkintilloch. E Dun 1B 18
Kirkland. Cumb 4F 7
Kirkland. Dum 2E 11
(nr. Kirkconnel)
Kirkland. Dum 4F 11
(nr. Moniaive)
Kirkland Guards. Cumb 4E 7
Kirklauchline. Dum 3B 4
Kirklinton. Cumb 2H 7
Kirkliston. Edin 1G 19
Kirkmabreck. Dum 3F 5
Kirkmaiden. Dum 5C 4
Kirkmichael. Per 2F 33
Kirkmichael. S Ayr 3A 10
Kirkmuirhill. S Lan 4C 18
Kirknewton. Nmbd 5G 21
Kirknewton. W Lot 2G 19
Kirkney. Abers 5A 50
Kirk of Shotts. N Lan 2D 18
Kirkoswald. S Ayr 3H 9
Kirkpatrick. Dum 4G 11
Kirkpatrick Durham. Dum 1A 6
Kirkpatrick-Fleming. Dum 1F 7
Kirkstile. Dum 4C 12
Kirkstyle. High 1G 59
Kirkton. Abers 2B 42
(nr. Alford)
Kirkton. Abers 1B 42
(nr. Insch)
Kirkton. Abers 4D 50
(nr. Turriff)
Kirkton. Ang 5B 34
(nr. Dundee)
Kirkton. Ang 4B 34
(nr. Forfar)
Kirkton. Ang 5H 41
(nr. Tarfside)
Kirkton. Dum 5G 11
Kirkton. Fife 1E 27
Kirkton. High 4E 55
(nr. Golspie)
Kirkton. High 1H 37
(nr. Kyle of Lochalsh)
Kirkton. High 4A 46
(nr. Lochcarron)
Kirkton. Bord 2E 13
Kirkton. S Lan 1G 11
Kirktonhill. W Dun 1G 17
Kirkton Manor. Bord 5H 19
Kirkton of Airlie. Ang 3A 34
Kirkton of Auchterhouse.
Ang 5A 34
Kirkton of Bourtie. Abers 1D 42
Kirkton of Collace. Per 5G 33
Kirkton of Craig. Ang 3E 35
Kirkton of Culsalmond.
Abers 5B 50
Kirkton of Durris. Abers 4C 42
Kirkton of Glenbuchat.
Abers 2G 41
Kirkton of Glenisla. Ang 2H 33
Kirkton of Kingoldrum. Ang 3A 34
Kirkton of Largo. Fife 3F 27
Kirkton of Lethendy. Per 4G 33
Kirkton of Logie Buchan.
Abers 1E 43
Kirkton of Maryculter. Abers 4D 42
Kirkton of Menmuir. Ang 2C 34
Kirkton of Monikie. Ang 5C 34
Kirkton of Oyne. Abers 1B 42
Kirkton of Rayne. Abers 5B 50
Kirkton of Skene. Abers 3D 42
Kirktown. Abers 2E 51
(nr. Fraserburgh)
Kirktown. Abers 3F 51
(nr. Peterhead)
Kirktown of Alvah. Abers 2B 50
Kirktown of Auchterless.
Abers 4C 50
Kirktown of Deskford. Mor 2A 50
Kirktown of Fetteresso.
Abers 5D 42
Kirktown of Mortlach. Mor 5G 49
Kirktown of Slains. Abers 1F 43
Kirkurd. Bord 4G 19
Kirkwall. Orkn 3D 64
Kirkwall Airport. Orkn 4D 64
Kirk Yetholm. Bord 1H 13
Kirn. Arg 1E 17
Kirriemuir. Ang 3A 34
Kirtlebridge. Dum 1F 7
Kirtleton. Dum 1F 7
Kirtomy. High 2A 58
Kishorn. High 4H 45
Kittybrowster. Aber 3E 43
Knapp. Per 5H 33
Knapperfield. High 3F 59
Knaven. Abers 4D 50
Knightswood. Glas 2A 18
Knock. Arg 5G 29
Knock. Mor 3A 50
Knockally. High 5E 59
Knockan. Arg 1B 22
Knockan. High 2H 53
Knockandhu. Mor 1F 41
Knockando. Mor 4E 49
Knockarthur. High 3E 55
Knockbain. High 3H 47
Knockbreck. High 2B 44
Knockdee. High 2E 59
Knockdolian. S Ayr 5G 9
Knockdon. S Ayr 2A 10
Knockenbaird. Abers 1B 42
Knockenkelly. N Ayr 1F 9
Knockentiber. E Ayr 5G 17
Knockfarrel. High 3G 47
Knockglass. High 2D 58
Knockie Lodge. High 2F 39
Knockinlaw. E Ayr 5H 17
Knockinnon. High 5E 59
Knockrome. Arg 1G 15
Knockshinnoch. E Ayr 2B 10
Knockvennie. Dum 1A 6
Knockvologan. Arg 2A 22
Knott. High 3C 44
Knowe. Dum 1E 5
Knowefield. Cumb 3H 7
Knowehead. Dum 4D 10
Knowes. E Lot 1D 20
Knoweside. S Ayr 2H 9
Knowles of Elrick. Abers 3B 50
Kyleakin. High 1G 37
Kyle of Lochalsh. High 1G 37
Kylerhea. High 1G 37
Kylesku. High 5D 56
Kyles Lodge. W Isl 2K 61
Kylesmorar. High 4H 37
Kylestrome. High 5D 56

L

Labost. W Isl 3G 63
Lacasaidh. W Isl 2E 62
Lacasdail. W Isl 4J 63
Ladybank. Fife 2E 27
Ladykirk. Bord 4F 21
Ladysford. Abers 2E 51
Laga. High 2H 29
Lagavulin. Arg 4F 15
Lagg. Arg 1G 15
Lagg. N Ayr 1E 9
Laggan. Arg 3D 14
Laggan. High 4D 38
(nr. Fort Augustus)
Laggan. High 4H 39
(nr. Newtonmore)
Laggan. Mor 5G 49
Lagganlia. High 3B 40
Lagganulva. Arg 4F 29
Laglingarten. Arg 3A 24
Laid. High 3F 57
Laide. High 4E 53
Laigh Fenwick. E Ayr 4H 17
Lairg. High 3C 54
Lairg Muir. High 3C 54
Laithes. Cumb 5H 7
Lamancha. Bord 3H 19
Lambden. Bord 4E 21
Lamberton. Bord 3G 21
Lambhill. Glas 2A 18
Laminess. Orkn 4J 65
Lamington. High 1A 48
Lamington. S Lan 5E 19
Lamlash. N Ayr 5D 16
Lamonby. Cumb 5H 7
Lanark. S Lan 4D 18
Landerberry. Abers 3C 42
Landhallow. High 5E 59
Lanehead. Nmbd 5G 13
Langais. W Isl 4J 61
Langal. High 2A 30
Langbank. Ren 1G 17
Langburnshiels. Bord 3E 13
Langdyke. Fife 3E 27
Langholm. Dum 5C 12
Langrigg. Cumb 4E 7
Langshaw. Bord 5C 20
Lanton. Nmbd 5G 21
Lanton. Bord 1F 13
Laphroaig. Arg 4E 15
Larachbeg. High 4H 29
Larbert. Falk 5H 25
Larel. High 3E 59
Largie. Abers 5B 50
Largiemore. Arg 5G 23
Largoward. Fife 3F 27
Largs. N Ayr 3F 17
Largue. Abers 4B 50
Largybeg. N Ayr 1F 9
Largymeanoch. N Ayr 1F 9
Largymore. N Ayr 1F 9
Larkfield. Inv 1F 17
Larkhall. S Lan 3C 18
Lary. Abers 3G 41
Lassodie. Fife 4C 26
Lasswade. Midl 2A 20
Latheron. High 5E 59
Latheronwheel. High 5E 59
Lathones. Fife 3F 27
Laudale House. High 3A 30
Lauder. Bord 4C 20
Laurencekirk. Abers 1E 35
Laurieston. Dum 2H 5
Laurieston. Falk 1E 19
Laverhay. Dum 4A 12
Laversdale. Cumb 2H 7
Law. S Lan 3D 18
Lawers. Per 5B 32
Laxfirth. Shet 1D 66
Laxo. Shet 6H 67
Leac a Li. W Isl 5C 62
Leachd. Arg 4H 23
Leachkin. High 4H 47
Leadburn. Midl 3H 19
Leaderfoot. Bord 5C 20
Leadhills. S Lan 2F 11
Lealt. Arg 4D 22
Lealt. High 2E 45
Leargybreck. Arg 1G 15
Leaths. Dum 2A 6
Leckfurin. High 3A 58
Leckgruinart. Arg 2D 14
Leckmelm. High 4G 53
Ledaig. Arg 5C 30
Ledgowan. High 3C 46
Ledmore. High 2H 53
Lednabirichen. High 4E 55
Lednagullin. High 2B 58
Leeans. Shet 2C 66
Leebotten. Shet 4D 66
Leetown. Per 1D 26
Legerwood. Bord 4C 20
Leirinmore. High 2F 57
Leishmore. High 4F 47
Leitfie. Per 4H 33
Leith. Edin 1H 19
Leitholm. Bord 4E 21
Lempitlaw. Bord 5E 21
Lenchie. Abers 5A 50
Lendalfoot. S Ayr 5G 9
Lendrick. Stir 3E 25
Lenimore. N Ayr 4B 16
Lennel. Bord 4F 21
Lennoxtown. E Dun 1B 18
Lentran. High 4G 47
Lenzie. E Dun 1B 18
Leochel Cushnie. Abers 2A 42
Leogh. Shet 1J 65
Lephenstrath. Arg 3B 8
Lephin. High 4A 44
Lephinchapel. Arg 4G 23
Lephinmore. Arg 4G 23
Lerwick. Shet 2D 66
Lerwick (Tingwall) Airport.
Shet 2D 66
Leslie. Abers 1A 42
Leslie. Fife 3D 26
Lesmahagow. S Lan 5D 18
Lessonhall. Cumb 3F 7
Leswalt. Dum 2B 4
Letham. Ang 4C 34
Letham. Falk 5H 25
Letham. Fife 2E 27
Lethanhill. E Ayr 2B 10
Lethenty. Abers 4D 50
Lettan. Orkn 3K 65
Letter. Abers 2C 42
Letterewe. High 1A 46
Letterfearn. High 1H 37
Lettermore. Arg 4F 29
Letters. High 5G 53
Leuchars. Fife 1F 27
Leumrabhagh. W Isl 3E 62
Levaneap. Shet 6H 67
Leven. Fife 3E 27
Levencorroch. N Ayr 1F 9
Levenhall. E Lot 1A 20
Levenwick. Shet 4D 66
Leverburgh. W Isl 6B 62
Levishie. High 2F 39
Lewiston. High 1G 39
Leylodge. Abers 2C 42
Leys. Per 5H 33
Leysmill. Ang 4D 34
Lhanbryde. Mor 2F 49
Liatrie. High 5D 46
Libberton. S Lan 4E 19
Liberton. Edin 2H 19
Liceasto. W Isl 5C 62
Liddel. Orkn 6D 64
Lienassie. High 1A 38
Liff. Ang 5A 34
Lilliesleaf. Bord 1E 13
Lilybank. Inv 1G 17
Limekilnburn. S Lan 3C 18
Lime Kiln Nook. Cumb 4G 7
Limekilns. Fife 5B 26
Limerigg. Falk 1D 18
Linburn. W Lot 2G 19
Lincluden. Dum 1C 6
Lindean. Bord 5B 20
Lindores. Fife 2D 26
Lingreabhagh. W Isl 6B 62
Lingyclose Head. Cumb 3G 7
Linicro. High 2C 44
Linklater. Orkn 6D 64
Linksness. Orkn 6B 64
(on Hoy)
Linksness. Orkn 3E 64
(on Mainland)
Linktown. Fife 4D 26
Linkwood. Mor 2F 49
Linlithgow. W Lot 1E 19
Linlithgow Bridge. Falk 1E 19
Linneraineach. High 3G 53
Linshiels. Nmbd 3H 13
Linsiadar. W Isl 1D 62
Linsidemore. High 4C 54
Linstock. Cumb 3H 7
Lintlaw. Bord 3F 21
Lintmill. Mor 2A 50
Linton. Bord 1G 13
Linwood. Ren 2H 17
Lionacleit. W Isl 6H 61
Lionacuidhe. W Isl 6H 61
Lional. W Isl 1K 63
Liquo. N Lan 3D 18
Litterty. Abers 3C 50
Little Ardo. Abers 5D 50
Little Ballinluig. Per 3E 33
Little Bampton. Cumb 3F 7
Little Blencow. Cumb 5H 7
Little Brechin. Ang 2C 34
Little Broughton. Cumb 5D 6
Little Clifton. Cumb 5D 6
Little Creich. High 5D 54
Little Crosthwaite. Cumb 5F 7
Little Dens. Abers 4F 51
Little Dunkeld. Per 4F 33
Littleferry. High 4F 55
Little Glenshee. Per 5E 33
Littlemill. Abers 4G 41
Littlemill. E Ayr 2B 10
Littlemill. High 4C 48
Little Orton. Cumb 3G 7
Little Rogart. High 3E 55
Little Scatwell. High 3E 47
Littlester. Shet 4J 67
Little Torboll. High 4E 55
Littletown. High 5E 55
Liurbost. W Isl 2E 62
Livingston. W Lot 2F 19
Livingston Village. W Lot 2F 19
Loan. Falk 1E 19
Loanend. Nmbd 3G 21
Loanhead. Midl 2H 19
Loaningfoot. Dum 3C 6
Loanreoch. High 1H 47
Loans. S Ayr 5G 17
Lochaber. Mor 3D 48
Loch a Charnain. W Isl 6J 61
Loch a Ghainmhich. W Isl 2D 62
Lochailort. High 5G 37
Lochaline. High 4H 29
Lochans. Dum 3B 4
Locharbriggs. Dum 5G 11
Lochardil. High 4H 47
Lochassynt Lodge. High 1G 53
Lochavich. Arg 2G 23
Lochawe. Arg 1A 24
Loch Baghasdail. W Isl 3C 60
Lochboisdale. W Isl 3C 60
Lochbuie. Arg 1D 22
Lochcarron. High 5H 45
Loch Choire Lodge. High 5H 57
Lochdochart House. Stir 1D 24
Lochdon. Arg 5A 30
Lochearnhead. Stir 1E 25
Lochee. D'dee 5A 34
Lochend. High 5G 47
(nr. Inverness)
Lochend. High 2F 59
(nr. Thurso)
Locherben. Dum 4G 11
Loch Euphort. W Isl 4J 61
Lochfoot. Dum 1B 6
Lochgair. Arg 4G 23
Lochgarthside. High 2G 39
Lochgelly. Fife 4C 26
Lochgilphead. Arg 5F 23
Lochgoilhead. Arg 3A 24
Loch Head. Dum 4E 5
Lochhill. Mor 2F 49
Lochindorb Lodge. High 5C 48
Lochinver. High 1F 53
Lochlane. Per 1H 25
Loch Loyal Lodge. High 4H 57
Lochluichart. High 2E 47
Lochmaben. Dum 5H 11
Lochmaddy. W Isl 4K 61
Loch nam Madadh. W Isl 4K 61
Lochore. Fife 4C 26
Lochportain. W Isl 3K 61
Lochranza. N Ayr 3C 16
Loch Sgioport. W Isl 1D 60
Lochside. Abers 2E 35
Lochside. High 5B 58
(nr. Achentoul)
Lochside. High 3B 48
(nr. Nairn)
Lochslin. High 5F 55
Lochstack Lodge. High 4D 56
Lochton. Abers 4C 42
Lochty. Fife 3G 27
Lochuisge. High 3A 30
Lochussie. High 3F 47
Lochwinnoch. Ren 3G 17
Lochyside. High 1E 31
Lockerbie. Dum 5A 12
Lockhills. Cumb 4H 7
Logan. E Ayr 1C 10
Loganlea. W Lot 2E 19
Loggie. High 4G 53
Logie. Ang 2D 34
Logie. Fife 1F 27
Logie. Mor 3D 48
Logie Coldstone. Abers 3H 41
Logie Pert. Ang 2D 34
Logierait. Per 3E 33
Lonbain. High 3F 45
Londubh. High 5D 52
Lone. High 4E 57
Lonemore. High 5E 55
(nr. Dornoch)
Lonemore. High 1G 45
(nr. Gairloch)
Longbar. N Ayr 3G 17
Longburgh. Cumb 3G 7
Longcroft. Cumb 3F 7
Longcroft. Falk 1C 18
Longdales. Cumb 4H 7
Longfield. Shet 5C 66
Longforgan. Per 1E 27
Longformacus. Bord 3D 20
Longhill. Abers 3F 51
Longhope. Orkn 5C 64
Longlands. Cumb 5F 7
Longmanhill. Abers 2C 50
Longmorn. Mor 3F 49
Longnewton. Bord 1E 13
Longniddry. E Lot 1B 20
Longpark. Cumb 2H 7
Longridge. W Lot 2E 19
Longriggend. N Lan 1D 18
Longside. Abers 4F 51
Longtown. Cumb 2G 7
Longyester. E Lot 2C 20
Lonmore. High 4B 44
Losgaintir. W Isl 5B 62
Lossiemouth. Mor 2F 49
Lossit. Arg 3C 14
Lothbeg. High 2G 55
Lothianbridge. Midl 2A 20
Lothianburn. Edin 2H 19
Lothmore. High 2G 55
Low Ardwell. Dum 4B 4
Low Ballochdoan. S Ayr 1B 4
Low Braithwaite. Cumb 4H 7
Low Coylton. S Ayr 2B 10
Low Crosby. Cumb 3H 7
Lower Arboll. High 5F 55
Lower Auchenreath. Mor 2G 49
Lower Badcall. High 4C 56
Lower Breakish. High 1F 37
Lower Diabaig. High 2G 45
Lower Dounreay. High 2C 58
Lower Gledfield. High 4C 54
Lower Killeyan. Arg 4D 14
Lower Largo. Fife 3F 27
Lower Lenie. High 1G 39
Lower Milovaig. High 3A 44
Lower Oakfield. Fife 4C 26
Lower Ollach. High 5E 45
Lower Pitkerrie. High 1B 48
Lowertown. Orkn 5D 64
Low Hesket. Cumb 4H 7
Lowick. Nmbd 5H 21
Low Lorton. Cumb 5E 7
Lownie Moor. Ang 4B 34
Lowood. Bord 5C 20
Low Row. Cumb 4E 7
Low Torry. Fife 5B 26
Low Valleyfield. Fife 5A 26
Low Whinnow. Cumb 3G 7
Lubcroy. High 3A 54
Lubinvullin. High 2G 57
Lucklawhill. Fife 1F 27
Ludag. W Isl 3C 60
Lugar. E Ayr 1C 10
Luggate Burn. E Lot 1D 20
Luggiebank. N Lan 1C 18
Lugton. E Ayr 3H 17
Luib. High 1E 37
Luib. Stir 1D 24
Lumphanan. Abers 3A 42
Lumphinnans. Fife 4C 26
Lumsdaine. Bord 2F 21
Lumsden. Abers 1H 41
Lunan. Ang 3D 34
Lunanhead. Ang 3B 34
Luncarty. Per 1B 26
Lundie. Ang 5H 33
Lundin Links. Fife 3F 27
Lunna. Shet 6H 67
Lunning. Shet 6J 67
Luss. Arg 4C 24
Lussagiven. Arg 5D 22
Lusta. High 3B 44
Luthermuir. Abers 2D 34
Luthrie. Fife 2E 27
Lybster. High 5F 59
Lyham. Nmbd 5H 21
Lylestone. N Ayr 4G 17
Lynaberack Lodge. High 4A 40
Lynchat. High 3A 40
Lyne. Bord 4H 19
Lyneholmeford. Cumb 1H 7
Lyne of Gorthleck. High 1G 39
Lyne of Skene. Abers 2C 42
Lyness. Orkn 5C 64
Lynwilg. High 2B 40
Lyth. High 2F 59
Lythes. Orkn 6D 64
Lythmore. High 2D 58

M

Mabie. Dum 1C 6
Macbiehill. Bord 3G 19
Macduff. Abers 2C 50
Machan. S Lan 3C 18
Macharioch. Arg 3C 8
Machrie. N Ayr 5B 16
Machrihanish. Arg 1B 8
Macmerry. E Lot 1B 20
Madderty. Per 1A 26
Maddiston. Falk 1E 19
Maggieknockater. Mor 4G 49
Maidens. S Ayr 3H 9
Mail. Shet 4D 66
Mains of Auchindachy.
Mor 4H 49
Mains of Auchnagatt. Abers 4E 51
Mains of Drum. Abers 4D 42
Mains of Edingight. Mor 3A 50
Mainsriddle. Dum 3C 6
Makerstoun. Bord 5D 20
Malacleit. W Isl 3H 61
Malcolmburn. Mor 3G 49
Maligar. High 2D 44
Mallaig. High 4F 37
Mallaig Bheag. High 4F 37
Malleny Mills. Edin 2G 19
Malt Lane. Arg 3H 23
Manais. W Isl 6C 62
Mangurstadh. W Isl 1B 62
Mannal. Arg 4A 28
Mannerston. Falk 1F 19
Mannofield. Aber 3E 43
Mansewood. Glas 2A 18
Mansfield. E Ayr 2D 10
Maraig. W Isl 4D 62
Marbhig. W Isl 6J 63
Margnaheglish. N Ayr 5D 16
Marishader. High 2D 44
Marjoriebanks. Dum 5H 11
Mark. Dum 3C 4
Markethill. Per 5H 33
Markinch. Fife 3D 26
Marnoch. Abers 3A 50
Marnock. N Lan 2C 18
Marrel. High 2H 55
Marrister. Shet 6J 67
Marshall Meadows. Nmbd 3G 21
Marwick. Orkn 2B 64
Marybank. High 3F 47
(nr. Dingwall)
Marybank. High 1A 48
(nr. Invergordon)
Maryburgh. High 3G 47
Maryhill. Glas 2A 18
Marykirk. Abers 2D 34
Marypark. Mor 5E 49
Maryport. Cumb 5D 6
Maryport. Dum 5C 4
Maryton. Ang 3A 34
(nr. Kirriemuir)
Maryton. Ang 3D 34
(nr. Montrose)
Marywell. Abers 4A 42
Marywell. Ang 4D 34
Masons Lodge. Abers 3D 42
Mastrick. Aber 3E 43
Mauchline. E Ayr 1B 10
Maud. Abers 4E 51
Mawbray. Cumb 4D 6
Maxton. Bord 5D 20
Maxwellheugh. Bord 5E 21
Maxwelltown. Dum 1C 6
Maybole. S Ayr 3A 10
Mayfield. Midl 2A 20
Mayfield. Per 1B 26
Maywick. Shet 4C 66
Meadowmill. E Lot 1B 20

Mealabost. W Isl 2J 63
(nr. Borgh)
Mealabost. W Isl 4J 63
(nr. Stornoway)
Mealasta. W Isl 2A 62
Mealrigg. Cumb 4E 7
Mealsgate. Cumb 4F 7
Meigle. Per 4H 33
Meikle Earnock. S Lan 3C 18
Meikle Kilchattan Butts. Arg 3D 16
Meikleour. Per 5G 33
Meikle Tarty. Abers 1E 43
Meikle Wartle. Abers 5C 50
Melby. Shet 1A 66
Melfort. Arg 2F 23
Melgarve. High 4F 39
Melkington. Nmbd 4F 21
Mellangaun. High 5D 52
Melldalloch. Arg 1C 16
Mellguards. Cumb 4H 7
Mellon Charles. High 4D 52
Mellon Udrigle. High 4D 52
Melrose. Bord 5C 20
Melsetter. Orkn 6B 64
Melvaig. High 5C 52
Melvich. High 2B 58
Memsie. Abers 2E 51
Memus. Ang 3B 34
Mennock. Dum 3F 11
Menstrie. Clac 4H 25
Merchiston. Edin 1H 19
Merkadale. High 5C 44
Merkland. S Ayr 4H 9
Merkland Lodge. High 1A 54
Methil. Fife 4E 27
Methilhill. Fife 4E 27
Methlick. Abers 5D 50
Methven. Per 1B 26
Mey. High 1F 59
Miabhag. W Isl 5C 62
Miabhaig. W Isl 4B 62
(nr. Cliasmol)
Miabhaig. W Isl 1B 62
(nr. Timsgearraidh)
Mial. High 1G 45
Micklethwaite. Cumb 3F 7
Mid Ardlaw. Abers 2E 51
Midbea. Orkn 3G 65
Mid Beltie. Abers 3B 42
Mid Calder. W Lot 2F 19
Mid Clyth. High 5F 59
Middlebie. Dum 1F 7
Middle Drums. Ang 3C 34
Middle Essie. Abers 3F 51
Middlemuir. Abers 4D 50
(nr. New Deer)
Middlemuir. Abers 3E 51
(nr. Strichen)
Middlesceugh. Cumb 4G 7
Middleton. Ang 4C 34
Middleton. Arg 4A 28
Middleton. Midl 3A 20
Middleton. Nmbd 5H 21
Middleton. Per 3C 26
Middleton Hall. Nmbd 5G 21
Midfield. High 2G 57
Mid Garrary. Dum 1G 5
Mid Ho. Shet 3J 67
Mid Kirkton. N Ayr 3E 17
Midland. Orkn 4C 64
Midlem. Bord 1E 13
Midton. Inv 1F 17
Midtown. High 5D 52
(nr. Poolewe)
Midtown. High 2G 57
(nr. Tongue)
Mid Walls. Shet 2A 66
Mid Yell. Shet 3J 67
Migdale. High 4D 54
Migvie. Abers 3H 41
Milesmark. Fife 5B 26
Milfield. Nmbd 5G 21
Millbank. High 2E 59
Millbeck. Cumb 5F 7
Millbounds. Orkn 1E 64
Millbreck. Abers 4F 51
Millden Lodge. Ang 1C 34
Milldens. Ang 3C 34
Millearn. Per 2A 26
Millerhill. Midl 2A 20
Millerston. N Lan 2B 18
Millfield. Abers 4H 41
Millhall. E Ren 3A 18
Millheugh. S Lan 3C 18
Millhouse. Arg 1C 16
Millhousebridge. Dum 5A 12
Millikenpark. Ren 2H 17
Mill Knowe. Arg 1C 8
Mill of Craigievar. Abers 2A 42
Mill of Fintray. Abers 2D 42
Mill of Haldane. W Dun 5D 24
Millport. N Ayr 3E 17
Milltimber. Aber 3D 42
Milltown. Abers 3F 41
(nr. Corgarff)
Milltown. Abers 2H 41
(nr. Lumsden)
Milltown. Dum 1G 7
Milltown. Mor 4A 50
Milltown of Aberdalgie. Per 1B 26
Milltown of Auchindoun. Mor 4G 49
Milltown of Campfield. Abers 3B 42
Milltown of Edinville. Mor 4F 49
Milltown of Towie. Abers 2H 41
Milnacraig. Ang 3H 33
Milnathort. Per 3C 26
Milngavie. E Dun 1A 18
Milnholm. Stir 5G 25
Milton. Ang 4A 34
Milton. Dum 1B 6
(nr. Crocketford)
Milton. Dum 3D 4
(nr. Glenluce)
Milton. E Ayr 1B 10
Milton. Glas 1A 18
Milton. High 3E 47
(nr. Achnasheen)
Milton. High 4G 45
(nr. Applecross)
Milton. High 5F 47
(nr. Drumnadrochit)
Milton. High 1A 48
(nr. Invergordon)
Milton. High 4G 47
(nr. Inverness)
Milton. High 3G 59
(nr. Wick)
Milton. Mor 2A 50
(nr. Cullen)
Milton. Mor 2E 41
(nr. Tomintoul)
Milton. Stir 3E 25
(nr. Aberfoyle)
Milton. Stir 4D 24
(nr. Drymen)
Milton. W Dun 1H 17
Milton Auchlossan. Abers 3A 42
Milton Bridge. Midl 2H 19
Milton Coldwells. Abers 5E 51
Miltonduff. Mor 2E 49
Milton Morenish. Per 5B 32
Milton of Auchinhove. Abers 3A 42
Milton of Balgonie. Fife 3E 27
Milton of Barras. Abers 1F 35
Milton of Campsie. E Dun 1B 18
Milton of Cultoquhey. Per 1H 25
Milton of Cushnie. Abers 2A 42
Milton of Finavon. Ang 3A 34
Milton of Gollanfield. High 3A 48
Milton of Lesmore. Abers 1H 41
Milton of Tullich. Abers 4G 41
Minard. Arg 4G 23
Mindrum. Nmbd 5F 21
Mingarrypark. High 2H 29
Mingary. High 2G 29
Mingearraidh. W Isl 2C 60
Minishant. S Ayr 2A 10
Minnigaff. Dum 2G 5
Mintlaw. Abers 4F 51
Minto. Bord 1E 13
Miodar. Arg 4B 28
Mirbister. Orkn 2C 64
Mireland. High 2G 59
Moarfield. Shet 2J 67
Moat. Cumb 1H 7
Mochrum. Dum 4E 5
Modsarie. High 2H 57
Moffat. Dum 3H 11
Mol-chlach. High 2D 36
Moll. High 5E 45
Mollinsburn. N Lan 1C 18
Monachyle. Stir 2D 24
Monar Lodge. High 4D 46
Moneydie. Per 1B 26
Moniaive. Dum 4E 11
Monifieth. Ang 5C 34
Monikie. Ang 5C 34
Monimail. Fife 2D 26
Monkhill. Cumb 3G 7
Monkshill. Abers 4C 50
Monkton. S Ayr 1A 10
Monktonhill. S Ayr 1A 10
Monreith. Dum 4E 5
Montford. Arg 2E 17
Montgarrie. Abers 2A 42
Montgarswood. E Ayr 1C 10
Montgreenan. N Ayr 4G 17
Montrave. Fife 3E 27
Montrose. Ang 3E 35
Monymusk. Abers 2B 42
Monzie. Per 1H 25
Moodiesburn. N Lan 1B 18
Moonzie. Fife 2E 27
Moorbrae. Shet 4H 67
Moorend. Dum 1F 7
Moorhouse. Cumb 3G 7
(nr. Carlisle)
Moorhouse. Cumb 3F 7
(nr. Wigton)
Moor of Granary. Mor 3D 48
Moor Row. Cumb 4E 7
Morangie. High 5E 55
Morar. High 4F 37
Morebattle. Bord 1G 13
Morefield. High 4G 53
Morenish. Per 5A 32
Morham. E Lot 1C 20
Morningside. Edin 1H 19
Morningside. N Lan 3D 18
Morrington. Dum 5F 11
Morton. Cumb 5H 7
(nr. Calthwaite)
Morton. Cumb 3G 7
(nr. Carlisle)
Morvich. High 3E 55
(nr. Golspie)
Morvich. High 1A 38
(nr. Shiel Bridge)
Moscow. E Ayr 4H 17
Mosedale. Cumb 5G 7
Moss. Arg 4A 28
Moss. High 2H 29
Mossatt. Abers 2H 41
Mossbank. Shet 5H 67
Mossblown. S Ayr 1B 10
Mossburnford. Bord 2F 13
Mossdale. Dum 1H 5
Mossedge. Cumb 2H 7
Mossend. N Lan 2C 18
Moss of Barmuckity. Mor 2F 49
Mosspark. Glas 2A 18
Mosspaul. Bord 4D 12
Moss Side. Cumb 3E 7
Moss-side. High 3B 48
Moss-side of Cairness. Abers 2F 51
Mosstodloch. Mor 3G 49
Motherby. Cumb 5H 7
Motherwell. N Lan 3C 18 & 84
Moulin. Per 3E 33
Mountain Cross. Bord 4G 19
Mountbenger. Bord 1C 12
Mountblow. W Dun 1H 17
Mountgerald. High 2G 47
Mount High. High 2H 47
Mount Lothian. Midl 3H 19
Mount Pleasant. Fife 2D 26
Mount Stuart. Arg 3E 17
Mouswald. Dum 1D 6
Mowhaugh. Bord 1H 13
Moy. High 5A 48
Moy Lodge. High 5F 39
Muasdale. Arg 4H 15
Muchalls. Abers 4E 43
Muchrachd. High 5D 46
Muckle Breck. Shet 6J 67
Mudale. High 5G 57
Mugdock. Stir 1A 18
Mugeary. High 5D 44
Muie. High 3D 54
Muirden. Abers 3C 50
Muirdrum. Ang 5C 34
Muiredge. Per 1D 26
Muirend. Glas 2A 18
Muirhead. Ang 5A 34
Muirhead. Fife 3D 26
Muirhead. N Lan 2B 18
Muirhouses. Falk 5B 26
Muirkirk. E Ayr 1D 10
Muir of Alford. Abers 2A 42
Muir of Fairburn. High 3F 47
Muir of Fowlis. Abers 2A 42
Muir of Miltonduff. Mor 3E 49
Muir of Ord. High 3G 47
Muir of Tarradale. High 3G 47
Muirshearlich. High 5C 38
Muirtack. Abers 5E 51
Muirton. High 2A 48
Muirton. Per 1C 26
Muirton of Ardblair. Per 4G 33
Muirtown. Per 2A 26
Muiryfold. Abers 3C 50
Mulben. Mor 3G 49
Mulindry. Arg 3E 15
Mulla. Shet 6H 67
Mullach Charlabhaigh. W Isl 3G 63
Munerigie. High 3D 38
Muness. Shet 2K 67
Mungasdale. High 4E 53
Mungrisdale. Cumb 5G 7
Munlochy. High 3H 47
Murieston. W Lot 2F 19
Murkle. High 2E 59
Murlaggan. High 4B 38
Murra. Orkn 4B 64
Murrayfield. Edin 1H 19
Murray, The. S Lan 3B 18
Murroes. Ang 5B 34
Murthly. Per 5F 33
Murton. Nmbd 4G 21
Musselburgh. E Lot 1A 20
Mutehill. Dum 4H 5
Muthill. Per 2H 25
Mybster. High 3E 59
Myrebird. Abers 4C 42
Myrelandhorn. High 3F 59

N

Naast. High 5D 52
Na Buirgh. W Isl 5B 62
Na Gearrannan. W Isl 3F 63
Nairn. High 3B 48
Navidale. High 2H 55
Nedd. High 5C 56
Neilston. E Ren 3H 17
Nemphlar. S Lan 4D 18
Nenthorn. Bord 5D 20
Neribus. Arg 3D 14
Nerston. S Lan 3B 18
Nesbit. Nmbd 5G 21
Ness of Tenston. Orkn 3B 64
Nethanfoot. S Lan 4D 18
Nether Blainslie. Bord 4C 20
Netherbrae. Abers 3C 50
Netherbrough. Orkn 3C 64
Netherburn. S Lan 4D 18
Netherby. Cumb 1G 7
Nether Careston. Ang 3C 34
Nether Dallachy. Mor 2G 49
Nether Durdie. Per 1D 26
Nether Howcleugh. Dum 2H 11
Nether Kinmundy. Abers 4F 51
Netherlaw. Dum 4A 6
Netherley. Abers 4D 42
Nethermill. Dum 5H 11
Nethermills. Mor 3A 50
Netherplace. E Ren 3A 18
Netherthird. E Ayr 2C 10
Netherton. Ang 3C 34
Netherton. Cumb 5D 6
Netherton. N Lan 3C 18
Netherton. Per 3G 33
Netherton. Stir 1A 18
Nethertown. High 1G 59
Nether Urquhart. Fife 3C 26
Nether Welton. Cumb 4G 7
Nethy Bridge. High 1D 40
Neuk, The. Abers 4C 42
New Abbey. Dum 2C 6
New Aberdour. Abers 2D 50
New Alyth. Per 4H 33
Newark. Orkn 3K 65
Newarthill. N Lan 3C 18
Newbattle. Midl 2A 20
Newbiggin. Cumb 5H 7
Newbigging. Ang 5B 34
(nr. Monikie)
Newbigging. Ang 4H 33
(nr. Newtyle)
Newbigging. Ang 5B 34
(nr. Tealing)
Newbigging. Edin 1G 19
Newbigging. S Lan 4F 19
New Bridge. Dum 1C 6
Newbridge. Edin 1G 19
Newburgh. Abers 1E 43
Newburgh. Fife 2D 26
Newby East. Cumb 3H 7
New Byth. Abers 3D 50
Newby West. Cumb 3G 7
Newcastleton. Bord 5D 12
New Cowper. Cumb 4E 7
Newcraighall. Edin 1A 20
New Cumnock. E Ayr 2D 10
New Deer. Abers 4D 50
New Elgin. Mor 2F 49
New Galloway. Dum 1H 5
Newhaven. Edin 1H 19
Newhouse. N Lan 2C 18
Newington. Edin 1H 19
New Kelso. High 4A 46
New Lanark. S Lan 4D 18
Newlandrig. Midl 2A 20
Newlands. Cumb 5G 7
Newlands. High 4A 48
Newlands of Geise. High 2D 58
Newlands of Tynet. Mor 2G 49
New Langholm. Dum 5C 12
New Leeds. Abers 3E 51
Newlot. Orkn 3E 64
New Luce. Dum 2C 4
Newmachar. Abers 2D 42
Newmains. N Lan 3D 18
New Mains of Ury. Abers 5D 42
Newmarket. W Isl 4J 63
New Mill. Abers 4C 50
Newmill. Mor 3H 49
Newmill. Bord 2D 12
Newmills. Fife 5B 26
Newmills. High 2H 47
Newmiln. Per 5G 33
Newmilns. E Ayr 5A 18
Newmore. High 3G 47
(nr. Dingwall)
Newmore. High 1H 47
(nr. Invergordon)
Newpark. Fife 2F 27
New Pitsligo. Abers 3D 50
Newport. High 1H 55
Newport-on-Tay. Fife 1F 27
New Prestwick. S Ayr 1A 10
New Rent. Cumb 5H 7
New Sauchie. Clac 4H 25
Newseat. Abers 5C 50
Newstead. Bord 5C 20
New Stevenston. N Lan 3C 18
Newton. Arg 4H 23
Newton. Dum 1F 7
(nr. Annan)
Newton. Dum 4A 12
(nr. Moffat)
Newton. High 2A 48
(nr. Cromarty)
Newton. High 4A 48
(nr. Inverness)
Newton. High 5D 56
(nr. Kylestrome)
Newton. High 4G 59
(nr. Wick)
Newton. Mor 2E 49
Newton. Bord 1F 13
Newton. Shet 3C 66
Newton. S Lan 2B 18
(nr. Glasgow)
Newton. S Lan 5E 19
(nr. Lanark)
Newton. W Lot 1F 19
Newtonairds. Dum 5F 11
Newton Arlosh. Cumb 3F 7
Newtongrange. Midl 2A 20
Newtonhill. Abers 4E 43
Newtonhill. High 4G 47
Newton Mearns. E Ren 3A 18
Newtonmore. High 4A 40
Newton of Ardtoe. High 1H 29
Newton of Balcanquhal. Per 2C 26
Newton of Beltrees. Ren 3G 17
Newton of Falkland. Fife 3D 26
Newton of Mountblairy. Abers 3C 50
Newton of Pitcairns. Per 2B 26
Newton Reigny. Cumb 5H 7
Newton Rigg. Cumb 5H 7
Newton Stewart. Dum 2F 5
Newton upon Ayr. S Ayr 1A 10
Newtown. Abers 2C 50
Newtown. Cumb 4D 6
(nr. Aspatria)
Newtown. Cumb 2H 7
(nr. Brampton)
New Town. E Lot 1B 20
Newtown. Falk 5A 26
Newtown. High 3E 39
Newtown. Nmbd 5H 21
Newtown. Shet 4H 67
Newtown St Boswells. Bord 5C 20
Newtyle. Ang 4H 33
New Winton. E Lot 1B 20
Niddrie. Edin 1H 19
Niddry. Edin 1F 19
Nigg. Aber 3E 43
Nigg. High 1B 48
Nigg Ferry. High 2A 48
Ninemile Bar. Dum 1B 6
Nine Mile Burn. Midl 3G 19
Nisbet. Bord 1F 13
Nisbet Hill. Bord 3E 21
Nitshill. E Ren 3A 18
Noness. Shet 4D 66
Nonikiln. High 1H 47
Nook. Cumb 1H 7
Noranside. Ang 2B 34
Norby. Shet 1A 66
Norham. Nmbd 4G 21
North Balfern. Dum 3F 5
North Ballachulish. High 2D 30
North Berwick. E Lot 5G 27
North Collafirth. Shet 4G 67
North Commonty. Abers 4D 50
North Corbelly. Dum 2C 6
North Craigo. Ang 2D 34
North Dronley. Ang 5A 34
Northdyke. Orkn 2B 64
North Erradale. High 5C 52
North Fearns. High 5E 45
North Feorline. N Ayr 1E 9
Northfield. Aber 3D 42
North Gluss. Shet 5G 67
North Hazelrigg. Nmbd 5H 21
North Kessock. High 4H 47
North Middleton. Midl 3A 20
Northmuir. Ang 3A 34
North Murie. Per 1D 26
North Ness. Orkn 5C 64
North Port. Arg 1H 23
North Queensferry. Fife 5C 26
North Roe. Shet 4G 67
North Ronaldsay Airport. Orkn 2K 65
North Row. Cumb 5F 7
North Sannox. N Ayr 4D 16
North Shian. Arg 4C 30
North Side. Cumb 5D 6
Northtown. Orkn 5D 64
North Town. Shet 5C 66
Northwall. Orkn 3K 65
North Water Bridge. Ang 2D 34
North Watten. High 3F 59
North Yardhope. Nmbd 3H 13
Norwick. Shet 1K 67
Noss. Shet 5C 66
Nostie. High 1H 37
Nunclose. Cumb 4H 7
Nunnerie. S Lan 2G 11
Nybster. High 2G 59

O

Oakbank. Arg 5A 30
Oakbank. W Lot 2F 19
Oakley. Fife 5B 26
Oakshaw Ford. Cumb 1H 7
Oape. High 3B 54
Oathlaw. Ang 3B 34
Oban. Arg 1F 23 & 84
Oban. W Isl 4C 62
Obsdale. High 2H 47
Ochiltree. E Ayr 1C 10
Ochtermuthill. Per 2H 25
Ochtertyre. Per 1H 25
Ockle. High 1G 29
Octofad. Arg 3D 14
Octomore. Arg 3D 14
Oddsta. Shet 3J 67
Odie. Orkn 5J 65
Okraquoy. Shet 3D 66
Old Aberdeen. Aber 3E 43
Oldany. High 5C 56
Old Blair. Per 2D 32
Old Bridge of Tilt. Per 2D 32
Old Bridge of Urr. Dum 2A 6
Old Dailly. S Ayr 4H 9
Old Deer. Abers 4E 51
Old Graitney. Dum 2G 7
Oldhall. High 3F 59
Oldhamstocks. E Lot 1E 21
Old Kilpatrick. W Dun 1H 17
Old Kinnernie. Abers 3C 42
Oldmeldrum. Abers 1D 42
Old Monkland. N Lan 2C 18
Old Pentland. Midl 2H 19
Old Philpstoun. W Lot 1F 19
Old Rayne. Abers 1B 42
Old Scone. Per 1C 26
Oldshore Beg. High 3C 56
Oldshoremore. High 3D 56
Old Town. Cumb 4H 7
Oldtown. High 5C 54
Old Town. Nmbd 4H 13
Oldtown of Ord. Abers 3B 50
Oldwall. Cumb 2H 7
Old Westhall. Abers 1B 42
Oldwhat. Abers 3D 50
Olgrinmore. High 3D 58
Ollaberry. Shet 4G 67
Olrig. High 2E 59
Omunsgarth. Shet 2C 66
Onich. High 2D 30
Onthank. E Ayr 5H 17
Opinan. High 1G 45
(nr. Gairloch)
Opinan. High 4D 52
(nr. Laide)
Orasaigh. W Isl 3E 62
Orbost. High 4B 44
Ord. High 2F 37
Ordale. Shet 2K 67
Ordhead. Abers 2B 42
Ordie. Abers 3H 41
Ordiquish. Mor 3G 49
Orgil. Orkn 4B 64
Ormacleit. W Isl 1C 60
Ormathwaite. Cumb 5F 7
Ormiscaig. High 4D 52
Ormiston. E Lot 2B 20
Ormsaigbeg. High 2F 29
Ormsaigmore. High 2F 29
Ormsary. Arg 1A 16
Orphir. Orkn 4C 64
Orthwaite. Cumb 5F 7
Orton. Mor 3G 49
Osclay. High 5F 59
Ose. High 4C 44
Oskaig. High 5E 45
Oskamull. Arg 4F 29
Osmondwall. Orkn 6C 64
Osnaburgh. Fife 2F 27
Ospisdale. High 5E 55
Otterburn. Nmbd 4H 13
Otterburn Camp. Nmbd 4H 13
Otterburn Hall. Nmbd 4H 13
Otter Ferry. Arg 5G 23
Otterswick. Shet 4J 67
Oughterby. Cumb 3F 7
Oughterside. Cumb 4E 7
Oulton. Cumb 3F 7
Ousdale. High 1H 55
Outertown. Orkn 3B 64
Overbister. Orkn 3J 65
Over Finlarg. Ang 4B 34
Overscaig. High 1B 54
Overton. Aber 2D 42
Overton. High 5F 59
Overtown. N Lan 3D 18
Oxgangs. Edin 2H 19
Oxnam. Bord 2G 13
Oxton. Bord 3B 20
Oykel Bridge. High 3A 54
Oyne. Abers 1B 42

P

Pabail Iarach. W Isl 4K 63
Pabail Uarach. W Isl 4K 63
Padanaram. Ang 3B 34
Paddockhole. Dum 5B 12
Paibeil. W Isl 4H 61
(on North Uist)
Paibeil. W Isl 5B 62
(on Taransay)
Paiblesgearraidh. W Isl 4H 61
Pairc Shiaboist. W Isl 3G 63
Paisley. Ren 2H 17 & 85
Palgowan. Dum 5A 10
Palnackie. Dum 3B 6
Palnure. Dum 2F 5
Panbride. Ang 5C 34
Pannanich. Abers 4G 41
Papa Stour Airport. Shet 1A 66
Papa Westray Airport. Orkn 2G 65
Papcastle. Cumb 5E 7
Papigoe. High 3G 59
Papil. Shet 3C 66
Papple. E Lot 1C 20
Park. Abers 4C 42
Park. Arg 4C 30
Park. Dum 4G 11
Parkburn. Abers 5C 50
Park End. Nmbd 5H 13
Parkgate. Cumb 4F 7
Parkgate. Dum 5H 11
Parkhall. W Dun 1H 17
Parkhead. Cumb 4G 7
Parkhead. Glas 2B 18
Parkneuk. Abers 1E 35
Parkside. N Lan 3D 18
Parsonby. Cumb 5E 7
Partick. Glas 2A 18
Parton. Cumb 3F 7
Parton. Dum 1H 5
Pathhead. Abers 2E 35
Pathhead. E Ayr 2D 10
Pathhead. Fife 4D 26
Pathhead. Midl 2A 20
Path of Condie. Per 2B 26
Pathstruie. Per 2B 26
Patna. E Ayr 2B 10
Pattiesmuir. Fife 5B 26
Pawston. Nmbd 5F 21
Paxton. Bord 3G 21
Peanmeanach. High 5G 37
Pearsie. Ang 3A 34
Peaston. E Lot 2B 20
Peastonbank. E Lot 2B 20
Peathill. Abers 2E 51
Peat Inn. Fife 3F 27
Peaton. Arg 5B 24
Peebles. Bord 4H 19
Peel. Bord 5B 20
Peinchorran. High 5E 45
Peinlich. High 3D 44
Pelutho. Cumb 4E 7
Pencaitland. E Lot 2B 20
Penicuik. Midl 2H 19
Penifiler. High 4D 44
Peninver. Arg 1C 8
Penkill. S Ayr 4H 9
Pennan. Abers 2D 50
Pennyghael. Arg 1C 22
Pennyvenie. E Ayr 3B 10
Penpont. Dum 4F 11
Penrith. Cumb 5H 7
Penruddock. Cumb 5H 7
Penston. E Lot 1B 20
Perceton. N Ayr 4G 17
Percyhorner. Abers 2E 51
Perth. Per 1C 26 & 85
Peterburn. High 5C 52
Peterculter. Aber 3D 42
Peterhead. Abers 4G 51
Petertown. Orkn 4C 64
Petteril Green. Cumb 4H 7
Pettinain. S Lan 4E 19
Pettycur. Fife 5D 26
Philiphaugh. Bord 1D 12
Philpstoun. W Lot 1F 19
Pickletillem. Fife 1F 27
Pierowall. Orkn 3G 65
Pilton. Edin 1H 19
Pinkerton. E Lot 1E 21
Pinmore. S Ayr 4H 9
Pinwherry. S Ayr 5G 9
Piperhill. High 3B 48
Pirnmill. N Ayr 4B 16
Pisgah. Stir 3G 25
Pitagowan. Per 2D 32
Pitcairn. Per 3D 32
Pitcairngreen. Per 1B 26
Pitcalnie. High 1B 48
Pitcaple. Abers 1C 42
Pitcox. E Lot 1D 20
Pitcur. Per 5H 33
Pitfichie. Abers 2B 42
Pitgrudy. High 4E 55
Pitkennedy. Ang 3C 34
Pitlessie. Fife 3E 27
Pitlochry. Per 3E 33
Pitmachie. Abers 1B 42
Pitmaduthy. High 1A 48

Pitmedden. Abers 1D 42
Pitnacree. Per 3E 33
Pitroddie. Per 1D 26
Pitscottie. Fife 2F 27
Pittentrail. High 3E 55
Pittenweem. Fife 3G 27
Pittulie. Abers 2E 51
Pitversie. Per 2C 26
Plaidy. Abers 3C 50
Plains. N Lan 2C 18
Plean. Stir 5H 25
Plockton. High 5H 45
Plocrapol. W Isl 5C 62
Plumbland. Cumb 5E 7
Plumpton. Cumb 5H 7
Plumptonfoot. Cumb 5H 7
Polbae. Dum 1D 4
Polbain. High 3F 53
Polbeth. W Lot 2F 19
Polchar. High 3B 40
Poles. High 4E 55
Polglass. High 3F 53
Polio. High 1A 48
Polla. High 3E 57
Polloch. High 2A 30
Pollok. Glas 2A 18
Pollokshaws. Glas 2A 18
Pollokshields. Glas 2A 18
Polmaily. High 5F 47
Polmont. Falk 1E 19
Polnessan. E Ayr 2B 10
Polnish. High 5G 37
Polskeoch. Dum 3D 10
Polton. Midl 2A 20
Polwarth. Bord 3E 21
Ponton. Shet 1C 66
Poolewe. High 5D 52
Pool o' Muckhart. Clac 3B 26
Porin. High 3E 47
Portachoillan. Arg 3A 16
Port Adhair Bheinn na Faoghla. W Isl 5H 61
Port Ann. Arg 5G 23
Port Appin. Arg 4C 30
Port Asgaig. Arg 2F 15
Port Askaig. Arg 2F 15
Portavadie. Arg 2C 16
Port Bannatyne. Arg 2D 16
Port Carlisle. Cumb 2F 7
Port Charlotte. Arg 3D 14
Port Driseach. Arg 1C 16
Port Dundas. Glas 2B 18
Port Ellen. Arg 4E 15
Port Elphinstone. Abers 1C 42
Portencalzie. Dum 1B 4
Portencross. N Ayr 4E 17
Port Erroll. Abers 5F 51
Portessie. Mor 2H 49
Port Glasgow. Inv 1G 17
Portgordon. Mor 2G 49
Portgower. High 2H 55
Porthalong. High 5C 44
Port Henderson. High 1G 45
Portincaple. Arg 4B 24
Portinnisherrich. Arg 2G 23
Portknockie. Mor 2H 49
Port Lamont. Arg 1D 16
Portlethen. Abers 4E 43
Portlethen Village. Abers 4E 43
Portling. Dum 3B 6
Port Logan. Dum 4B 4
Portmahomack. High 5G 55
Port Mholair. W Isl 4K 63
Port Mor. High 1F 29
Portnacroish. Arg 4C 30
Portnahaven. Arg 3C 14
Portnalong. High 5C 44
Portnaluchaig. High 5F 37
Portnancon. High 2F 57
Port Nan Giuran. W Isl 4K 63
Port nan Long. W Isl 3J 61
Port Nis. W Isl 1K 63
Portobello. Edin 1A 20
Port of Menteith. Stir 3E 25
Portormin. High 5E 59
Portpatrick. Dum 3B 4
Port Ramsay. Arg 4B 30
Portree. High 4D 44
Portskerra. High 2B 58
Portsonachan. Arg 1H 23
Portsoy. Abers 2A 50
Porttannachy. Mor 2G 49
Portuairk. High 2F 29
Port Wemyss. Arg 3C 14
Port William. Dum 4E 5
Potarch. Abers 4B 42
Potterton. Abers 2E 43
Poundland. S Ayr 5G 9
Powfoot. Dum 2E 7
Powmill. Per 4B 26
Pressen. Nmbd 5F 21
Preston. E Lot 1C 20
(nr. East Linton)
Preston. E Lot 1A 20
(nr. Prestonpans)
Preston. Bord 3E 21
Prestonmill. Dum 3C 6
Prestonpans. E Lot 1A 20
Prestwick. S Ayr 1A 10
Priesthill. Glas 2A 18
Priestland. E Ayr 5A 18
Primsidemill. Bord 1H 13
Prior Muir. Fife 2G 27
Prospect. Cumb 4E 7
Provanmill. Glas 2B 18
Pulpit Hill. Arg 1F 23
Pumpherston. W Lot 2F 19

Q

Quarrier's Village. Inv 2G 17
Quarrywood. Mor 2E 49
Quartalehouse. Abers 4E 51
Quarter. N Ayr 2E 17
Quarter. S Lan 3C 18
Queenzieburn. N Lan 1B 18
Quendale. Shet 5C 66
Quholm. Orkn 3B 64
Quilquox. Abers 5E 51
Quindry. Orkn 5D 64
Quothquan. S Lan 5E 19
Quoyloo. Orkn 2B 64
Quoyness. Orkn 4B 64
Quoys. Shet 6H 67
(on Mainland)
Quoys. Shet 1K 67
(on Unst)

R

Raby. Cumb 3E 7
Rachan Mill. Bord 5G 19
Racks. Dum 1D 6
Rackwick. Orkn 5A 64
(on Hoy)
Rackwick. Orkn 3G 65
(on Westray)
Radernie. Fife 2F 27
Rafford. Mor 3D 48
Raggra. High 4G 59
Raigbeg. High 1B 40
Rait. Per 1D 26
Ralia. High 4A 40
Ramasaig. High 4A 44
Ramnageo. Shet 2K 67
Ramsburn. Mor 3A 50
Ramscraigs. High 5E 59
Ramstone. Abers 2B 42
Ranais. W Isl 5J 63
Ranfurly. Ren 2G 17
Rangag. High 4E 59
Rankinston. E Ayr 2B 10
Rannoch School. Per 3A 32
Rannoch Station. Per 3H 31
Ranochan. High 5H 37
Raploch. Stir 4G 25
Rapness. Orkn 3H 65
Rascarrel. Dum 4A 6
Rashfield. Arg 5A 24
Ratagan. High 2A 38
Rathen. Abers 2F 51
Rathillet. Fife 1E 27
Ratho. Edin 1G 19
Ratho Station. Edin 1G 19
Rathven. Mor 2H 49
Rattar. High 1F 59
Ratten Row. Cumb 4G 7
Rattray. Abers 3F 51
Rattray. Per 4G 33
Raughton. Cumb 4G 7
Raughton Head. Cumb 4G 7
Ravenstruther. S Lan 4E 19
Raylees. Nmbd 4H 13
Rearquhar. High 4E 55
Reaster. High 2F 59
Reawick. Shet 2C 66
Reay. High 2C 58
Rechullin. High 3H 45
Redburn. High 4C 48
Redcastle. High 4G 47
Red Dial. Cumb 4F 7
Redding. Falk 1E 19
Reddingmuirhead. Falk 1E 19
Redesdale Camp. Nmbd 4H 13
Redesmouth. Nmbd 5H 13
Redford. Ang 4C 34
Redfordgreen. Bord 2C 12
Redhill. Abers 3C 42
Redhouses. Arg 2E 15
Redland. Orkn 2C 64
Redmain. Cumb 5E 7
Redpath. Bord 5C 20
Redpoint. High 2G 45
Reemshill. Abers 4C 50
Regoul. High 3B 48
Reiff. High 2E 53
Reinigeadal. W Isl 4D 62
Reisque. Abers 1D 42
Reiss. High 3G 59
Relugas. Mor 4C 48
Renfrew. Ren 2A 18
Renton. W Dun 1G 17
Resaurie. High 4A 48
Rescobie. Ang 3C 34
Resipole. High 2A 30
Resolis. High 2H 47
Rest and be thankful. Arg 3B 24
Reston. Bord 2F 21
Rheindown. High 4G 47
Rhemore. High 3G 29
Rhenetra. High 3D 44
Rhian. High 2C 54
Rhian Breck. High 3C 54
Rhicarn. High 1F 53
Rhiconich. High 3D 56
Rhicullen. High 1H 47
Rhidorroch. High 4G 53
Rhifail. High 4A 58
Rhilochan. High 3E 55
Rhiroy. High 5G 53
Rhitongue. High 3H 57
Rhonehouse. Dum 3A 6
Rhu. Arg 5B 24
Rhubadach. Arg 1D 16
Rhubha Stoer. High 5B 56
Rhue. High 4F 53
Rhunahaorine. Arg 4A 16
Rhuvoult. High 3D 56
Rhynd. Per 1C 26
Rhynie. Abers 1H 41
Ribigill. High 3G 57
Riccarton. E Ayr 5H 17
Rickarton. Abers 5D 42
Rickerby. Cumb 3H 7
Ridsdale. Nmbd 5H 13
Riemore Lodge. Per 4F 33
Rigg. Dum 2F 7
Riggend. N Lan 1C 18
Rigside. S Lan 5D 18
Rimsdale. High 4A 58
Ringasta. Shet 5C 66
Ringford. Dum 3H 5
Rinmore. Abers 2H 41
Rinnigill. Orkn 5C 64
Riof. W Isl 1C 62
Rireavach. High 4F 53
Risabus. Arg 4E 15
Rispond. High 2F 57
Roadhead. Cumb 1H 7
Roadmeetings. S Lan 4D 18
Roadside. High 2E 59
Roadside of Catterline. Abers 1F 35
Roadside of Kinneff. Abers 1F 35
Roag. High 4B 44
Roberton. Bord 2D 12
Roberton. S Lan 1G 11
Robertstown. Mor 4F 49
Rob Roy's House. Arg 2A 24
Rochester. Nmbd 4H 13
Rockcliffe. Cumb 2G 7
Rockcliffe. Dum 3B 6
Rockcliffe Cross. Cumb 2G 7
Rockfield. High 5G 55
Roddenloft. E Ayr 1B 10
Roesound. Shet 6G 67
Rogart. High 3E 55
Roghadal. W Isl 6B 62
Roman Camp. W Lot 1F 19
Romannobridge. Bord 4G 19
Romesdal. High 3D 44
Ronaldsvoe. Orkn 5D 64
Rootfield. High 3G 47
Rootpark. S Lan 3E 19
Rora. Abers 3F 51
Rorandle. Abers 2B 42
Rosebank. S Lan 4D 18
Rosehall. High 3B 54
Rosehearty. Abers 2E 51
Roseisle. Mor 2E 49
Rosemarkie. High 3A 48
Rosemount. Per 4G 33
Rosewell. Midl 2H 19
Roshven. High 1A 30
Roskhill. High 4B 44
Rosley. Cumb 4G 7
Roslin. Midl 2H 19
Rosneath. Arg 5B 24
Ross. Dum 4H 5
Ross. Per 1G 25
Ross. Bord 2G 21
Rosskeen. High 2H 47
Rossland. Ren 1H 17
Roster. High 4F 59
Rosyth. Fife 5C 26
Rothes. Mor 4F 49
Rothesay. Arg 2D 16
Rothienorman. Abers 5C 50
Rothiesholm. Orkn 5J 65
Rottal. Ang 2A 34
Rough Haugh. High 4A 58
Roughsike. Cumb 1H 7
Roundyhill. Ang 3A 34
Rowanburn. Dum 1H 7
Rowanhill. Abers 3F 51
Rowardennan. Stir 4C 24
Roxburgh. Bord 5E 21
Roybridge. High 5D 38
Ruaig. Arg 4B 28
Ruarach. High 1A 38
Ruchazie. Glas 2B 18
Ruckcroft. Cumb 4H 7
Ruglen. S Ayr 3H 9
Ruilick. High 4G 47
Ruisaurie. High 4F 47
Ruisigearraidh. W Isl 2K 61
Rumbling Bridge. Per 4B 26
Rumford. Falk 1E 19
Runtaleave. Ang 2H 33
Ruskie. Stir 3F 25
Russland. Orkn 3C 64
Rutherglen. S Lan 2B 18
Ruthrieston. Aber 3E 43
Ruthven. Abers 4A 50
Ruthven. Ang 4H 33
Ruthven. High 5B 48
(nr. Inverness)
Ruthven. High 4A 40
(nr. Kingussie)
Ruthwaite. Cumb 5F 7
Ruthwell. Dum 2E 7
Rychraggan. High 5F 47

S

Saasaig. High 3F 37
Saddell. Arg 5A 16
Saighdinis. W Isl 4J 61
St Abbs. Bord 2G 21
St Andrews. Fife 2G 27 & 86
St Ann's. Dum 4H 11
St Boswells. Bord 5D 20
St Catherines. Arg 3A 24
St Colmac. Arg 2D 16
St Combs. Abers 2F 51
St Cyrus. Abers 2E 35
St David's. Per 1A 26
St Fergus. Abers 3F 51
St Fillans. Per 1F 25
St Helens. Cumb 5D 6
St John's Town of Dalry. Dum 5D 10
St Katherines. Abers 5C 50
St Madoes. Per 1C 26
St Margaret's Hope. Orkn 5D 64
St Martins. Per 5G 33
St Mary's. Orkn 4D 64
St Monans. Fife 3G 27
St Ninians. Stir 4H 25
St Quivox. S Ayr 1A 10
St Vigeans. Ang 4D 34
Salen. Arg 4G 29
Salen. High 2H 29
Saligo. Arg 2D 14
Saline. Fife 4B 26
Sallachan. High 2C 30
Sallachy. High 3C 54
(nr. Lairg)
Sallachy. High 5A 46
(nr. Stromeferry)
Salmond's Muir. Ang 5C 34
Salsburgh. N Lan 2D 18
Salta. Cumb 4D 6
Saltburn. High 2A 48
Saltcoats. N Ayr 4F 17
Saltness. Orkn 6B 64
Saltness. Shet 2B 66
Salum. Arg 4B 28
Samalaman. High 1H 29
Samhia. W Isl 4H 61
Samsonlane. Orkn 5J 65
Samuelston. E Lot 1B 20
Sanaigmore. Arg 1D 14
Sand. High 4E 53
Sand. Shet 2C 66
Sandaig. Arg 4A 28
Sandaig. High 3G 37
Sandale. Cumb 4F 7
Sandavore. High 5D 36
Sanday Airport. Orkn 3J 65
Sandbank. Arg 5A 24
Sandend. Abers 2A 50
Sandford. S Lan 4C 18
Sandfordhill. Abers 4G 51
Sandgreen. Dum 3G 5
Sandhaven. Abers 2E 51
Sandhead. Dum 3B 4
Sandness. Shet 1A 66
Sandsound. Shet 2C 66
Sandvoe. Shet 3G 67
Sandwick. Orkn 3B 64
(on Mainland)
Sandwick. Orkn 6D 64
(on South Ronaldsay)
Sandwick. Shet 4D 66
(on Mainland)
Sandwick. Shet 6J 67
(on Whalsay)
Sandyhills. Dum 3B 6
Sandystones. Bord 1E 13
Sangobeg. High 2F 57
Sangomore. High 2F 57
Sanna. High 2F 29
Sanndabhaig. W Isl 4J 63
(on Isle of Lewis)
Sanndabhaig. W Isl 6J 61
(on South Uist)
Sannox. N Ayr 4D 16
Sanquhar. Dum 2E 11
Sarclet. High 4G 59
Sauchen. Abers 2B 42
Saucher. Per 5G 33
Saughtree. Bord 4E 13
Saval. High 3C 54
Scadabhagh. W Isl 5C 62
Scaladal. W Isl 3C 62
Scalasaig. Arg 4A 22
Scaleby. Cumb 2H 7
Scaleby Hill. Cumb 2H 7
Scales. Cumb 5G 7
Scalloway. Shet 3C 66
Scalpaigh. W Isl 5D 62
Scalpay House. High 1F 37
Scamodale. High 1B 30
Scaniport. High 5H 47
Scapa. Orkn 4D 64
Scar. Orkn 3J 65
Scarasta. W Isl 5B 62
Scardroy. High 3D 46
Scarfskerry. High 1F 59
Scarinish. Arg 4B 28
Scarvister. Shet 2C 66
Scatness. Shet 6C 66
Scatwell. High 3E 47
Scaur. Dum 3B 6
Scolpaig. W Isl 3H 61
Scone. Per 1C 26
Sconser. High 5E 45
Scoonie. Fife 3E 27
Scoraig. High 4F 53
Scotby. Cumb 3H 7
Scotlandwell. Per 3C 26
Scotsburn. High 1A 48
Scotsburn. Mor 2F 49
Scotsdike. Cumb 1G 7
Scotstoun. Glas 2A 18
Scotstown. High 2B 30
Scottas. High 3G 37
Scourie. High 4C 56
Scourie More. High 4C 56
Scousburgh. Shet 5C 66
Scrabster. High 1D 58
Scremerston. Nmbd 4H 21
Scuggate. Cumb 1H 7
Seafield. High 5G 55
Seafield. Midl 2H 19
Seafield. S Ayr 1A 10
Seafield. W Lot 2F 19
Seamill. N Ayr 4E 17
Seaside. Per 1D 26
Seater. High 1G 59
Seaton. Cumb 5D 6
Seatown. Abers 2A 50
Seatown. Mor 2A 50
(nr. Cullen)
Seatown. Mor 1F 49
(nr. Lossiemouth)
Seaville. Cumb 3E 7
Sebergham. Cumb 4G 7
Second Coast. High 4E 53
Sefster. Shet 1C 66
Seggat. Abers 4C 50
Seilebost. W Isl 5B 62
Seisiadar. W Isl 4K 63
Selkirk. Bord 1D 12
Sellafirth. Shet 3J 67
Semblister. Shet 1C 66
Setter. Shet 4H 67
Settiscarth. Orkn 3C 64
Sgallairidh. W Isl 5B 60
Sgarasta Mhor. W Isl 5B 62
Sgiogarstaigh. W Isl 1K 63
Sgreadan. Arg 4A 22
Shandon. Arg 5B 24
Shandwick. High 1B 48
Shannochie. N Ayr 1E 9
Shawhead. Dum 1B 6
Shawwood. E Ayr 1C 10
Shearington. Dum 2D 6
Shebster. High 2D 58
Sheddocksley. Aber 3D 42
Shedog. N Ayr 5C 16
Sheigra. High 2C 56
Shennanton. Dum 2E 5
Shenval. Mor 1F 41
Sheppardstown. High 4E 59
Sheriffston. Mor 2F 49
Shettleston. Glas 2B 18
Shiel Bridge. High 2A 38
Shieldaig. High 1H 45
(nr. Charlestown)
Shieldaig. High 3H 45
(nr. Torridon)
Shieldhill. Dum 5H 11
Shieldhill. Falk 1D 18
Shieldhill. S Lan 4F 19
Shieldmuir. N Lan 3C 18
Shielfoot. High 2H 29
Shielhill. Abers 3F 51
Shielhill. Ang 3B 34
Shillford. E Ren 3H 17
Shillmoor. Nmbd 3H 13
Shinness. High 2C 54
Shires Mill. Fife 5A 26
Shiskine. N Ayr 1E 9
Shoresdean. Nmbd 4G 21
Shoreswood. Nmbd 4G 21
Shore, The. Fife 2D 26
Shotton. Nmbd 5F 21
Shotts. N Lan 2D 18
Shulishadermor. High 4D 44
Shulista. High 1D 44
Shurrery. High 3D 58
Siabost. W Isl 3G 63
Siabost bho Dheas. W Isl 3G 63
Siabost bho Thuath. W Isl 3G 63
Siadar. W Isl 2H 63
Siadar Uarach. W Isl 2H 63
Sibbaldbie. Dum 5A 12
Sibster. High 3G 59
Siddick. Cumb 5D 6
Sighthill. Edin 1G 19
Sildinis. W Isl 3D 62
Silloth. Cumb 3E 7
Sills. Nmbd 3H 13
Sillyearn. Mor 3A 50
Silverbank. Abers 4C 42
Silverburn. Midl 2H 19
Silverhillocks. Abers 2C 50
Silverton. W Dun 1H 17
Simprim. Bord 4F 21
Sinclairston. E Ayr 2B 10
Sinclairtown. Fife 4D 26
Sinnahard. Abers 2H 41
Skail. High 4A 58
Skaill. Orkn 3B 64
Skaills. Orkn 4E 64
Skares. E Ayr 2C 10
Skateraw. E Lot 1E 21
Skaw. Shet 6J 67
Skeabost. High 4D 44
Skeabrae. Orkn 2B 64
Skelberry. Shet 5C 66
(nr. Boddam)
Skelberry. Shet 4G 67
(nr. Housetter)
Skelbo. High 4E 55
Skelbo Street. High 4E 55
Skelfhill. Bord 3D 12
Skellister. Shet 1D 66
Skelmorlie. N Ayr 2E 17
Skelpick. High 3A 58
Skelton. Cumb 5H 7
Skelwick. Orkn 3G 65
Skeroblingarry. Arg 1C 8
Skerray. High 2H 57
Skerricha. High 3D 56
Skerries Airport. Shet 5K 67
Skiall. High 2D 58
Skinburness. Cumb 3E 7
Skinflats. Falk 5A 26
Skinidin. High 4B 44
Skinnet. High 2G 57
Skipness. Arg 3B 16
Skiprigg. Cumb 4G 7
Skirling. Bord 5F 19
Skirza. High 2G 59
Skitby. Cumb 2H 7
Skroo. Shet 1J 65
Skulamus. High 1F 37
Skullomie. High 2H 57
Skye of Curr. High 1C 40
Slackhead. Mor 2H 49
Slacks of Cairnbanno. Abers 4D 50
Slamannan. Falk 1D 18
Slickly. High 2F 59
Sliddery. N Ayr 1E 9
Sligachan. High 1D 36
Slochd. High 1B 40
Slockavullin. Arg 4F 23
Sluggan. High 1B 40
Smailholm. Bord 5D 20
Smallburn. E Ayr 1D 10
Smallholm. Dum 1E 7
Smeircleit. W Isl 3C 60
Smerral. High 5E 59
Smirisary. High 1H 29
Smithfield. Cumb 2H 7
Smithstown. High 1G 45
Smithton. High 4A 48
Smoogro. Orkn 4C 64
Snaigow House. Per 4F 33
Sniseabhal. W Isl 1C 60
Sockbridge. Cumb 5H 7
Sodom. Shet 6J 67
Solas. W Isl 3J 61
Sorbie. Dum 4F 5
Sordale. High 2E 59
Sorisdale. Arg 2D 28
Sorn. E Ayr 1C 10
Sornhill. E Ayr 5A 18
Sortat. High 2F 59
Soulby. Cumb 5H 7
Sound. Shet 2D 66
(nr. Lerwick)
Sound. Shet 1C 66
(nr. Tresta)
Sourhope. Bord 1H 13
Sourin. Orkn 1D 64
South Alloa. Falk 4H 25
Southannan. N Ayr 3F 17
South Balfern. Dum 4F 5
South Ballachulish. High 3D 30
South Broomage. Falk 5H 25
South Clunes. High 4G 47
South Creagan. Arg 4C 30
Southdean. Bord 3F 13
Southend. Arg 3B 8
Southerfield. Cumb 4E 7
Southerhouse. Shet 3C 66
Southerness. Dum 3C 6
South Erradale. High 1G 45
South Feorline. N Ayr 1E 9
South Garvan. High 1C 30
South Gluss. Shet 5G 67
South Hazelrigg. Nmbd 5H 21
South Kessock. High 4H 47
South Kirkton. Abers 3C 42
South Ledaig. Arg 5C 30
South Newton. N Ayr 3C 16
South Port. Arg 1H 23
Southpunds. Shet 5D 66
South Queensferry. Edin 1G 19
Southside. Orkn 2E 64
Southtown. Orkn 5D 64
South View. Shet 2C 66
Southwaite. Cumb 4H 7
Soval Lodge. W Isl 2E 62
Sowerby Row. Cumb 4G 7
Soyal. High 4C 54
Sparket. Cumb 5H 7
Spean Bridge. High 5D 38
Speybank. High 3B 40
Spey Bay. Mor 2G 49
Speybridge. High 1D 40
Speyview. Mor 4F 49
Spinningdale. High 5D 54
Spittal. Dum 3E 5
Spittal. E Lot 1B 20
Spittal. High 3E 59
Spittal. Nmbd 3H 21
Spittalfield. Per 4G 33
Spittal of Glenmuick. Abers 5G 41
Spittal of Glenshee. Per 1G 33
Spittal-on-Rule. Bord 1E 13
Spott. E Lot 1D 20
Springburn. Glas 2B 18
Springfield. Dum 2G 7
Springfield. Fife 2E 27
Springfield. High 2H 47
Springholm. Dum 1B 6
Springside. N Ayr 5G 17
Sprouston. Bord 5E 21
Sprunston. Cumb 4G 7
Sraid Ruadh. Arg 4A 28
Srannda. W Isl 6B 62
Sronphadruig Lodge. Per 1C 32
Sruth Mor. W Isl 4K 61
Stadhlaigearraidh. W Isl 1C 60
Staffin. High 2D 44
Stainburn. Cumb 5D 6
Stainton. Cumb 3G 7
(nr. Carlisle)
Stainton. Cumb 5H 7
(nr. Penrith)
Stair. E Ayr 1B 10
Stamperland. E Ren 3A 18
Stand. N Lan 2C 18
Standburn. Falk 1E 19
Standingstone. Cumb 4F 7
Stane. N Lan 3D 18
Stanecastle. N Ayr 5G 17
Stanhope. Bord 5G 19
Stanley. Per 5G 33
Stannersburn. Nmbd 5G 13
Stanydale. Shet 1B 66
Staoinebrig. W Isl 1C 60
Stapleton. Cumb 1H 7
Star. Fife 3E 27
Staxigoe. High 3G 59
Steelend. Fife 4B 26
Steele Road. Bord 4E 13
Stein. High 3B 44
Steinmanhill. Abers 4C 50
Stemster. High 2E 59
(nr. Halkirk)
Stemster. High 2D 58
(nr. Westfield)
Stenhouse. Edin 1H 19
Stenhousemuir. Falk 5H 25
Stenscholl. High 2D 44
Stenso. Orkn 2C 64
Stenton. E Lot 1D 20
Steòrnabhagh. W Isl 4J 63
Stepford. Dum 5F 11
Stepps. N Lan 2B 18
Stevenston. N Ayr 4F 17
Stewarton. Arg 2B 8
Stewarton. E Ayr 4H 17
Stichill. Bord 5E 21
Stirling. Abers 4G 51
Stirling. Stir 4G 25 & 87
Stittenham. High 1H 47
Stobo. Bord 5G 19
Stobo Castle. Bord 5G 19
Stobs Castle. Bord 3E 13
Stockdalewath. Cumb 4G 7
Stoer. High 1F 53
Stonebyres. S Lan 4D 18
Stonefield. Arg 5C 30
Stonefield. S Lan 3B 18
Stonehaugh. Nmbd 5G 13

…s 5D **42**
…Lan 4C **18**
…W Lot 2E **19**
…k. *Dum* 3B **4**
…wood. *Aber* 2D **42**
Sto…ybreck. *Shet* 1J **65**
Stormontfield. *Per* 1C **26**
Stornoway. *W Isl* 4J **63**
Stornoway Airport. *W Isl* 4J **63**
Stotfield. *Mor* 1F **49**
Stoul. *High* 4G **37**
Stove. *Orkn* 4J **65**
Stove. *Shet* 4D **66**
Stow. *Bord* 4B **20**
Straad. *Arg* 2D **16**
Strachan. *Abers* 4B **42**
Straid. *S Ayr* 4G **9**
Straiton. *Edin* 2H **19**
Straiton. *S Ayr* 3A **10**
Straloch. *Per* 2F **33**
Stranraer. *Dum* 2B **4**
Strath. *High* 1G **45**
(nr. Gairloch)
Strath. *High* 3F **59**
(nr. Wick)
Strathan. *High* 4A **38**
(nr. Fort William)
Strathan. *High* 1F **53**
(nr. Lochinver)
Strathan. *High* 2G **57**
(nr. Tongue)
Strathan Skerray. *High* 2H **57**
Strathaven. *S Lan* 4C **18**
Strathblane. *Stir* 1A **18**
Strathcanaird. *High* 3G **53**
Strathcarron. *High* 4A **46**
Strathcoil. *Arg* 5H **29**
Strathdon. *Abers* 2G **41**
Strathkinness. *Fife* 2F **27**
Strathmashie House. *High* 4G **39**
Strathmiglo. *Fife* 2D **26**
Strathmore Lodge. *High* 4E **59**
Strathpeffer. *High* 3F **47**
Strathrannoch. *High* 1E **47**
Strathtay. *Per* 3E **33**
Strathvaich Lodge. *High* 1E **47**
Strathwhillan. *N Ayr* 5D **16**
Strathy. *High* 1H **47**
(nr. Invergordon)
Strathy. *High* 2B **58**
(nr. Melvich)
Strathyre. *Stir* 2E **25**
Stravithie. *Fife* 2G **27**
Strichen. *Abers* 3E **51**
Stroanfreggan. *Dum* 4D **10**
Stromeferry. *High* 5H **45**
Stromemore. *High* 5H **45**
Stromness. *Orkn* 4B **64**
Stronachie. *Per* 3B **26**
Stronachlachar. *Stir* 2D **24**
Stronchreggan. *High* 1D **30**
Strone. *Arg* 5A **24**
Strone. *High* 1G **39**
(nr. Drumnadrochit)
Strone. *High* 3A **40**
(nr. Kingussie)
Stronenaba. *High* 5D **38**
Stronganess. *Shet* 2J **67**
Stronmilchan. *Arg* 1A **24**
Stronsay Airport. *Orkn* 5J **65**
Strontian. *High* 2B **30**
Struan. *High* 5C **44**
Struan. *Per* 2D **32**
Struanmore. *High* 5C **44**
Strutherhill. *S Lan* 3C **18**
Struy. *High* 5E **47**
Stuartfield. *Abers* 4E **51**
Suainebost. *W Isl* 1K **63**
Suardail. *W Isl* 4J **63**
Succoth. *Abers* 5H **49**
Succoth. *Arg* 3B **24**
Suisnish. *High* 5E **45**
Sulaisiadar. *W Isl* 4K **63**
Sullom. *Shet* 5G **67**
Sumburgh. *Shet* 6D **66**
Sumburgh Airport. *Shet* 5C **66**
Summerhill. *Aber* 3G **43**
Sunderland. *Cumb* 5E **7**
Sunnylaw. *Stir* 4G **25**
Sutors of Cromarty. *High* 2B **48**
Swanbister. *Orkn* 4C **64**
Swarister. *Shet* 4J **67**
Swiney. *High* 5F **59**
Swinhill. *S Lan* 4C **18**
Swinister. *Shet* 4G **67**
Swinside Hall. *Bord* 2G **13**
Swinton. *Bord* 4F **21**
Swordale. *High* 2G **47**
Swordly. *High* 2A **58**
Symbister. *Shet* 6J **67**
Symington. *S Ayr* 5G **17**
Symington. *S Lan* 5E **19**
Syre. *High* 4H **57**

T

Tabost. *W Isl* 3E **62**
(nr. Cearsiadar)
Tabost. *W Isl* 1K **63**
(nr. Suainebost)
Tacleit. *W Isl* 1C **62**
Taigh a Ghearraidh. *W Isl* 3H **61**
Taigh Bhuirgh. *W Isl* 5B **62**
Tain. *High* 5E **55**
(nr. Invergordon)
Tain. *High* 2F **59**
(nr. Thurso)
Tairbeart. *W Isl* 5C **62**
Talisker. *High* 5C **44**
Talladale. *High* 1A **46**
Talla Linnfoots. *Bord* 1A **12**
Tallaminnock. *S Ayr* 4B **10**
Tallentire. *Cumb* 5E **7**
Talmine. *High* 2G **57**
Tandlehill. *Ren* 2H **17**
Tangasdale. *W Isl* 4B **60**
Tangwick. *Shet* 5F **67**
Tankerness. *Orkn* 4E **64**
Tannach. *High* 4G **59**
Tannadice. *Ang* 3B **34**
Tannochside. *N Lan* 2C **18**
Taobh a Chaolais. *W Isl* 3C **60**
Taobh a Deas Loch Aineort.
W Isl 2C **60**
Taobh a Ghlinne. *W Isl* 3E **62**
Taobh a Tuath Loch Aineort.
W Isl 2C **60**
Taobh Tuath. *W Isl* 2K **61**
Tarbert. *Arg* 5D **22**
(on Jura)
Tarbert. *Arg* 2B **16**
(on Kintyre)
Tarbert. *W Isl* 5C **62**
Tarbet. *Arg* 3C **24**
Tarbet. *High* 4G **37**
(nr. Mallaig)
Tarbet. *High* 4C **56**
(nr. Scourie)
Tarbolton. *S Ayr* 1B **10**
Tarbrax. *S Lan* 3F **19**
Tarfside. *Ang* 1B **34**
Tarland. *Abers* 3H **41**
Tarlogie. *High* 5E **55**
Tarns. *Cumb* 4E **7**
Tarrel. *High* 5F **55**
Tarsappie. *Per* 1C **26**
Tarskavaig. *High* 3E **37**
Tarves. *Abers* 5D **50**
Tarvie. *High* 3F **47**
Tavool House. *Arg* 1B **22**
Tayinloan. *Arg* 4H **15**
Taynish. *Arg* 5E **23**
Taynuilt. *Arg* 5D **30**
Tayport. *Fife* 1F **27**
Tay Road Bridge. *Fife* 1F **27**
Tayvallich. *Arg* 5E **23**
Tealing. *Ang* 5B **34**
Teangue. *High* 3F **37**
Teanna Machair. *W Isl* 4H **61**
Tempar. *Per* 3B **32**
Templand. *Dum* 5H **11**
Temple. *Glas* 2A **18**
Temple. *Midl* 3A **20**
Templehall. *Fife* 4D **26**
Tenandry. *Per* 2E **33**
Tenga. *Arg* 4G **29**
Terregles. *Dum* 1C **6**
Teviothead. *Bord* 3D **12**
Tewel. *Abers* 5H **42**
Thackthwaite. *Cumb* 5G **7**
Thankerton. *S Lan* 5E **19**
Thethwaite. *Cumb* 4G **7**
Thirlestane. *Bord* 4C **20**
Thomas Close. *Cumb* 4H **7**
Thomastown. *Abers* 4C **50**
Thomshill. *Mor* 3F **49**
Thornby. *Cumb* 3F **7**
Thornhill. *Dum* 4F **11**
Thornhill. *Stir* 4F **25**
Thornington. *Nmbd* 5F **21**
Thornliebank. *E Ren* 3A **18**
Thornroan. *Abers* 5D **50**
Thornthwaite. *Cumb* 5F **7**
Thornton. *Ang* 4A **34**
Thornton. *Fife* 4D **26**
Thornton. *Nmbd* 4G **21**
Thorntonhall. *S Lan* 3A **18**
Thorntonloch. *E Lot* 1E **21**
Thrashbush. *N Lan* 2C **18**
Threapland. *Cumb* 5E **7**
Threlkeld. *Cumb* 5G **7**
Throsk. *Stir* 4H **25**
Throughgate. *Dum* 5F **11**
Thrumster. *High* 4G **59**
Thundergay. *N Ayr* 4B **16**
Thursby. *Cumb* 3G **7**
Thurso. *High* 2E **59**
Thurso East. *High* 2E **59**
Thurstonfield. *Cumb* 3G **7**
Tibbermore. *Per* 1B **26**
Tifty. *Abers* 4C **50**
Tigerton. *Ang* 2C **34**
Tighnabruaich. *Arg* 1C **16**
Tillathrowie. *Abers* 5H **49**
Tillery. *Abers* 1E **43**
Tillicoultry. *Clac* 4A **26**
Tillybirloch. *Abers* 3B **42**
Tillyfourie. *Abers* 2B **42**
Timsgearraidh. *W Isl* 1C **62**
Tingwall. *Orkn* 2D **64**
Tinwald. *Dum* 5H **11**
Tipperty. *Abers* 1E **43**
Tiree Airport. *Arg* 4B **28**
Tirinie. *Per* 2D **32**
Tiroran. *Arg* 1B **22**
Tirril. *Cumb* 5H **7**
Tirryside. *High* 2C **54**
Toab. *Orkn* 4E **64**
Toab. *Shet* 5C **66**
Tobermory. *Arg* 3G **29**
Toberonochy. *Arg* 3E **23**
Tobha-Beag. *W Isl* 4K **61**
Tobha Beag. *W Isl* 1C **60**
Tobha Mor. *W Isl* 1C **60**
Tobhtarol. *W Isl* 1C **62**
Tobson. *W Isl* 1C **62**
Tocher. *Abers* 5B **50**
Todhills. *Cumb* 2G **7**
Tofts. *High* 2G **59**
Tokavaig. *High* 2F **37**
Tolastadh a Chaolais. *W Isl* 1C **62**
Tollie. *High* 3G **47**
Tollie Farm. *High* 1H **45**
Tolm. *W Isl* 4J **63**
Tolstadh bho Thuath. *W Isl* 3K **63**
Tomachlaggan. *Mor* 1E **41**
Tomaknock. *Per* 1H **25**
Tomatin. *High* 1B **40**
Tombuidhe. *Arg* 3H **23**
Tomdoun. *High* 3C **38**
Tomich. *High* 1E **39**
(nr. Cannich)
Tomich. *High* 1A **48**
(nr. Invergordon)
Tomich. *High* 3D **54**
(nr. Lairg)
Tomintoul. *Mor* 2E **41**
Tomnavoulin. *Mor* 1F **41**
Tomsleibhe. *Arg* 5H **29**
Tongland. *Dum* 3H **5**
Tongue. *High* 3G **57**
Torbeg. *N Ayr* 1D **8**
Torbothie. *N Lan* 2D **18**
Tore. *High* 3H **47**
Torgyle. *High* 2E **39**
Torinturk. *Arg* 2B **16**
Torlum. *W Isl* 5H **61**
Torlundy. *High* 1E **31**
Tormitchell. *S Ayr* 4H **9**
Tormore. *High* 3E **37**
Tormore. *N Ayr* 5B **16**
Tornagrain. *High* 4A **48**
Tornaveen. *Abers* 3B **42**
Torness. *High* 1G **39**
Torpenhow. *Cumb* 5F **7**
Torphichen. *W Lot* 1E **19**
Torphins. *Abers* 3B **42**
Torra. *Arg* 3E **15**
Torran. *High* 4E **45**
Torrance. *E Dun* 1B **18**
Torrans. *Arg* 1B **22**
Torranyard. *E Ayr* 4G **17**
Torridon. *High* 3A **46**
Torrin. *High* 1E **37**
Torrisdale. *Arg* 5A **16**
Torrisdale. *High* 2H **57**
Torrish. *High* 2G **55**
Torroble. *High* 3C **54**
Torroy. *High* 4C **54**
Torry. *Aber* 3E **43**
Torryburn. *Fife* 5B **26**
Torthorwald. *Dum* 1D **6**
Torvaig. *High* 4D **44**
Torwood. *Falk* 5H **25**
Toscaig. *High* 5G **45**
Totaig. *High* 3B **44**
Totardor. *High* 5C **44**
Tote. *High* 4D **44**
Totegan. *High* 2B **58**
Totronald. *Arg* 3C **28**
Totscore. *High* 2C **44**
Toulvaddie. *High* 5F **55**
Toward. *Arg* 2E **17**
Towie. *Abers* 2H **41**
Towiemore. *Mor* 4G **49**
Townend. *W Dun* 1H **17**
Towngate. *Cumb* 4H **7**
Townhead. *Cumb* 5D **6**
Townhead. *Dum* 4H **5**
Townhead of Greenlaw. *Dum* 2A **6**
Townhill. *Fife* 5C **26**
Town Yetholm. *Bord* 1H **13**
Trabboch. *E Ayr* 1B **10**
Tradespark. *High* 3B **48**
Tradespark. *Orkn* 4D **64**
Tranent. *E Lot* 1B **20**
Trantlebeg. *High* 3B **58**
Trantlemore. *High* 3B **58**
Traquair. *Bord* 5A **20**
Treaslane. *High* 3C **44**
Tressady. *High* 3D **54**
Tressait. *Per* 2D **32**
Tresta. *Shet* 3K **67**
(on Fetlar)
Tresta. *Shet* 1C **66**
(on Mainland)
Trinafour. *Per* 2C **32**
Trinity. *Ang* 2D **34**
Trinity. *Edin* 1H **19**
Trislaig. *High* 1D **30**
Trochry. *Per* 4E **33**
Trondavoe. *Shet* 5G **67**
Troon. *S Ayr* 5G **17**
Troqueer. *Dum* 1C **6**
Troutbeck. *Cumb* 5G **7**
Trumaisgearraidh. *W Isl* 3J **61**
Trumpan. *High* 2B **44**
Tulchan. *Per* 1A **26**
Tullibardine. *Per* 2A **26**
Tullibody. *Clac* 4H **25**
Tullich. *Arg* 2H **23**
Tullich. *High* 4A **46**
(nr. Lochcarron)
Tullich. *High* 1B **48**
(nr. Tain)
Tullich. *Mor* 4G **49**
Tullich Muir. *High* 1A **48**
Tulliemet. *Per* 3E **33**
Tulloch. *Abers* 5D **50**
Tulloch. *High* 4D **54**
(nr. Bonar Bridge)
Tulloch. *High* 5E **39**
(nr. Fort William)
Tulloch. *High* 2C **40**
(nr. Grantown-on-Spey)
Tulloch. *Per* 1B **26**
Tullochgorm. *Arg* 4G **23**
Tullybeagles Lodge. *Per* 5F **33**
Tullymurdoch. *Per* 3G **33**
Tullynessle. *Abers* 2A **42**
Tummel Bridge. *Per* 3C **32**
Tunga. *W Isl* 4J **63**
Turfholm. *S Lan* 5D **18**
Turnberry. *S Ayr* 3H **9**
Turnhouse. *Edin* 1G **19**
Turriff. *Abers* 4C **50**
Turtory. *Mor* 4B **50**
Tushielaw. *Bord* 2C **12**
Twatt. *Orkn* 2B **64**
Twatt. *Shet* 1C **66**
Twechar. *E Dun* 1C **18**
Tweedmouth. *Nmbd* 3G **21**
Tweedsmuir. *Bord* 1H **11**
Twynholm. *Dum* 3H **5**
Tyndrum. *Stir* 5G **31**
Tynehead. *Midl* 3A **20**
Tyninghame. *E Lot* 1D **20**
Tynron. *Dum* 4F **11**
Tyrie. *Abers* 2E **51**

U

Uachdar. *W Isl* 5J **61**
Uags. *High* 5G **45**
Uddingston. *S Lan* 2B **18**
Uddington. *S Lan* 5D **18**
Udny Green. *Abers* 1D **42**
Udny Station. *Abers* 1E **43**
Udston. *S Lan* 3C **18**
Udstonhead. *S Lan* 4C **18**
Ugadale. *Arg* 1C **8**
Uidh. *W Isl* 5B **60**
Uig. *Arg* 3C **28**
Uig. *High* 2C **44**
(nr. Balgown)
Uig. *High* 3A **44**
(nr. Dunvegan)
Uigshader. *High* 4D **44**
Uisken. *Arg* 2A **22**
Ulbster. *High* 4G **59**
Uldale. *Cumb* 5F **7**
Ullapool. *High* 4G **53**
Ullinish. *High* 5C **44**
Ulsta. *Shet* 4H **67**
Ulva House. *Arg* 5F **29**
Unapool. *High* 5D **56**
Underhoull. *Shet* 2J **67**
Unthank. *Cumb* 4G **7**
(nr. Carlisle)
Unthank. *Cumb* 5H **7**
(nr. Penrith)
Unthank End. *Cumb* 5H **7**
Uphall. *W Lot* 1F **19**
Uphall Station. *W Lot* 1F **19**
Uplawmoor. *E Ren* 3H **17**
Uppat. *High* 3F **55**
Upper Badcall. *High* 4C **56**
Upper Bighouse. *High* 3B **58**
Upper Boddam. *Abers* 5B **50**
Upper Bogside. *Mor* 3F **49**
Upper Boyndlie. *Abers* 2E **51**
Upper Breakish. *High* 1F **37**
Upper Cuttlehill. *Abers* 4H **49**
Upper Dallachy. *Mor* 2G **49**
Upper Derraid. *High* 5D **48**
Upper Diabaig. *High* 2H **45**
Upper Dochcarty. *High* 2G **47**
Upper Dounreay. *High* 2C **58**
Upper Gills. *High* 1G **59**
Upper Glenfintaig. *High* 5D **38**
Upper Hindhope. *Bord* 3G **13**
Upper Kirkton. *Abers* 5C **50**
Upper Kirkton. *N Ayr* 3E **17**
Upper Knockando. *Mor* 4E **49**
Upper Knockchoilum. *High* 2F **39**
Upper Largo. *Fife* 3F **27**
Upper Latheron. *High* 5E **59**
Upper Lenie. *High* 1G **39**
Upper Lochton. *Abers* 4C **42**
Upper Lybster. *High* 5F **59**
Upper Milovaig. *High* 4A **44**
Upper Neepaback. *Shet* 4J **67**
Upper Ollach. *High* 5E **45**
Upper Rusko. *Dum* 2G **5**
Upper Sandaig. *High* 2G **37**
Upper Sanday. *Orkn* 4E **64**
Upper Skelmorlie. *N Ayr* 2E **17**
Upper Sonachan. *Arg* 1H **23**
Upper Tillyrie. *Per* 3C **26**
Uppertown. *High* 1G **59**
Uppertown. *Orkn* 5D **64**
Upper Urquhart. *Fife* 3C **26**
Upsettlington. *Bord* 4F **21**
Upton. *Cumb* 5G **7**
Urafirth. *Shet* 5G **67**
Uragaig. *Arg* 4A **22**
Urchany. *High* 4B **48**
Ure. *Shet* 5F **67**
Urgha. *W Isl* 5C **62**
Urquhart. *Mor* 2F **49**
Urray. *High* 3G **47**
Usan. *Ang* 3E **35**
Uyeasound. *Shet* 2J **67**

V

Valsgarth. *Shet* 1K **67**
Valtos. *High* 2E **45**
Vatsetter. *Shet* 4J **67**
Vatten. *High* 4B **44**
Vaul. *Arg* 4B **28**
Veensgarth. *Shet* 2D **66**
Veness. *Orkn* 2E **64**
Vidlin. *Shet* 6H **67**
Viewpark. *N Lan* 2C **18**
Village Bay. *High* 3B **44**
Voe. *Shet* 6H **67**
(nr. Hillside)
Voe. *Shet* 4G **67**
(nr. Swinister)
Voxter. *Shet* 5G **67**
Voy. *Orkn* 3B **64**

W

Wadbister. *Shet* 2D **66**
Wag. *High* 1H **55**
Walby. *Cumb* 2H **7**
Walkerburn. *Bord* 5A **20**
Walkerton. *Fife* 3D **26**
Wallaceton. *Dum* 5F **11**
Wallacetown. *Shet* 1C **66**
Wallacetown. *S Ayr* 1A **10**
(nr. Ayr)
Wallacetown. *S Ayr* 3H **9**
(nr. Dailly)
Walls. *Shet* 2B **66**
Wallyford. *E Lot* 1A **20**
Walnut Grove. *Per* 1C **26**
Walston. *S Lan* 4F **19**
Walton. *Cumb* 2H **7**
Wampool. *Cumb* 3F **7**
Wandel. *S Lan* 1G **11**
Wanlockhead. *Dum* 2F **11**
Wardhouse. *Abers* 5A **50**
Warenton. *Nmbd* 5H **21**
Wark. *Nmbd* 5E **21**
(nr. Coldstream)
Wark. *Nmbd* 5H **13**
(nr. Hexham)
Warmanbie. *Dum* 2E **7**
Warse. *High* 1G **59**
Warwick. *Cumb* 3H **7**
Warwick Bridge. *Cumb* 3H **7**
Wasbister. *Orkn* 1C **64**
Watchhill. *Cumb* 4E **7**
Waterbeck. *Dum* 1F **7**
Waterfoot. *E Ren* 3A **18**
Waterhead. *E Ayr* 2C **10**
Waterhead. *S Ayr* 4A **10**
Waterheads. *Bord* 3H **19**
Waterloo. *High* 1F **37**
Waterloo. *N Lan* 3D **18**
Waterloo. *Per* 5F **33**
Waterside. *Cumb* 4F **7**
Waterside. *E Ayr* 3B **10**
(nr. Ayr)
Waterside. *E Ayr* 4H **17**
(nr. Kilmarnock)
Waterside. *E Dun* 1B **18**
Waterstein. *High* 4A **44**
Watten. *High* 3F **59**
Wattston. *N Lan* 1C **18**
Waulkmill. *Abers* 4B **42**
Waverbridge. *Cumb* 4F **7**
Waverton. *Cumb* 4F **7**
Wedderlairs. *Abers* 5D **50**
Weem. *Per* 4D **32**
Weetwood Hall. *Nmbd* 5H **21**
Wellbank. *Ang* 5B **34**
Welldale. *Dum* 2E **7**
Wells of Ythan. *Abers* 5B **50**
Wellwood. *Fife* 5B **26**
Welton. *Cumb* 4G **7**
Wemyss Bay. *Inv* 1E **17**
West Allerdean. *Nmbd* 4G **21**
West Arthurlie. *E Ren* 3H **17**
West Barns. *E Lot* 1D **20**
West Bennan. *N Ayr* 1E **9**
West Burnside. *Abers* 1E **35**
West Burrafirth. *Shet* 1B **66**
West Calder. *W Lot* 2F **19**
West Clyne. *High* 3F **55**
West Croftmore. *High* 2C **40**
West Cullerlie. *Abers* 3C **42**
West Culvennan. *Dum* 2D **4**
West Curthwaite. *Cumb* 4G **7**
West Dunnet. *High* 1F **59**
West End. *S Lan* 4E **19**
Wester Aberchalder. *High* 2G **39**
Wester Balgedie. *Per* 3C **26**
Wester Brae. *High* 2H **47**
Wester Culbeuchly. *Abers* 2B **50**
Westerdale. *High* 3E **59**
Wester Dechmont. *W Lot* 1F **19**
Wester Fearn. *High* 5D **54**
Wester Galcantray. *High* 4B **48**
Wester Gruinards. *High* 4C **54**
Westerloch. *High* 3G **59**
Wester Mandally. *High* 3D **38**
Wester Quarff. *Shet* 3D **66**
Wester Rarichie. *High* 1B **48**
Wester Shian. *Per* 5D **32**
Wester Skeld. *Shet* 2B **66**
Westerton. *Ang* 3D **34**
Westerwick. *Shet* 2B **66**
Westfield. *Cumb* 5C **6**
Westfield. *High* 2D **58**
Westfield. *N Lan* 1C **18**
Westfield. *W Lot* 1E **19**
Westfields of Rattray. *Per* 4G **33**
Westhall Terrace. *Ang* 5B **34**
West Helmsdale. *High* 2H **55**
West Heogaland. *Shet* 5F **67**
Westhill. *Abers* 3D **42**
Westhill. *High* 4A **48**
West Horton. *Nmbd* 5H **21**
West Houlland. *Shet* 1B **66**
West Hynish. *Arg* 5A **28**
Westing. *Shet* 2J **67**
West Kilbride. *N Ayr* 4F **17**
West Langwell. *High* 3D **54**
West Learmouth. *Nmbd* 5F **21**
West Lingo. *Fife* 3F **27**
Westlinton. *Cumb* 2G **7**
West Linton. *Bord* 3G **19**
West Mains. *Per* 2A **26**
Westmoor End. *Cumb* 5D **6**
West Muir. *Ang* 2C **34**
(nr. Brechin)
Westmuir. *Ang* 3A **34**
(nr. Forfar)
West Murkle. *High* 2E **59**
Westness. *Orkn* 2C **64**
Westnewton. *Cumb* 4E **7**
Westnewton. *Nmbd* 5G **21**
Weston. *S Lan* 4F **19**
Westown. *Per* 1D **26**
West Pitcorthie. *Fife* 3G **27**
West Plean. *Stir* 5H **25**
Westray Airport. *Orkn* 2G **65**
Westrigg. *W Lot* 2E **19**
Westruther. *Bord* 3D **20**
West Saltoun. *E Lot* 2B **20**
West Sandwick. *Shet* 4H **67**
Westside. *Orkn* 2C **64**
West Strathan. *High* 2G **57**
West Tarbert. *Arg* 2B **16**
Westward. *Cumb* 4F **7**
West Wemyss. *Fife* 4E **27**
Westwood. *S Lan* 3B **18**
West Woodburn. *Nmbd* 5H **13**
West Woodside. *Cumb* 4G **7**
West Yell. *Shet* 4H **67**
Wetheral. *Cumb* 3H **7**
Wethersta. *Shet* 6G **67**
Weydale. *High* 2E **59**
Whauphill. *Dum* 4F **5**
Whelpo. *Cumb* 5G **7**
Whigstreet. *Ang* 4B **34**
Whinnyfold. *Abers* 5F **51**
Whitburn. *W Lot* 2E **19**
Whitchester. *Bord* 3E **21**
Whitebog. *High* 2A **48**
Whitebridge. *High* 2F **39**
Whitecairns. *Abers* 2E **43**
White Corries. *High* 3F **31**
Whitecraig. *E Lot* 1A **20**
Whitecross. *Falk* 1E **19**
Whiteface. *High* 5E **55**
Whitefaulds. *S Ayr* 3H **9**
Whiteford. *Abers* 1C **42**
Whitehall. *Orkn* 5J **65**
Whitehill. *N Ayr* 3F **17**
Whitehills. *Abers* 2B **50**
Whitehills. *Ang* 3B **34**
Whitehouse. *Abers* 2B **42**
Whitehouse. *Arg* 2B **16**
Whiteinch. *Glas* 2A **18**
Whitekirk. *E Lot* 5G **27**
Whitemire. *Mor* 3C **48**
Whiteness. *Shet* 2D **66**
Whiterashes. *Abers* 1D **42**
Whiterow. *High* 4G **59**
Whiterow. *Mor* 3D **48**
Whiteside. *W Lot* 2E **19**
Whitestone. *Abers* 4B **42**
Whitestones. *Abers* 3D **50**
Whitewreath. *Mor* 3F **49**
Whitfield. *D'dee* 5B **34**
Whithorn. *Dum* 4F **5**
Whiting Bay. *N Ayr* 1F **9**
Whitletts. *S Ayr* 1A **10**
Whitrigg. *Cumb* 3F **7**
(nr. Kirkbride)
Whitrigg. *Cumb* 5F **7**
(nr. Torpenhow)
Whitsome. *Bord* 3F **21**
Whitton. *Bord* 1G **13**
Whygate. *Nmbd* 5G **13**
Wick. *High* 3G **59**
Wick. *Shet* 3D **66**
(on Mainland)
Wick. *Shet* 2J **67**
(on Unst)
Wick Airport. *High* 3G **59**
Widewall. *Orkn* 5D **64**
Wiggonby. *Cumb* 3F **7**
Wigton. *Cumb* 4F **7**
Wigtown. *Dum* 3F **5**
Wildmanbridge. *S Lan* 3D **18**
Wilkhaven. *High* 5G **55**
Wilkieston. *W Lot* 2G **19**
Williamsetter. *Shet* 4C **66**
Wilsontown. *S Lan* 3E **19**
Wilton. *Bord* 2E **13**
Winchburgh. *W Lot* 1F **19**
Windhill. *High* 4G **47**
Windyedge. *Abers* 4E **43**
Windygates. *Fife* 3E **27**
Windyknowe. *W Lot* 2E **19**
Winless. *High* 3G **59**
Winscales. *Cumb* 5D **6**
Wishaw. *N Lan* 3D **18**
Wiston. *S Lan* 5E **19**
Wolfhill. *Per* 5G **33**
Wolsty. *Cumb* 3E **7**
Woodhall. *Inv* 1G **17**
Woodhaven. *Fife* 1F **27**
Woodhead. *Abers* 2E **51**
(nr. Fraserburgh)
Woodhead. *Abers* 5C **50**
(nr. Fyvie)
Woodlands. *Abers* 4C **42**
Woodrow. *Cumb* 4F **7**
Woodside. *Aber* 3E **43**
Woodside. *Cumb* 5D **6**
Woodside. *Dum* 1D **6**
Woodside. *Fife* 3F **27**
Woodside. *Per* 5H **33**
Woodwick. *Orkn* 2C **64**
Wooler. *Nmbd* 5G **21**
Woolfords. *S Lan* 3F **19**
Work. *Orkn* 3D **64**
Workington. *Cumb* 5C **6**
Wormit. *Fife* 1E **27**
Wreay. *Cumb* 4H **7**
Wyng. *Orkn* 5C **64**
Wythop Mill. *Cumb* 5E **7**
Wyvis Lodge. *High* 1F **47**

Y

Yanwath. *Cumb* 5H **7**
Yarrow. *Nmbd* 5G **13**
Yarrow. *Bord* 1C **12**
Yarrow Feus. *Bord* 1C **12**
Yarrow Ford. *Bord* 5B **20**
Yearngill. *Cumb* 4E **7**
Yeavering. *Nmbd* 5G **21**
Yesnaby. *Orkn* 3B **64**
Yett. *N Lan* 3C **18**
Yett. *S Ayr* 1B **10**
Yetts o' Muckhart. *Clac* 3B **26**
Yieldshields. *S Lan* 3D **18**
Yinstay. *Orkn* 3E **64**
Yoker. *Glas* 2A **18**
Yonder Bognie. *Abers* 4A **50**
Yonderton. *Abers* 5E **51**
Ythanbank. *Abers* 5E **51**
Ythanwells. *Abers* 5B **50**

HOW TO USE THE PLACES OF INTEREST INDEX

This is an index to selected features shown on the map pages in Scotland only.
The index reference is to the square in which the symbol (or its pointer) appears; the text may be in a different square e.g. Ardchattan Priory (remains of) — 5C **30** is to be found in square 5C on page **30**.
The page number is shown in bold type.

Entries shown without an index reference have the name of the appropriate town plan on which they appear. The extent of these town plans are indicated on the main pages by a blue box.
Terms such as 'museum', 'country park' etc. are omitted from the text on the map; a key to the various map symbols used can be found on page 2 in the reference.
Any category in the index that does not have its own symbol in the reference will be depicted by a dot. Visitor & Information Centres use the tourist information centre blue symbol.

Entries in italics are not named on the map but are shown with a symbol.
Entries in italics and enclosed in brackets are not shown on the map.
For both these types of entry, the nearest village or town name is given, where that name is not already included in the name of the place of interest.

Places of interest that are open for the summer season only are shown with an S after the index reference.

Opening times for places of interest vary considerably depending on the season, day of week or the ownership of the property. Please check with the nearest tourist information centre listed below before starting your journey.

NTS, National Trust for Scotland Property - Always open.   NTS, National Trust for Scotland Property- Restricted opening.   NP, National Park Property - Always open.

Tourist Information Centre (Open All Year)

Aberdeen Visitor Information Centre, Tel: 01224 288828
Aberfeldy — 4D **32**, Tel: 01887 820276
Aberfoyle — 3E **25**, Tel: 08707 200604
Abington, M74, Junction 13, Abington — 1G **11**, Tel: 01864 502436
Alva — 4H **25**, Tel: 08707 200605
Arbroath — 4D **34**, Tel: 01241 872609
Auchterarder — 2A **26**, Tel: 01764 663450
Aviemore, Tel: 01479 810363
Ayr, Tel: 0845 22 55 121
Ballater — 4G **41**, Tel: 013397 55306
Blairgowrie — 4G **33**, Tel: 01250 872960
Bowmore — 3E **15**, Tel: 08707 200617
Braemar — 4E **41**, Tel: 013397 41600
Brodick — 5D **16**, Tel: 0845 22 55 121
Brora — 3F **55**, Tel: 0845 22 55 121
Callander — 3F **25**, Tel: 08707 200628
Campbeltown — 1C **8**, Tel: 08707 200609
Craignure — 5A **30**, Tel: 08707 200610
Crieff — 1H **25**, Tel: 01764 652578
Dornoch — 5E **55**, Tel: 0845 22 55 121
Drumnadrochit — 1G **39**, Tel: 0845 22 55 121
Dumbarton, Milton — 1H **17**, Tel: 08707 200612
Dumfries, Tel: 01387 253862
Dundee, Tel: 01382 527527
Dunfermline, Tel: 01383 720999
Dunkeld — 4F **33**, Tel: 01350 727688
Dunoon — 1E **17**, Tel: 08707 200629
Edinburgh Airport Tourist Information Desk — 1G **19**, Tel: 0845 22 55 121
Edinburgh & Scotland Information Centre, Tel: 0845 22 55 121
Elgin — 2F **49**, Tel: 01343 542666
Falkirk — 08707 200614
Forth Bridges, North Queensferry — 5C **26**, Tel: 01383 417759
Fort William — 0845 22 55 121
Glasgow Airport Tourist Information Desk, Paisley — 2H **17**, Tel: 0141 848 4440
Glasgow, Tel: 0141 204 4400
Hamilton Services, M74 (Northbound), Hamilton, Tel: 01698 285590
Heart of Scotland, Kinross — 3B **26**, Tel: 01557 863680
Inveraray — 3H **23**, Tel: 08707 200616
Inverness, Tel: 0845 22 55 121
Inverurie — 1C **42**, Tel: 01467 625800
Jedburgh — 1F **13**, Tel: 0870 608 0404
Kelso — 5E **21**, Tel: 0870 608 0404
Kirkcaldy, Tel: 01592 267775
Kirkwall — 3D **64**, Tel: 01856 872856
Lanark — 4D **18**, Tel: 01555 661661
Largs — 3F **17**, Tel: 0845 22 55 121
Lerwick — 2D **66**, Tel: 08701 999 440
Loch Lomond — 5C **24**, Tel: 08707 200631
Melrose — 5C **20**, Tel: 0870 608 0404 (general)
Newtonmore — 4A **40**, Tel: 01540 670157
North Berwick — 5G **27**, Tel: 0845 22 55 121
Oban, Tel: 08707 200630
Paisley, Tel: 0141 889 0711
Peebles — 4H **19**, Tel: 0870 608 0404
Perth, Tel: 01738 450600
Pitlochry — 3E **33**, Tel: 01796 472215 / 472751
Portree — 4D **44**, Tel: 0845 22 55 121
Rothesay — 2D **16**, Tel: 08707 200619
St Andrews, Tel: 01334 472021
Stirling (Pirnhall), M9, Junction 9, Stirling — 5H **25**, Tel: 08707 200621
Stirling (Dumbarton Road), Tel: 08707 200620
Stornoway — 4J **63**, Tel: 01851 703088
Stranraer — 2B **4**, Tel: 01776 702595
Stromness — 4B **64**, Tel: 01856 850716
Sumburgh — 5C **66**, Tel: 01595 693 434

Tourist Information Centre (Summer Season Only)

Alford — 2A **42**, S, Tel: 019755 62052
Anstruther, Anstruther Easter — 3G **27**, S, Tel: 01333 311073
Ardgartan — 3B **24**, S, Tel: 08707 200606
Balloch — 5C **24**, S, Tel: 08707 200607
Banchory — 4B **42**, S, Tel: 01330 822000
Banff — 2B **50**, S, Tel: 01261 812419
Biggar — 5F **19**, S, Tel: 01899 221066
Bo'ness — 5A **26**, S, Tel: 08707 200608
Brechin, Haughmuir — 2C **34**, S, Tel: 01356 623050
Carnoustie — 3G **34**, S, Tel: 01241 852258
Castlebay — 5B **60**, S, Tel: 01871 810336
Castle Douglas — 2A **6**, S, Tel: 01556 502611
Crail — 3H **27**, S, Tel: 01333 450859
Crathie — 4F **41**, S, Tel: 013397 42414
Daviot Wood, Inverness — 4A **48**, S, Tel: 0845 22 55 121
Drymen — 5D **24**, S, Tel: 08707 200611
Dufftown — 4G **49**, S, Tel: 01340 820501
Dunbar — 1D **20**, S, Tel: 0845 22 55 121
Dunblane — 3G **25**, S, Tel: 08707 200613
Dunvegan — 4B **44**, S, Tel: 0845 22 55 121
Durness — 2F **57**, S, Tel: 0845 22 55 121
Eyemouth — 2G **21**, S, Tel: 0870 608 0404
Forfar — 3B **34**, S, Tel: 01307 467876
Forres — 3D **48**, S, Tel: 01309 672938

Fort Augustus — 3E **39**, S, Tel: 0845 22 55 121
Fraserburgh — 2F **51**, S, Tel: 01346 518315
Gatehouse of Fleet — 3H **5**, S, Tel: 01557 814212
Grantown-on-Spey — 1D **40**, S, Tel: 0845 22 55 121
Gretna Information Centre, Gretna Green — 2G **7**, S, Tel: 0161 337834
Hawick — 2E **13**, S, Tel: 0870 608 0404
Helensburgh — 5B **24**, S, Tel: 08707 200615
Huntly — 4A **50**, S, Tel: 01466 792255
John o'Groats — 1G **59**, S, Tel: 0845 22 55 121
Kilchoan — 2F **29**, S, Tel: 0845 22 55 121
Killin — 5A **32**, S, Tel: 08707 200627
Kirkcudbright — 3H **5**, Tel: 01557 330494
Kirriemuir — 3A **34**, S, Tel: 01575 574097
Linlithgow — 1F **19**, S, Tel: 01506 844600
Lochboisdale — 3C **60**, S, Tel: 01878 700286
Lochgilphead — 5F **23**, S, Tel: 08707 200618
Lochinver — 1F **53**, S, Tel: 0845 22 55 121
Lochmaddy — 4K **61**, S, Tel: 01876 500321
Melrose — 5C **20**, S, Tel: 0870 608 0404
Moffat — 3H **11**, S, Tel: 01683 220620
Montrose — 3E **35**, S, Tel: 01674 672000
Newtongrange — 2A **20**, S, Tel: 0845 22 55 121
Newton Stewart — 2F **5**, S, Tel: 01671 402431
North Kessock — 4H **47**, S, Tel: 0845 22 55 121
Old Craighall, Musselburgh — 1A **20**, S, Tel: 0845 22 55 121
Selkirk — 1D **12**, S, Tel: 0870 608 0404
Stonehaven — 5D **42**, S, Tel: 01569 762806
Strathpeffer — 3F **47**, Tel: 01997 421415
Strontian — 2B **30**, S, Tel: 0845 22 55 121
Tarbert (Harris) — 5C **62**, S, Tel: 01859 502011

Loch View

Tarbert — 2B **16**, S, Tel: 08707 200624
Tarbet (Loch Lomond) — 3C **24**, S, Tel: 08707 200623
Thurso — 2E **59**, Tel: 0845 22 55 121
Tobermory — 3G **29**, S, Tel: 08707 200625
Tomintoul — 2E **41**, S, Tel: 01807 580285
Tyndrum — 5G **31**, S, Tel: 08707 200626
Ullapool — 4G **53**, S, Tel: 0845 22 55 121

Visitor Centre/Information Centre (National Trust for Scotland)

Ben Lawers Visitor Centre, Killin NTS — 5B **32**, Tel: 01567 820988 / 820397
Crathes Castle Visitor Centre, Banchory NTS — 4C **42**, Tel: 01330 844525
Culloden Visitor Centre, Inverness NTS — 4A **48**, Tel: 01463 790607
Culzean Castle Visitor Centre, Maybole NTS — 2H **9**, Tel: 0870 118 1945
Glencoe Visitor Centre NTS — 3E **31**, Tel: 01855 811307 811729
Glenfinnan Visitor Centre NTS — 5A **38**, Tel: 01397 722250
Inverewe Visitor Centre, Poolewe NTS — 5D **52**, Tel: 01445 781200
Killiecrankie Visitor Centre, Pitlochry NTS — 2E **33**, Tel: 01796 473233
Morvich Farm Countryside Centre, Inverinate NTS — 1A **38**, Tel: 01599 511231
Pitmedden Garden Visitor Centre, Ellon NTS — 1D **42**, Tel: 01651 842352
St Abb's Head National Nature Reserve Visitor Centre NTS — 2G **21**, Tel: 01890 771443
Threave Garden Visitor Centre, Castle Douglas NTS — 2A **6**, Tel: 01556 502575

Torridon Countryside Centre NTS — 3A **46**, Tel: 01445 791368
Town House Visitor Centre, Culross NTS — 5A **26**, Tel: 01383 880359

Abbey/Friary/Priory

See also Cathedral, Church/Chapel

Arbroath Abbey (remains of) — 4D **34**
Ardchattan Priory (remains of) — 5C **30**
Balmerino Abbey (remains of) NTS — 1E **27**
Beauly Priory (remains of) — 4G **47**
Cambuskenneth Abbey (remains of), Stirling — 4H **25**
Cross Kirk Friary (remains of) — 4H **19**
Crossraguel Abbey (remains of) — 3H **9**, S
Culross Abbey (remains of) — 5A **26**
Deer Abbey (remains of) — 4E **51**
Dryburgh Abbey (remains of) — 5C **20**
Dundrennan Abbey (remains of) — 4A **6**
Dunfermline Abbey (remains of) — **Dunfermline**
Fort Augustus Abbey — 3E **39**
Glenluce Abbey (remains of) — 3C **4**
Holyrood Abbey remains of, Canongate — **Edinburgh**
Inchcolm Abbey (remains of) — 5C **26**
Inchmahome Priory (remains of) — 3E **25**, S
Iona Abbey & Nunnery — 3A **22**
Jedburgh Abbey (remains of) — 2F **13**
Kelso Abbey (remains of) — 5E **21**
Kilwinning Abbey (remains of) — 4G **17**

Lindores Abbey (remains of) — 2D **26**
Melrose Abbey (remains of) — 5C **20**
Paisley Abbey Church — **Paisley**
Pluscarden Abbey — 3E **49**
Restenneth Priory (remains of) — 3B **34**
St. Ebba and Coldingham Priory (remains of) — 2G **21**
Sweetheart Abbey (remains of) — 2C **6**
Whithorn Priory (remains of) — 4F **5**

Animal Collection

See also Farm Park, Wildlife Park, Zoo

(Amazonia — 3C **18**)
Belwade Farm — 4A **42**
Cairngorm Reindeer Centre — 3C **40**
Fairways Heavy Horse Centre — 1C **26**
Galloway Wild Boar Park — 4C **4**
Glen Finart Deer Farm — 5A **24**
Glengoulandie Deer Park — 3C **32**
Hazelhead Park Pets Corner & 'Walk-in' Aviary — 3D **42**
Kingspark Llama Farm — 1H **55**
Kylerhea Otter Haven — 1G **37**
Monreith Animal World — 5E **5**
Mossburn Animal Centre — 1D **6**
(Ostrich Kingdom, Collessie — 2D **26**)
Reediehill Deer Farm — 2D **26**
Scottish Deer Centre, The — 2E **27**
Skye Serpentarium — 1F **37**
Strathspey Highland Pony Centre — 1D **40**
Tullochville Farm Heavy Horse Centre — 4C **32**

Aquarium

Deep Sea World — 5C **26**
Logan Fish Pond — 4B **4**
Macduff Marine Aquarium — 2C **50**
Mallaig Marine World — 4F **37**
St Andrews Aquarium — **St Andrews**
Scottish Sealife Sanctuary — 4C **30**

Arboretum/Botanical Garden

See also Garden

Benmore Botanic Garden — 5A **24**, S
Cruickshank Botanic Garden — 3E **43**
(Dalzell Arboretum, Motherwell — 3C 18)
Dawyck Botanic Garden — 5G **19**
(Dundee University Botanic Garden — 1E 27)
Glasgow Botanic Gardens — 2A **18**
Kilmun Arboretum — 5A **24**
Kirroughtree Forest Garden — 2F **5**
(Lael Forest Garden, Ullapool — 5G 53)
(Leckmelm Arboretum & Garden — 4G 53)
Linn Botanic Gardens — 5B **24**
Logan Botanic Garden — 4B **4**, S
Mabie Forest Arboretum — 1C **6**
Mount Stewart House Victorian Pinetum — 3E **17**
Royal Botanic Garden — 1H **19**
St Andrews Botanic Garden — **St Andrews**
(Scone Palace Pinetum — 1C 26)

Art Gallery

Aberdeen Art Gallery — **Aberdeen**
Aberdeen Arts Centre — **Aberdeen**
(An Tuireann Arts Centre, Portree — 4D 44)
Broughton Place — 5G **19**
Castle Douglas Art Gallery — 2A **6**
Centre for Contemporary Arts, Glasgow — **Glasgow**
Clachanmore Art Gallery — 4B **4**
Collins Gallery, Glasgow — **Glasgow**
Dean Gallery, The, Edinburgh — 1H **19**
(Designs Gallery, Castle Douglas — 2A 6)
Duff House Country Gallery — 2B **50**
Dundee Contemporary Arts Centre — **Dundee**
Edinburgh City Art Centre — **Edinburgh**
Edinburgh Stills Gallery — 1H **19**
Fergusson Gallery — **Perth**
Fife Contemporary Art & Craft — **St Andrews**
Flat Cat Gallery — 4C **20**
Fruitmarket Gallery, The, Edinburgh — **Edinburgh**
Gallery of Modern Art — **Glasgow**
Glasgow Vennel Gallery, Irvine — 5G **17**
Gracefield Arts Centre — **Dumfries**
Harbour Cottage Gallery — 3H **5**
Hunterian Gallery, Glasgow — 2A **18**
Inverleith House — 1H **19**
Lantern Gallery of Fine Art, The — 2F **49**
Laurence Broderick Sculpture Exhibition — 2G **37**
Lighthouse, The, Scotland's Centre for Architecture, Design & the City, Glasgow — **Glasgow**
Lillie Art Gallery, Milngavie — 1A **18**
Lyth Arts Centre — 2F **59**
McEwan Gallery, The — 4G **41**
(Maclaurin Galleries, Alloway — 2A 10)
Meffan, The — 3B **34**
(National Gallery of Scotland — Edinburgh)
Old Manse Gallery — 1B **42**
(Open Eye Gallery — Edinburgh)
(Patriothall Gallery, Stockbridge — Edinburgh)
Peacock Visual Arts — **Aberdeen**
Peebles Gallery — 4H **19**
(Peter Anson Gallery, Buckie — 2H 49)
(Pier Art Centre, Stromness — 4B 64)
Project Ability — **Glasgow**
(Queen's Gallery, The — Edinburgh)
(Royal Scottish Academy, Edinburgh — Edinburgh)
Scone Studios — 1C **26**
Scottish Antique & Arts Centre — 5H **33**
(Scottish Gallery, The — Edinburgh)
Scottish National Gallery of Modern Art — 1H **19**
(Scottish National Portrait Gallery, Edinburgh — Edinburgh)
Stenton Gallery — 1D **20**
Syllavethy Gallery — 2A **42**
(Talbot Rice Gallery, Edinburgh — Edinburgh)
(Tolbooth Art Centre, Kirkcudbright — 3H 5)
Tolquhon Gallery — 1D **42**

Aviary/Bird Garden

(Cluanie Park, Beauly — 4F 47)
Cowal Bird Garden — 1E **17**
Edinburgh Bird of Prey Centre — 2A **20**
Scottish Centre for Falconry — 3C **26**
Wings Over Nevis Falconry Centre — 1E **31**

Battle Site

Ancrum Moor Battle Site (1545) — 1F **13**
Auldearn Battle Site (1645) — 3C **48**
Bannockburn Battle Site (1314) — 4H **25**
Bothwell Bridge Battle Site (1679) — 3C **18**
Carbisdale Battle Site (1650) — 4C **54**
Culloden Battle Site (1746) NTS — 4A **48**
Dunbar Battle Site (1650) — 1D **20**
Dupplin Battle Site (1332) — 2B **26**
Falkirk Battle Site (1746) — 1D **18**
(Glencoe Massacre (1692) NTS — 3E 31)
Glenlivet Battle Site (1594) — 1F **41**
Glen Shiel Battle Site (1719) NTS — 2A **38**
Glen Trool Battle Site (1307) — 1F **5**
Harlaw Battle Site (1411) — 1C **42**
Inverlochy Battle Site (1645) — 1E **31**
Killiecrankie Battle Site (1689) — 2E **33**
Rapploch Moss Battle Site (1307) — 1G **5**
Selkirk Battle Site (1645) — 1D **12**
Sheriffmuir Battle Site (1715) — 3H **25**
Tibbermore Battle Site (1644) — 1B **26**

Bridge

Ayr Auld Brig — **Ayr**
Big Water of Fleet Viaduct — 2G **5**
(Bow Brig, Elgin — 2E 49)
(Brechin Bridge — 3C 34)
Bridge of Alvah — 2B **50**
Bridge of Dee — 3E **43**
Bridge of Oich — 3E **39**
Brig O' Balgownie — 3E **43**
Brig O'Doon — 2A **10**
(Charleston of Aberlour Packhorse Bridge — 4F 49)
Craigellachie Bridge — 4F **49**
(Craigmin Bridge, Drybridge — 2H 49)
Devorgilla Bridge (Old Bridge) — **Dumfries**
(Dunkeld Bridge — 4F 33)
Glenfinnan Viaduct — 5A **38**
Invercauld Bridge — 4E **41**
(Keith Auld Brig — 3H 49)
Laigh Milton Viaduct — 5G **17**
Ruthrieston Packhorse Bridge — 3E **43**
Spey Viaduct — 2G **49**
Stirling Old Bridge — **Stirling**
Stow Pack Bridge — 4B **20**
Tay Rail Bridge — 1E **27**
Tay Road Bridge — 1F **27**
Tomnavoulin Packhorse Bridge — 1F **41**
Wade's Bridge — 4D **32**

Butterfly Farm

(Drumpellier Butterfly House, Coatbridge — 2C 18)
(Edinburgh Butterfly & Insect World — 2A 20)
Tropic House, The — 2F **5**

Castle

See also Castle & Garden, Fortress

Affleck Castle — 5B **34**
Alloa Tower NTS — 4H **25**, S
Ayton Castle (Eyemouth) — 2G **21**
Balvaird Castle — 2C **26**
Balvenie Castle — 4G **49**, S
Blackness Castle — 5B **26**
Bothwell Castle — 3B **18**
Braemar Castle — 4E **41**
Brodie Castle NTS — 3C **48**, S
Broughty Castle — 5B **34**
(Buittle Castle, Dalbeattie — 2B 6)
Burleigh Castle — 3C **26**, S
Cadzow Castle — 3C **18**
Caerlaverock Castle — 2D **6**
Cardoness Castle — 3G **5**
Carnassarie Castle — 3F **23**
Carsluith Castle — 3F **5**
Castle Leod — 3F **47**, S
Castle of Old Wick — 4G **59**
Castle of St John — 2B **4**
Castle Stuart — 4A **48**
Cessford Castle — 1G **13**
Clackmannan Tower — 4A **26**
Claypotts Castle — 5B **34**
Colzium Castle — 1C **18**
Corgarff Castle — 3F **41**
Coulter Motte — 5F **19**
Craig Castle — 1H **41**, S
Craigievar Castle NTS — 3A **42**, S
Craignethan Castle — 4D **18**
Crichton Castle — 2A **20**, S
Crookston Castle, Pollok — 2A **18**
Cubbie Roo's Castle — 2D **64**
Dean Castle — 5H **17**
Delgatie Castle — 3C **50**, S
Doune Castle — 3G **25**
Druchtag Motte — 4E **5**
Drumcoltran Tower — 2B **6**
Duart Castle — 5A **30**, S
Duffus Castle — 2E **49**
Dumbarton Castle — 1H **17**
Dundonald Castle — 5G **17**, S
Dunnottar Castle — 5D **42**
Dunskey Castle — 3B **4**
Dunstaffnage Castle — 5B **30**
Edinburgh Castle — **Edinburgh**
Eilean Donan Castle — 1H **37**
Elcho Castle — 1C **26**, S
Fast Castle (Eyemouth) — 1F **21**
Ferniehirst Castle — 2F **13**
Glenbuchat Castle — 2G **41**
Greenan Castle — 2A **10**
Hailes Castle — 1C **20**
Hawick Castle — 2D **12**
Hermitage Castle — 4E **13**, S
Huntingtower Castle — 1B **26**
Huntly Castle — 4A **50**
Inveraray Castle — 3H **23**, S
Inverlochy Castle — 1E **31**
Kilchurn Castle — 1A **24**, S
Kildrummy Castle — 2H **41**, S
Lauriston Castle — 2E **35**
Linlithgow Palace — 1F **19**
Loch Doon Castle — 4B **10**
Lochleven Castle — 3C **26**, S
Lochmaben Castle — 5H **11**
Lochranza Castle — 3C **16**
MacLellan's Castle — 3H **5**, S
Menstrie Castle — 4H **25**
Mote of Urr — 2B **6**
Muness Castle — 2K **67**
Neidpath Castle — 4H **19**
Newark Castle (Port Glasgow) — 1G **17**, S
Noltland Castle — 3G **65**
Orchardton Tower — 3B **6**
Peel of Lumphanan — 3A **42**
Preston Tower NTS — 1A **20**
Ravenscraig Castle — 4D **26**
Red Castle — 3D **34**
Rothesay Castle — 2D **16**
Roxburgh Castle — 5E **21**
St Andrews Castle — **St Andrews**
Scalloway Castle — 3D **66**

Scotstarvit Tower — 2E **27**, S
Skipness Castle — 3C **16**
Smailholm Tower — 5D **20**
Stirling Castle — **Stirling**
Strathaven Castle — 4C **18**
Strome Castle NTS — 5H **45**
Sween Castle — 1A **16**
Tantallon Castle — 5G **27**
Threave Castle — 2A **6**, S
Tolquhon Castle — 1D **42**
Urquhart Castle — 1G **39**
Wark Castle — 5F **21**

Castle & Garden

See also Castle, Fortress

Aberdour Castle — 5C **26**
Ballindalloch Castle — 5E **49**, S
Brodick Castle & Garden NTS — 5D **16**, S
Castle Campbell — 4A **26**
Castle Fraser NTS — 2C **42**, S
Castle Menzies — 4D **32**, S
Castle of Mey — 1F **59**, S
Cawdor Castle — 4B **48**, S
Comlongon Castle — 2D **6**
Craigmillar Castle — 1H **19**
Craigston Castle — 3C **50**, S
Crathes Castle NTS — 4C **42**
Dirleton Castle — 5G **27**
Drum Castle NTS — 3C **42**, S
Dunrobin Castle — 3F **55**, S
Dunvegan Castle — 4B **44**
Edzell Castle — 2C **34**
Floors Castle & Gardens — 5E **21**
Fyvie Castle NTS — 5C **50**, S
Glamis Castle — 4A **34**
Kilravock Castle — 4B **48**
Lauriston Castle — 1H **19**
Sorn Castle — 1C **10**, S
Thirlestane Castle — 4C **20**

Cathedral

See also Abbey, Church/Chapel

Aberdeen Cathedral — **Aberdeen**
Aberdeen RC Cathedral — **Aberdeen**
Aberdeen St Machars Cathedral — 3E **43**
(Aberdeen St Machar's Cathedral Transepts (remains of) — 3E 43)
Ayr RC Cathedral — 1A **10**
Brechin Cathedral — 3C **34**
Dornoch Cathedral — 4E **55**
Dunblane Cathedral — 3G **25**
Dundee Cathedral — **Dundee**
Dundee RC Cathedral — **Dundee**
Dunkeld Cathedral (remains of) — 4F **33**
Edinburgh RC Cathedral — **Edinburgh**
Edinburgh St Giles' Cathedral — **Edinburgh**
Edinburgh St. Mary's Episcopal Cathedral — 1H **19**
Elgin Cathedral (remains of) — 2F **49**
Fortrose Cathedral (remains of) — 3A **48**
Glasgow St Mungo's Cathedral — **Glasgow**
Inverness Cathedral — **Inverness**
Kirkwall Cathedral — 3D **64**
Millport Cathedral — 3E **17**
Motherwell RC Cathedral — **Motherwell**
Oban RC Cathedral — **Oban**
Paisley RC Cathedral — **Paisley**
Perth Cathedral — **Perth**
St Andrews Cathedral (remains of) — **St Andrews**
(St Andrew's RC Cathedral (Glasgow) — Glasgow)
St Mary's Episcopal Cathedral (Glasgow) — 2A **18**

Children's Play Centre

Big Adventure, The — 2H **17**
(Jungle Kids, Dundee — 5A 34)
Kid'z Play — 1A **10**
Pirate Pete's — **Ayr**
Scotia Kids — 5C **20**

Church/Chapel/Holy Well

See also Abbey, Cathedral

Arbuthnott Church — 1E **35**
Ayr Auld Kirk — **Ayr**
Blackfriars Chapel — **St Andrews**
Canongate Kirk — **Edinburgh**
Castle Semple Collegiate Church — 2G **17**
Chapel Finian — 4D **4**
Church of Kilarow, Bowmore — 3E **15**
Church of St Magnus — 1D **64**
Crathie Church — 4F **41**
Deskford Church — 2A **50**
Dundee St Mary's Tower — **Dundee**
Dunglass Collegiate Church, Cockburnspath — 1E **21**
Dunstaffnage Chapel — 5B **30**
Durisdeer Church — 3F **11**
Edrom Church — 3F **21**
Eileach an Naoimh Monastery — 3D **22**
Eynhallow Church, Eynhallow Island — 2C **64**
Fordyce Church — 2A **50**
Govan Old Parish Church — 2A **18**
Greyfriars Tolbooth & Highland Kirk — **Edinburgh**
Haddington St Martin's Kirk — 1C **20**
(Haddington St Mary's Church — 1C 20)
Hamilton Old Parish Church — **Hamilton**
Hermitage Chapel — 4D **12**
Hilton of Cadboll Chapel — 1B **48**
Inchkenneth Chapel — 5F **29**
Innerpeffray Chapel — 2A **26**
Italian Chapel, The — 4D **64**
Keills Chapel — 5D **22**
Kilmory Knap Chapel — 1A **16**
Kinkell Church — 2C **42**
Kirk Alloway — 2A **10**
Kirkconnel Church — 1F **7**

(Kirk of St Nicholas, Aberdeen — **Aberdeen**)
Lincluden Collegiate Church — 1C **6**
Mackintosh Church, The — 2A **18**
Maison Dieu Chapel, Brechin — 3C **34**
Maybole Collegiate Church — 3A **10**
Morthlach Parish Church, Kirkton of Mortlach — 5G **49**
Muthill Old Church & Tower — 2H **25**
Orphir Church — 4C **64**
Pierowall Church — 3G **65**
(Restalrig Collegiate Church — 1H **19**)
Rosslyn Chapel, Roslin — 2H **19**
St Blane's Church — 3D **16**
St Bride's Church, Douglas — 5D **18**
St Bridget's Kirk — 5C **26**
St Clement's Church — 6B **62**
St Conan's Church — 2B **44**
St Cormac's Chapel — 1H **15**
(St Duthus Chapel, Tain — 5E **55**)
St Duthus Collegiate Church, Tain — 5E **55**
St John's Kirk — **Perth**
St Mary's Chapel — 2D **58**
St Mary's Chapel — 2D **64**
St Mary's Chapel, Rothesay — 2D **16**
St Mary's Church — 3D **32**
St Mary's Church — **St Andrews**
St Mary's Collegiate Church, Crail — 3H **27**
St Mary's Kirk — 1H **41**
St Moluag's Chapel — 5E **45**
St Ninian's Chapel, Fochabers — 2G **49**
St Ninian's Chapel — 5F **5**
St Peter's Kirk — 2E **49**
St Rule's Church — **St Andrews**
St Serf's Church & Dupplin Cross — 2B **26**
St Triduana's Chapel — 1H **19**
Seton Collegiate Church — 1B **20**, S
Skipness Chapel — 3C **16**
Stirling Church of the Holy Rude — **Stirling**
Stow Old Kirk and Bishop's Palace (remains of) — 4B **20**
Torphichen Preceptory — 1E **19**
Tullibardine Chapel — 2A **26**
Westside Church — 3G **65**

Country Park

Aden Country Park, Mintlaw — 4E **51**
Almondell & Calderwood Country Park, Broxburn — 2F **19**
Balloch Castle Country Park — 5C **24**
Balmedie Country Park — 2E **43**
Beecraigs Country Park — 1E **19**
Black Isle Wildlife & Country Park — 3H **47**
Bonaly Country Park — 2H **19**
Bowhill Country Park & Courtyard — 1D **12**
Brimmond & Elrick Country Park — 2D **42**
Brodick Castle Country Park NTS — 5D **16**
Calderglen Country Park — 3B **18**
Camperdown Country Park — 5A **34**
Cathkin Braes Country Park — 3B **18**
Chatelherault Country Park — 3C **18**
Clatto Country Park — 5A **34**
Craigtoun Country Park — 2F **27**
Crombie Country Park — 4C **34**
Culzean Castle Country Park NTS — 3H **9**
Dalkeith Country Park — 2A **20**
Dalzell Estate, Motherwell — 3C **18**
Danestone Country Park, Woodside — 3E **43**
(Dean Castle Country Park, Kilmarnock — 5H **17**)
Drumlanrig Castle Country Park — 3F **11**
Drumpellier Country Park, Coatbridge — 2C **18**
Eglinton Country Park — 4G **17**
Forfar Loch Country Park — 3B **34**
Gartmorn Dam Country Park — 4A **26**
Gleniffer Braes Country Park — 2H **17**
Haddo Country Park — 5D **50**
Haughton Country Park — 2A **42**
Hirsel Country Park, The — 4F **21**
John Muir Country Park — 1D **20**
Lochore Meadows Country Park — 4C **26**
Loirston Country Park — 3E **43**
Millbuies Country Park — 3F **49**
Monikie Country Park — 5C **34**
Mugdock Country Park, Strathblane — 1A **18**
Muiravonside Country Park — 1E **19**
Muirshiel Country Park — 2G **17**
Palacerigg Country Park — 1C **18**
Pentland Hills Country Park, Penicuik — 2H **19**
Plean Country Park — 5H **25**
Polkemmet Country Park — 2E **19**
Pollok Country Park, Glasgow — 2A **18**
Strathclyde Country Park, Motherwell — 3C **18**
Townhill Country Park — 5B **26**
Vogrie Country Park, Gorebridge — 2A **20**

Distillery

(Aberfeldy Distillery — 4D **32**)
Ardbeg Distillery — 4F **15**
Auchentoshan Distillery — 1H **17**
Balblair Distillery — 5E **55**
(Ben Nevis Distillery, Fort William — 1E **31**)
(Blair Athol Distillery, Pitlochry — 3E **33**)
Bowmore Distillery — 3E **15**
Cardhu Distillery — 4E **49**
Clynelish Distillery — 3F **55**
Cragganmore Distillery — 5E **49**
Dallas Dhu Historic Distillery — 3D **48**
Dalwhinnie Distillery — 5H **39**
Edradour Distillery — 3E **33**
Fettercairn Distillery — 1D **34**
Glendronach Distillery — 4B **50**
Glenfarclas Distillery — 5F **49**
Glenfiddich Distillery — 4G **49**
Glengoyne Distillery — 5E **25**
Glen Grant Distillery — 4F **49**
Glenkinchie Distillery — 2B **20**
Glenlivet Distillery — 1E **41**
Glenmorangie Distillery — 5E **55**
Glen Ord Distillery — 3G **47**
Glenturret Distillery — 1H **25**
Highland Park Distillery — 4D **64**
Isle of Arran Distillery — 4C **16**
Oban Distillery — **Oban**
Royal Lochnagar Distillery — 4F **41**
Scapa Distillery — 4D **64**

Strathisla Distillery — 3H **49**
Talisker Distillery — 5C **44**
Tobermory Distillery — 3G **29**
Tomatin Distillery — 1A **40**

Earthwork

See also Hill Fort, Prehistoric Monument

Antonine Wall (Allandale) — 1D **18**
Antonine Wall (Bar Hill), Twechar — 1C **18**
Antonine Wall (Callendar Park) — **Falkirk**
Antonine Wall (Croy Hill) — 1C **18**
Antonine Wall (Dullatur, Tollpark & Garnhill) — 1C **18**
Antonine Wall (Falkirk) — 5H **25**
(Antonine Wall (Polmonthill) — 1E **19**)
Antonine Wall (Rough Castle) — 1D **18**
Antonine Wall (Seabegs Wood), Bonnybridge — 1D **18**
Antonine Wall (Watling Lodge), Falkirk — 1D **18**
Deer Dyke — 1D **34**
Scot's Dyke — 1G **7**

Farm Park/Open Farm

See also Animal Collection, Wildlife Park, Zoo

Ayrshire Rare Breeds Centre — 2C **10**
Barholm Mains Open Farm — 3F **5**
Boreland Farm Park — 4C **32**
(Brechin Castle Centre — 3C **34**)
Choraidh Croft Farm Park — 3F **57**
Cloverleaf Fibre Stud — 3B **50**
Craig Highland Farm — 5H **45**
Cream o' Galloway Visitor Centre — 3H **5**
Cullerlie Farm Park — 3C **42**
Doonies Farm — 3E **43**
Drum Farm Centre — 1G **39**
Drummond Trout Farm — 1G **25**
Dunaverig Farmlife Centre — 3F **25**
Fife Animal Park — 2D **26**
(Gorgie City Farm — 1H **19**)
Heads of Ayr Farm Park — 2H **9**
Highland & Rare Breeds Farm — 2H **53**
Hillcroft Open Farm — 5C **44**
Isle of Mull Angora Rabbit Farm — 1B **22**
Jedforest Deer & Farm Park — 2F **13**
(Kelton Mains Open Farm, Castle Douglas — 2A **6**)
(Lochinch Farm, Aberdeen — 3E **43**)
Mabie Farm Park — 1C **6**
(Newparks Farm, Loan — 1E **19**)
Noah's Ark 2x2 Country Activity Centre — 3A **42**
Oban Rare Breeds Farm Park — 1F **23**
Peel Farm — 3H **33**
Praytis Farm Park — 3E **27**
West Highland Dairy — 5H **45**
Working Sheepdogs — 3B **40**

Forest Park/National Park

Cairngorms National Park, The NP — 3D **40**
Galloway Forest Park — 5B **10**
Glenmore Forest Park — 3C **40**
Loch Lomond & The Trossachs National Park NP — 2D **24**
Queen Elizabeth Forest Park — 4D **24**
Tay Forest Park — 3A **32**

Forest Walk/Nature Trail

See also Nature Reserve

Aberfeldy Nature Trail — 4D **32**
Abernethy Forest (Boat of Garten) Forest Walks — 2C **40**
Abernethy Forest Forest Walks — 2C **40**
Achany Forest Forest Walks — 4C **54**
Achindarroch Forest Walk — 3D **30**
Achmelvich Nature Trail, Lochinver — 1F **53**
Achriabhach Forest Walks — 2E **31**
(Aden Country Park Tree Trail, Old Deer — 4E **51**)
Aden Nature Trail — 4E **51**
Aldie Burn Forest Walks — 1A **48**
Allanreid Forest Walk — 1F **41**
Allean Forest Forest Walk — 3D **32**
Allean Forest Forest Walks — 2D **32**
Allt Na Criche Forest Walk — 2E **39**
Alva Glen Nature Trail — 4H **25**
Ardcastle Wood Forest Trails, Lochgair — 4G **23**

Ardentinny Forest Trail — 5A **24**
Ardery Wood Forest Walk — 2A **30**
Ardgartan Forest walks — 3B **24**
Ardmore Forest Walk — 3F **29**
Ariundle Nature Trail — 2B **30**
Aros Park Trails, Tobermory — 3G **29**
Atholl Estate Nature Trail — 2D **32**
Attadale Garden Woodland Walks — 5A **46**
(Avich Falls Trail, Dalavich — 2G **23**)
Balblair Forest Forest Walks — 4D **54**
Balleich Forest Trails — 3E **25**
Balmacara Forest Walks NTS — 1H **37**
Balmaha Forest Walks — 4D **24**
Balquhidder Forest Walks — 1E **25**
Balranald Nature Trail — 3H **61**
(Banff Woodland Walk — 2B **50**)
(Barhill Wood Walks, Kirkcudbright — 3H **5**)
Baron's Haugh Nature Trails, Motherwell — 3C **18**
Barony College Countryside Walks — 5H **11**
Beinn Eighe Nature Trails — 2B **46**
Bellanoch Forest Walks — 4E **23**
Benderloch Forest Walks — 5C **30**
Ben Lawers Nature Trail NTS — 5B **32**
Bennachie Forest Forest Walks — 1B **42**
Bennachie Forest Forest Walks — 1B **42**
Bennan Forest Walk, Mossdale — 1H **5**
Bennybeg Nature Trail — 2H **25**
Bin Forest Forest Walks, The — 4A **50**
Birnam Hill Walk — 5F **33**
(Birnam Walk — 4F **33**)
Black Gates Forest Trail — 5A **24**
Blackmuir Wood Trails — 3F **47**
Black Wood of Rannoch Forest Walks, Kinloch Rannoch — 3A **32**
Borgie Forest Forest Walk — 3H **57**
Braan Walk, Dunkeld NTS — 4F **33**
Bracklinn Falls Forest Walk — 3F **25**
Braeloine Nature Trail — 4H **41**
Bridge of Brown Forest Walk, Tomintoul — 1E **41**
Bridge of Coe Forest Walk — 3E **31**
Brimmond Hill Forest Walks — 3D **42**
Brodick Castle Trails NTS — 5D **16**
Brodie Castle Woodland Walk — 3C **48**
Caerlaverock Trails — 2D **6**
Caerlaverock Wildfowl & Wetlands Nature Trail — 2D **6**
(Cairngorms Nature Trail, Aviemore — 2B **40**)
Cairnsmore of Fleet Walk — 2G **5**
Calderglen Country Park Nature Trails — 3B **18**
Cambus O' May Forest Walks — 4H **41**
Camperdown Country Park Forest Trails — 5A **34**
Canonbie Forest Walks — 1G **7**
Carbisdale Forest Walks, Culrain — 4C **54**
Cardrona Walks — 5H **19**
Carradale Forest Walks — 5B **16**
Carron Valley Forest Forest Walks, Stirling — 5G **25**
Castle Fraser Woodland Walk NTS — 2C **42**
Castle O'er Forest Walk — 4B **12**
Cathkin Braes Country Park Walks, Carmunnock — 3B **18**
Cawdor Castle Nature Trails — 4B **48**
Chatelherault Woodland Walks — 3C **18**
Clatteringshaws Forest Trail — 1G **5**

Cleanhill Wood Woodland Walks — 3B **50**
Cluanie Park Nature Trail, Beauly — 4F **47**
Clunes Forest Forest Walks — 5C **38**
Contin Forest Trails — 3F **47**
Cornalees Bridge Nature Trail — 1F **17**
Corrychurrachan Forest Walk — 2D **30**
Countesswells Forest Walks — 3D **42**
Countesswells Forest Walks — 3D **42**
Craigellachie Nature Trail — **Aviemore**
Craighall Burn Nature Trail, Ceres — 2F **27**
Craigieburn Forest Walks — 3A **12**
Craig Phadraig Forest Walk — 4H **47**
Craig Phadrig Forest Walk — 4H **47**
Craigvinean Forest Walk — 4F **33**
Craik Forest Woodland Walks — 3C **12**
Crathes Castle Trails NTS — 4C **42**
(Crieff Nature Trail — 1H **25**)
Crinan Canal Forest Walks, Bellanoch — 4F **23**
Crinan Forest Walk — 4E **23**
Crombie Country Park Discovery Trail — 4C **34**
Culag Wood Nature Trail — 1F **53**
Culbin Forest Forest Walk (Cloddymoss), Forres — 3C **48**
Culbin Forest Forest Walk (Kingsteps) — 3C **48**
Culbin Forest Forest Walk (Welhill) — 2C **48**
Culloden Forest Walk — 4A **48**
Culzean Castle Country Park Woodland Walks NTS — 3H **9**
Dalavich Oakwood Forest Trail — 2G **23**
Dalbeattie Forest Walks — 3B **6**
Dalzell Country Park Trails, Motherwell — 3C **18**
Darnaway Forest Forest Walk — 3C **48**
Darnaway Forest Forest Walk — 3D **48**
Daviot Wood Forest Walk — 4H **47**

Linlithgow

Den of Maidencraig Woodland Walks, Aberdeen — 3D **42**
Doach Wood Walks — 3A **6**
Dog Falls Forest Walk — 1D **38**
Doon Hill Forest Walk — 3E **25**
Doune Ponds Nature Trail — 3G **25**
Drinnie's Wood Woodland Walks, Fetterangus — 3E **51**
Drum Castle Woodland Walks NTS — 3C **42**
Drumlanrig Castle Nature Trails — 4F **11**
Drummond Hill Forest Walks, Kenmore — 4C **32**
Drumpellier Country Park Nature Trail, Coatbridge — 2C **18**
Drumtochty Forest Forest Walks, Auchenblae — 1D **34**
Dunmore Trail NTS — 3E **33**
Dunnet Links Forest Walks — 2F **59**
Dunniker Nature Trail, Kirkcaldy — 4D **26**
Dunnottar Woodland Park Forest Walks — 5D **42**
East Aquhorthies Forest Walks — 1C **42**
Edenstown Forest Walks, Freuchie — 3D **26**
Falls of Clyde Wildlife Reserve Nature Trail — 4D **18**
Farigaig Forest Forest Walks — 1G **39**
Faskally Forest Walks — 3E **33**
Fassfern Forest Walks, Corpach — 1D **30**
Ferry Wood Forest Walks, Lairg — 3C **54**
Fleet Oakwoods Forest Walk — 3H **5**
Foggieton Forest Walks — 3D **42**
Forest of Ae Walks — 4G **11**
Forfar Loch Nature Trail — 3B **34**
Fungarth & Atholl Woods Walks, Dunkeld — 4F **33**
Garioch Forest Walks, Chapel of Garioch — 1B **42**
Glamis Castle Nature Trail — 4A **34**
Glenashdale Forest Walk, Whiting Bay — 1F **9**
Glenborrodale Nature Trail — 2H **29**
Glen Donich Forest Walk — 3B **24**
Glengarry Forest Forest Walks — 3D **38**
Glenhurich Forest Forest Walk — 2A **30**
Glenloy Forest Forest Walk — 5C **38**
Glenloy Oakwood Walk — 5C **38**
(Glenmore Forest Forest Walks (Allt Mor), Aviemore — 3C **40**)
Glenmore Forest Forest Walks (Glenmore), Aviemore — 3C **40**
Glenmore Forest Forest Walks (Herons Field), Aviemore — 2C **40**
Glenmullie Nature Trail, Tomintoul — 2E **41**
Glen Nant Forest Trails — 1H **23**
Glen Nature Trail, The, Glenburn — 2H **17**
Glen Nevis Forest Forest Walks, Fort William — 1E **31**
Glenrigh Forest Forest Walks — 2D **30**
Glenrothes Nature Trail — 3D **26**
Glentress Forest Walks — 4H **19**
Glen Trool Forest Trails — 1E **5**
Hart Fell Forest Walks — 5B **12**
Haughton Country Park Nature Trails — 2A **42**
Hazelbank Forest Walk, Sorbie — 4F **5**
Highland Boundary Fault Trail, The — 3E **25**
Hills Wood Forest Walk — 1C **6**
Hirsel Country Park Nature Trails, The — 4F **21**
Hopetoun House Nature Trail — 1F **19**
House of Dun Woodland Walks NTS — 2D **34**
House of The Binns Woodland Walks NTS — 1F **19**
Inchewan Walk — 4F **33**
(Insh Marshes Nature Trail, Kingussie — 3B **40**)
Inshriach Forest Forest Walks (Feshiebridge) — 3B **40**
Inshriach Forest Forest Walks (Uath Lochan) — 3B **40**
Inverinan Glen Forest Walk — 2G **23**
Inversnaid Nature Trail — 2C **24**
Inver Walk — 4F **33**
Ken-Dee Marshes Nature Trail — 2H **5**
Kilcamb Wood Forest Walk — 2B **30**
Killiecrankie Nature Trail NTS — 2E **33**
Killiecrankie Trails — 2E **33**
Kilmun Forest Walks — 5A **24**
Kincardine Forest Walk — 5D **54**
Kindrogan Wood Forest Trail, Straloch — 2F **33**
Kinnoull Hill Woodland Walks (Jubilee) — 1C **26**
Kinnoull Hill Woodland Walks (Quarry) — 1C **26**
Kirkhill Forest Forest Walks — 2D **42**
Kirkhill Forest Forest Walks — 2D **42**
Kirroughtree Forest Garden Trail — 2F **5**
Kirroughtree Forest Walk — 2F **5**
Kirroughtree Forest Walks — 2F **5**
(Knockan Crag Trail, Inverlochy — 2H **53**)
Knockman Wood Forest Walk — 2F **5**
Lael Forest Garden Walks — 5H **53**
Laggan Wood Forest Walk, Comrie — 1G **25**
(Larch Walk, Dunkeld — 4F **33**)
Lauder Forest Walks — 4A **24**
Laurieston Forest Walks — 2H **5**
Leanachan Forest Walks — 1E **31**
Leiterfearn Forest Forest Walk, Invergarry — 4E **39**
Leith Hall Trails NTS — 1A **42**
Lemahamish Forest Trails — 4E **25**
Leny Forest Walk — 3E **25**
Letham Glen Nature Trail — 3E **27**
Linn of Tummel Nature Trail, Killiecrankie NTS — 2E **33**
Linn Park Nature Trail — 3A **18**
Loch an Eilein Forest Walk, Aviemore — 3B **40**
Loch Ard Forest Forest Walks, Aberfoyle — 4E **25**
Lochletter Wood Forest Walks, Balnain — 1F **39**
(Loch Leven Lochside Trail, Ballachulish — 2D **30**)
Loch Lomond Nature Trail — 4D **24**
Lochore Meadows Country Park Woodland Trail — 4C **26**
Loch Riddon Forest Trails, Rothesay — 1D **16**
Loch Ruthven Nature Trail — 1H **39**
Loch Trool Forest Trail — 1E **5**
Lochwinnoch Nature Trail — 3G **17**
Lower Woodend Forest Walk, Chapel of Garioch — 2B **42**
Mabie Forest Walks — 1C **6**
Malleny Woodland Walks NTS — 2G **19**
Meall Buidhe Forest Walks — 5D **16**
Megget Reservoir Walk — 1B **12**
Mersehead Nature Trails — 3C **6**
(Millbuies Country Park Nature Trail, Elgin — 3F **49**)
Milton Forest Trail — 3E **25**
Monamore Forest Walks — 1F **9**
Moncreiffe Hill Forest Walk — 2C **26**
Morinsh Forest Trail — 5F **49**
Morrone Birkwood Nature Trails — 4E **41**
Mugdock Country Park Nature Trail, Strathblane — 1A **18**
Muiravonside Country Park Walk — 1E **19**
Muir of Dinnet Trails — 4H **41**
Muirshiel Country Park Trails — 2G **17**
Newcastleton Forest Trail — 5E **13**
North Berwick Nature Trail — 5G **27**
Oape Forest Walk, Invercassley — 3B **54**
Ochil Hills Woodland Trails — 4H **25**
Ord Hill Archaeology Trail, Lairg — 3C **54**
Ord Hill Forest Trails — 4H **47**
Penninghame Forest Walk — 2E **5**
Pitcairn Nature Walks, Glenrothes — 3D **26**
Plean Country Park Trails — 5H **25**

Plodda Falls Forest Walks — 1D **38**
Polmaddy Interpretative Trail — 5C **10**
Port Ann Forest Walk — 5G **23**
Portree Forest Forest Walks — 4D **44**
Potterland Forest Walk — 3B **6**
Pressmennan Wood Forest Trail, Stenton — 1D **20**
Puck's Glen Walk — 5A **24**
Quarrelwood Woodland Walks, Elgin — 2F **49**
Quarrymill Woodland Park Woodland Walks — 1C **26**
Queen Elizabeth Forest Park Forest Trails — 3E **25**
Raasay Forest Forest Walks, Inverarish — 5E **45**
Raasay Forest Walks, Inverarish — 5E **45**
Raelees Wood Forest Walk — 5B **20**
Rannoch Forest Forest Walks — 3B **32**
Ravenscraig Park Nature Trail — 4E **27**
Ravens Rock Forest Walk — 3C **54**
Reelig Glen Forest Walk — 4G **47**
Revack Estate Woodland Walks — 1D **40**
River Affric Forest Walk — 1C **38**
River Oich Forest Walks (River Oich) — 3E **39**
River Oich Forest Walk (Torr Dhuin) — 3E **39**
Rùm Nature Trails — 4D **36**
Rob Roy's Cave Walk — 3A **24**
Rogie Falls Forest Walk — 3F **47**
Rosal Forest Trail — 4H **57**
Roseisle Forest Trails — 2E **49**
Rothiemurchus Estate Nature Trail — 2C **40**
Rumster Forest Forest Walks, Lybster — 5F **59**
Salen Woods Forest Walks — 2H **29**
Sands of Forvie Walks — 1F **43**
Scolty Forest Walks — 4B **42**
Scone Palace Woodland Walks — 1C **26**
Screel Hill Forest Walk, Auchencairn — 3A **6**
Seaton Cliffs Nature Trail — 4D **34**
Seaton Park Woodland Walks — 3E **43**
Shooting Greens Forest Walks — 4B **42**
Signal Rock Forest Walks NTS — 3E **31**
Silverbridge Forest Trails — 2E **47**
Skelbo Wood Forest Walk — 4E **55**
Slattadale Forest Forest Walk, Gairloch — 1H **45**
Stinchar Bridge Forest Walks — 4A **10**
Strathmashie Forest Forest Walks — 4G **39**
Strathyre Forest Forest Trails — 2E **25**
Stroan Loch Forest Trail, Mossdale — 1H **5**

Lighthouse at Sunset

Tain Hill Forest Walk — 5E **55**
Talnotry Forest Trails — 1F **5**
Templeton Wood Trails, Birkhill — 5A **34**
Tentsmuir Forest Forest Walk, Tayport — 1F **27**
Threave Trails, Castle Douglas NTS — 2A **6**
Tillicoultry Nature Trail — 4A **26**
Timber Walk — 2G **23**
Tomintoul Country Walk — 2E **41**
Torrieston Forest Walks — 3E **49**
Trumland Bird Sanctuary Nature Trail — 2D **64**
Tummel Bridge Forest Walk, Keltneyburn — 3C **32**
Vane Farm Nature Trail — 4C **26**
Victoria Falls Forest Walks — 1H **45**
Weem Forest Forest Walk — 4D **32**
West Auchavaich Forest Walk, Chapeltown — 1F **41**
Whiteash Hill Wood Forest Walks, Fochabers — 3G **49**
White Cow Wood Forest Walk — 3E **51**
Wiston Nature Trail — 5E **19**
Wood of Cree Nature Trail — 1E **5**
Wood of Ordiequish Forest Walks, Fochabers — 3G **49**
(Woodside Nature Trail — 3E **43**)
Yair Hill Forest Nature Trail — 5B **20**

Fortress

See also Castle, Castle & Garden

Fort Charlotte — 2D **66**
Fort George — 3A **48**
Hackness Martello Tower and Battery — 5C **64**
White Castle Fort — 2D **20**

Garden

See also Historic Building & Garden

Abriachan Garden & Nursery — 5G **47**
Achamore Gardens — 4H **15**
Achiltibuie Hydroponicum — 3F **53**
(Achnacloich Garden, Connel — 5C **30**)
An Cala Garden — 2E **23**
Annahill Gardens, Kilmarnock — 5H **17**
Appin House Garden — 4C **30**
Arbigland Gardens — 3C **6**

Arbuthnott House Garden — 1E **35**
Ardanaiseig Gardens — 1H **23**
Ardchattan Gardens, Connel — 5C **30**
Ardencraig Gardens — 2E **17**
(Ardfearn Nursery, Bunchrew — 4H **47**)
Ardkinglas Woodland Garden — 2A **24**
Ardmaddy Castle Gardens — 2E **23**
Ardtornish Estate Garden — 4H **29**
Arduaine Garden NTS — 2E **23**
Ardwell Gardens — 4C **4**, S
(Armadale Castle Garden, Ardvasar — 3F **37**, S)
Attadale Garden — 5A **46**
(Balcarres Garden, Colinsburgh — 3F **27**)
Bargany Gardens — 3H **9**
Barguillean's Angus Garden — 1G **23**
Beatrix Potter Garden — 4F **33**
Belleisle Estate & Gardens, Alloway — 2A **10**
Bell's Cherrybank Gardens — 1B **26**
Bogside Organic Gardeners at Woodside — 1F **13**
Bolfracks Garden — 4D **32**
Branklyn Garden, Perth NTS — 1C **26**
Brin Herb Nursery — 1H **39**
Bught Floral Hall Gardens — 4H **47**
Cally Gardens — 3H **5**
Cambo Gardens — 2H **27**
Candacraig Nursery Gardens — 2G **41**
Castle Kennedy & Lochinch Gardens — 2C **4**, S
Cluny House Gardens — 3D **32**
Coiltie Garden — 1F **39**
Colleonard Sculpture Garden — 2B **50**
Colonsay House Gardens — 4A **22**
Colzium House Garden — 1C **18**, S
Craigieburn Garden — 3A **12**, S
(Craiglochan Gardens, Moffat — 3A **12**)
Crarae Garden NTS — 4G **23**
Crichton, The — 1C **6**
Crinan Hotel Garden — 4E **23**
Crossways Garden — 1H **17**
Dochfour Gardens — 5H **47**
Druimneil House Garden — 4C **30**
Drummond Castle Gardens — 2H **25**, S
Dunskey Gardens — 3B **4**
Duthie Park Winter Gardens, Aberdeen — 3E **43**
(Elgin Biblical Garden — 2F **49**)

Finlaystone Country Estate — 1G **17**
Galloway House Gardens — 4F **5**, S
(Geilston Garden, Cardross NTS — 1G **17**)
Glamaig Garden — 5E **45**
Glenarn Garden — 5B **24**, S
Glenfeochan Gardens — 1F **23**
Glenwhan Gardens — 3C **4**, S
Grant Park Rose Garden — 3D **48**
Greenbank Garden NTS — 3A **18**
Harmony Garden, Melrose NTS — 5C **20**
Hazlehead Park — 3D **42**
House of Pitmuies Garden — 4C **34**
Innes House Gardens — 2F **49**
Inshriach Nursery — 3B **40**
Inveresk Lodge Garden NTS — 1A **20**
Inverewe Garden NTS — 5D **52**
Johnston Gardens — 3E **43**
Jura House Garden — 2F **15**
Kailzie Gardens — 5H **19**
Kildrummy Castle Garden — 2H **41**
(Kilmory Castle Garden — 1A **16**)
Kilmory Woodland Park — 5F **23**
Kinlochlaich Gardens — 4C **30**
Kinross House Garden — 3C **26**, S
Lochalsh Woodland Garden NTS — 1G **37**
Logan House Garden — 4B **4**
Malleny Garden NTS — 2G **19**
Megginch Castle Gardens — 1D **26**, S
Mertoun Gardens — 5D **20**
Monreith House Garden — 4E **5**
Monteviot House Garden — 1F **13**, S
(Persley Walled Garden, Aberdeen — 3E **43**)
Pineapple Garden — 5H **25**
Pitmedden Garden NTS — 1D **42**, S
Priorwood Garden, Melrose NTS — 5C **20**
Revack Estate Garden — 1D **40**
St Mary's Pleasance — 1C **20**
Sea View Garden — 4F **53**
Silverburn Park, Leven — 3E **27**
Sir Douglas Bader Disabled Garden — 2E **27**
Speyside Heather Centre — 1C **40**
Stobhall — 5G **33**
(Stonefield Castle Gardens — 5C **30**)
Suntrap Garden — 1G **19**
Teviot Game Fare Smokery & Watergardens — 1G **13**
Union Terrace Gardens — **Aberdeen**
Viewpark Gardens, Bellshill — 2C **18**
Warmanbie Walled Garden — 2E **7**

Hill Figure

White Horse of Strichen — 3E **51**
White Stag of Strichen — 3E **51**

Hill Fort

See also Earthwork, Prehistoric Monument

Barsalloch Fort — 4E **5**
Black Hill Hill Fort NTS — 4D **18**
Brown Caterhuns Hill Fort — 2C **34**
Burnswark — 1E **7**
Castlelaw Hill Fort — 2H **19**
Chesters Hill Fort — 1C **20**
Craig Phadrig Hill Fort — 4H **47**
Dum Doarduit — 1G **39**
Dunadd Fort — 4F **23**
Dun Creich — 5D **54**
Dun Gerashader Hill Fort — 4D **44**
Dun Mhor Hill Fort — 5C **44**
*(Dunnideer Hill Fort, Insch — 1B **42**)*
Dunsinane Hill Hill Fort — 5H **33**
Dun Skudiburgh Hill Fort — 2C **44**
Fort Fiddes — 2D **50**
*(Knockfarrel Hill Fort, Strathpeffer — 3G **47**)*
Mote of Mark NTS — 3B **6**
Ord Hill Hill Fort — 4H **47**
Pirn Hill Fort — 5A **20**
Tap O'Noth — 1H **41**
Torr a'Chaisteal Fort — 1E **9**
White Caterhuns Hill Fort — 2C **34**

Historic Building

See also Historic Building & Garden

Abbotsford — 5C **20**
Abernethy Round Tower — 2C **26**, S
Aikwood Tower — 1D **12**
Argyll's Lodging — **Stirling**
Arniston House — 3A **20**, S
Bachelors' Club NTS — 1B **10**, S
*(Bishop's Palace, Kirkwall — 3D **64**)*
Black House — 3H **63**
Boath Doocot NTS — 3C **48**
Brechin Cathedral Round Tower — 3C **34**
*(Burns Cottage, Alloway — 2A **10**)*
*(Chatelherault House, Ferniegair — 3C **18**)*
*Corstorphine Dovecot — 1H **19***
Crail Tolbooth — 3H **27**
Dalmeny House — 1G **19**
Dunfermline Palace — **Dunfermline**
Dunkitterick Cottage (Murray's Birthplace) — 1G **5**
Earl's Palace — 2B **64**
*(Earl's Palace, Kirkwall — 3D **64**)*
Ellisland Farm — 5G **11**
Finavon Doocot NTS — 3B **34**
*(Georgian House, The NTS — 1H **19**, S)*
Gladstone's Land NTS — **Edinburgh**, S
Glasgow City Chambers — **Glasgow**
*(Greenhill Covenanters' House, Biggar — 5F **19**)*
Greenknowe Tower — 4D **20**
*Holmwood House, Cathcart NTS — 3A **18**, S*
Hutchesons' Hall, Glasgow NTS — **Glasgow**
John Knox House, Edinburgh — **Edinburgh**
Lennoxlove House — 1C **20**, S
Maggie's Hoosie — 2F **51**
Mar's Wark — **Stirling**
*(Maybole Castle — 3A **10**)*
Mid Steeple — **Dumfries**
Moirlanich Longhouse NTS — 5A **32**
Monzie Castle — 1H **25**
Mounthooley Doocot — 2E **51**
*(New Elgin Doo'cot — 2F **49**)*
*(Old Buittle Tower, Dalbeattie — 2B **6**)*
Phantassie Doocot NTS — 1C **20**
*(Preston Doocot, Prestonpans NTS — 1A **20**)*
Provan Hall NTS — 2B **18**
Ruthven Barracks — 4A **40**
Spynie Palace — 2F **49**
Stirling Guildhall — **Stirling**
Study, The NTS — 5A **26**
Tealing Dovecot — 5B **34**
Tenement House, The, Glasgow NTS — **Glasgow**
Trades Hall, Glasgow — **Glasgow**
Traquair — 5A **20**
*Westquarter Dovecot, Laurieston — 1E **19***

Historic Building & Garden

See also Historic Building, Garden

Balmoral Castle — 4F **41**, S
Blair Castle — 2D **32**
Blairquhan Castle — 3A **10**, S
Bowhill House (Selkirk) — 1D **12**
Broughton House NTS — 3H **5**, S
Culross Palace NTS — 5A **26**
Culzean Castle NTS — 2H **9**, S
Drumlanrig Castle — 4F **11**, S
Dunninald — 3E **35**
Falkland Palace NTS — 3D **26**, S
Gosford House — 1B **20**, S
Haddo House NTS — 5D **50**
Hill House, The NTS — 5B **24**, S
Hill of Tarvit Mansionhouse & Garden NTS — 2E **27**, S
Hopetoun House — 1F **19**, S
House of Dun NTS — 3D **34**, S
House of The Binns NTS — 1F **19**, S
Kelburn Castle — 3F **17**, S
Kellie Castle NTS — 3G **27**
Leith Hall NTS — 1A **42**, S
Manderston — 3F **21**
Maxwelton House — 5F **11**
Mellerstain — 5D **20**
Mount Stuart — 3E **17**, S
*(Newhailes NTS — 1A **20**)*
Palace of Holyroodhouse — **Edinburgh**
Paxton House & Country Park — 3G **21**
*Pollok House, Glasgow NTS — 2A **18***
Rammerscales House — 1D **6**, S
*Rozelle House, Alloway — 2A **10***
Scone Palace — 1C **26**, S
Stevenson House — 1C **20**
Threave NTS — 2A **6**
Torosay Castle — 5A **30**

Horse Racecourse

Ayr Racecourse — **Ayr**
Hamilton Park Racecourse — **Hamilton**
Kelso Racecourse — 5E **21**
Musselburgh Racecourse — 1A **20**
Perth Racecourse — **Perth**

Industrial Monument

See also Mine, Windmill

*(Aberfeldy Watermill — 4D **32**)*
Aldie Watermill — 5E **55**
Barry Mill NTS — 5C **34**
*(Blair Atholl Watermill — 2D **32**)*
Bonawe Iron Furnace — 5D **30**
Click Mill — 2C **64**
Dalgarven Mill — 4F **17**
James Pringle Weavers of Inverness — 4H **47**
Kirkdale Water Driven Sawmill & Nature Trail — 3G **5**
Lochcarron Weavers — 5H **45**
Lower City Mills — **Perth**
Mill of Benholm, The — 2F **35**
Mill on the Fleet — 3H **5**
*(Muiravonside Lime Kiln, Loan — 1E **19**)*
Neptune's Staircase — 1E **31**
New Abbey Corn Mill — 2C **6**
Old Mills — 2F **49**
Preston Mill NTS — 1C **20**
Sandhaven Meal Mill — 2E **51**
*(Skye Woollen Mill, Portree — 4D **44**)*
*(Spean Bridge Woollen Mill — 5D **38**)*
Tormiston Mill — 3C **64**
Wanlockhead Beam Engine — 2F **11**

Leisure Park/Leisure Pool

See also Theme Park

Clyde Muirshiel Regional Park — 3G **17**

Lighthouse

*Ailsa Craig Lighthouse — 4F **9***
*Aird Laimisiadair Lighthouse, Borghastan — 3F **63***
Ardnamurchan Point Lighthouse — 2F **29**
*Ardrishaig Lighthouse — 5F **23***
*Ardrossan Lighthouse — 4F **17***
*Ardtreck Point Lighthouse, Portnalong — 5C **44***
*Ayr Lighthouse — 1A **10***
*Baa Taing Lighthouse, Hillswick — 5F **67***
*Barns Ness Lighthouse, Dunbar — 1E **21***
*Beamer Lighthouse, Queensferry — 5C **26***
*Bell Rock (Inchcape) Lighthouse, Bell Rock Island — 5E **35***
*Berneray Lighthouse, Berneray Island — 6A **60***
*Black Head Lighthouse, Portpatrick — 3A **4***
*Bound Skerry Lighthouse, Housay — 5K **67***
*Branderburgh Lighthouse, Lossiemouth — 1F **49***
*Broti Ber Lighthouse, Muckle Skerry — 1H **59***
Brough of Birsay Lighthouse — 2B **64**
*Buchanness Lighthouse, Boddam — 4G **51***
*Butt of Lewis (Rhuba Robhanais) Lighthouse, Coig Peighinnean — 1K **63***
*Cailleach Head Lighthouse, Badrallach — 4E **53***
*Cairn Point Lighthouse, Cairnryan — 2B **4***
*Calf of Cava Lighthouse — 4C **64***
*Cantick Head Lighthouse, Osmondwall — 6C **64***
Cape Wrath Lighthouse — 1D **56**
*Carnoustie High Lighthouse — 5C **34***
*Carnoustie Low Lighthouse — 5C **34***
*Carragh an t-Sruith Lighthouse, Feolin Ferry — 1F **15***
*Carraig Fhada Lighthouse, Port Ellen — 4E **15***
*Chanonry Point Lighthouse, Fortrose — 3A **48***
*Cloch Point Lighthouse, Gourock — 1F **17***
*Corpach Lighthouse — 1D **30***
*Corran Point Lighthouse — 2D **30***
*Corsewall Point Lighthouse, Kirkcolm — 1A **4***
*Crammag Head Lighthouse, Kirkmaiden — 5B **4***
*Cromarty Lighthouse — 2A **48***
*Duncansby Head Lighthouse, John o' Groats — 1H **59***
Dunnet Head Lighthouse — 1F **59**
*East Landing Lighthouse, Bass Rock — 5H **27***
*Eileach an Naoimh Lighthouse — 3D **22***
*Eilean a Chait Lighthouse, Plockton — 5H **45***
*Eilean A'chuirn Lighthouse, Eilean a'Churin — 4F **15***
*Eilean Ban Lighthouse, Kyle of Lochalsh — 1G **37***
*Eilean Beag Lighthouse, Crowlin Islands — 5F **45***
*Eilean Dubh Lighthouse, Tighnabruaich — 1D **16***
*Eilean Mor Lighthouse, Sandaig Islands — 2G **37***
*Eilean Musdile Lighthouse — 5A **30***
*Eilean Sionnach Lighthouse, Ornsay — 2G **37***
*Eilean Trodday Lighthouse — 1D **44***
*Elie Lighthouse — 4F **27***
*Eriboll Lighthouse — 2F **57***
*Esha Ness Lighthouse, West Heogaland — 5F **67***
*Eyre Point Lighthouse — 5E **45***
*Fidra Lighthouse — 5G **27***
*Fife Ness Lighthouse, Crail — 2H **27***
*Fladda Lighthouse — 2E **23***
*Fort Augustus Lighthouse — 3E **39***
*Fraserburgh Harbour Lighthouse — 2F **51***
*Fugla Ness Lighthouse, Hamnavoe — 3C **66***
*Gairlochy Lighthouse, Loch Lochy — 5C **38***
*Girdleness Lighthouse, Aberdeen — 3E **43***
*Glas Eileanan Lighthouse — 5A **30***
*Gordonsburgh Lighthouse, Buckie — 2H **49***
*Heisker (Monach) Islands Lighthouse — 4F **61***
*Hestan Island Lighthouse, Auchencairn — 3B **6***
*Inch Garvie Lighthouse, North Queensferry — 1G **19***
*Inchkeith Lighthouse, Inchkeith Island — 5D **26***
*Island Davaar Lighthouse — 1C **8***
Isle of May Lighthouse — 4H **27**
*Kingscross Point Lighthouse, Holy Island — 1F **9***
*Kinnaird Head Castle Lighthouse & Museum, Fraserburgh — 2E **51***
*Kirkabister Ness Lighthouse — 3D **66***
*Kyle Rhea Lighthouse, Kylerhea — 1G **37***
*Lady Isle Lighthouse — 1H **9***
*Little Cumbrae Island Lighthouse, Millport — 3E **17***
*Little Ross Lighthouse — 4H **5***
*Loch a Bhraige Lighthouse, Island of Rona — 2F **45***
*Mc Arthur's Head Lighthouse, Port Askaig — 3F **15***
*Mathers Head Lighthouse, Stonybreck — 2H **65***
*Muckle Flugga Lighthouse, Herma Ness — 1K **67***
Mull of Galloway Lighthouse — 5C **4**
*Mull of Kintyre Lighthouse, Southend — 3A **8***
*Na Cuiltean Lighthouse — 2G **15***
*Neist Point Lighthouse, Waterstein — 4A **44***
*Ness Lighthouse, The, Papa Stronsay — 4J **65***
*Newhaven Lighthouse — 1H **19***
*Newhaven Old Lighthouse — 1H **19***
*Nizz Lighthouse, The, Vaasetter — 1J **65***
*Noss Head Lighthouse, Staxigoe — 3G **59***
*Noup Head Lighthouse, Rackwick — 3F **65***
*Oigh-sgeir Lighthouse — 4A **36***
*Orsay Lighthouse — 3C **14***
*Ousbacky Lighthouse, Overton — 5F **59***
Oxcars Lighthouse — 5D **26**
*Pillar Rock Point Lighthouse, Holy Island — 1F **9***
*Pladda Lighthouse — 2F **9***
*Point of Oxan Lighthouse, Graemsay — 4B **64***
*Point of Sinsoss Lighthouse, Hollandstoun — 2K **65***
*Point of Sleat Lighthouse, Aird of Sleat — 4E **37***
*(Port Askaig Lighthouse — 2F **15**)*
*Port of Leith Lighthouse, Newhaven — 1H **19***
*Rattray Head Lighthouse, Crimond — 3G **51***
*Rhu Stoer Lighthouse, Rubha Stoer — 5B **56***
*Rhuvaal Lighthouse, Bunnahabhain — 1F **15***
*Rose Ness Lighthouse, Cornquoy — 5E **64***
*Ruadh Sgeir Lighthouse — 4E **23***
*Rubha Airnis, Stornoway (Steornabhagh) — 4J **63***
*Rubha an Fhigheadair Lighthouse, North Uist (Uibhista A Tuath) — 4K **61***
*Rubha an Iasgaich Lighthouse, Eilean Chathastail — 5D **36***
*Rubha an t-Siumpain Lighthouse, Brocair — 4K **63***
*Rubha Cadail Lighthouse, Rhue — 4F **53***
*Rubha Dubh Lighthouse, Scalasaig — 4A **22***
*Rubha Nan Gall Lighthouse, Tobermory — 3G **29***
*Rubh'an Duin Lighthouse, Port Charlotte — 3D **14***
*Rubh an Eorna Lighthouse, Ceann a Bhaigh — 5D **62***
*Rubha Reidh Lighthouse, Melvaig — 4C **52***
*Rubha Sheallacro Lighthouse, South Uist (Uibhist A Deas) — 1D **60***
*Saeva Ness Lighthouse, Balfour — 3D **64***
*St Abb's Head Lighthouse, St Abbs — 2G **21***
*Sanda Island Lighthouse — 3C **8***
*Scarf Skerry Lighthouse, Uppertown — 5D **64***
*Scarinish Lighthouse — 4B **28***
*Scrabster Lighthouse — 1E **59***
*Scurdie Ness Lighthouse, Montrose — 3E **35***
*Skerry of Vasa Lighthouse — 3D **64***
*Skervuile Lighthouse — 1H **15***
*South Taing Lighthouse, Auskerry — 6J **65***
*Start Point Lighthouse, Lettan — 3K **65***
*Strathy Point Lighthouse, Totegan — 2B **58***
*Suil Ghorm Lighthouse, Coll — 2D **28***
Sumburgh Head Lighthouse — 6D **66**
*Swilkie Point Lighthouse, Nethertown — 1G **59***
*Taing of Sandside Lighthouse, Graemsay — 4B **64***
*Tarbat Ness Lighthouse, Wilkhaven — 5G **55***
*Tayport Lighthouse — 1F **27***
*Tayport Old Lighthouse — 1F **27***
*Todhead Lighthouse, Crawton — 1F **35***
*Tor Ness Lighthouse, Melsetter — 6B **64***
*Toward Point Lighthouse — 2E **17***
*Troon Lighthouse — 5G **17***
*Turnberry Point Lighthouse — 3G **9***
*Waternish Point Lighthouse, Trumpan — 2B **44***

Long Distance Footpath

West Highland Way (Fort William) — **Fort William**

Mine/Cave

See also Industrial Monument

Birkhill Fireclay Mine — 1E **19**
Bruce's Cave — 1F **7**
Covesea Caves — 1E **49**
Fingal's Cave NTS — 5E **29**
Inchnadamph Bone Caves — 2H **53**
Lecht Iron Mine — 2F **41**
Lochnell Lead Mine — 2F **11**
Ossian's Cave NTS — 4F **33**
Ossian's Cave NTS — 3E **31**
Prince Charles's Cave — 2E **37**
Rob Roy's Cave — 3D **24**
St Columba's Cave — 1A **16**
St Fillan's Cave — 3G **27**
St Margaret's Cave — **Dunfermline**
St Ninian's Cave — 5F **5**
Smoo Cave — 2F **57**
Uamh Shomhairle — 2E **31**
Wemyss Caves — 4E **27**

Monument/Folly

Aberdeen Mercat Cross — **Aberdeen**
Albert Memorial — **Edinburgh**
Alexander III Monument — 5D **26**
Allan Ramsay Monument — 3H **19**
American Monument, The — 4D **14**
Black Watch Memorial, The — 4D **32**
Boswell Mausoleum — 1C **10**
*(Bothwell Bridge Monument — 3C **18**)*
Bruce's Stone — 5B **10**
Burns Mausoleum — **Dumfries**
*(Burns Monument, Alloway — 2A **10**)*
Burns Monument, Edinburgh — **Edinburgh**
Burns Monument — **Kilmarnock**
Cameronian Regiment Monument — 5D **18**
Cameronians' Regimental Memorial NTS — 5D **18**
*(Clermiston Tower, Corstorphine — 1H **19**)*

Cobb Memorial — 1G **39**
Commando Memorial — 5D **38**
Culloden Battlefield Memorial Cairn NTS — 4A **48**
Culsh Monument — 4D **50**
*(Cumberland Stone, Inverness NTS — 4A **48**)*
Cunninghame Graham Memorial NTS — 4E **25**
David Bell Memorial — 4A **10**
Donald Murchison's Monument — 1G **37**
Duchess of Gordon's Monument — 3B **40**
Dugald Stewart Monument — **Edinburgh**
Duke of Gordon's Monument — 3B **40**
Duke of Sutherland Monument — 3F **55**
Duncan Ban MacIntyre Monument — 1A **24**
Dundee Law War Memorial — 5A **34**
Fettercairn Arch — 1D **34**
Flora Macdonald Monument — 1C **44**
*(Flora Macdonald Statue, Inverness — **Inverness**)*
Fyrish Monument — 2H **47**
Gavin Maxwell Memorial — 4E **5**
General Burnett Monument — 4B **42**
George Buchanan Obelisk — 5E **25**
Glenfinnan Monument NTS — 5A **38**
Greyfriars Bobby, Edinburgh — **Edinburgh**
Hamilton Mausoleum — **Hamilton**
Harlaw Monument — 1C **42**
*(Hector Macdonald Memorial, Dingwall — 3G **47**)*
*(Highland Mary's Statue, Dunoon — 1E **17**)*
Hopetoun Monument — 1C **20**
Hume Castle — 4E **21**
*(James Gavin Memorial Stone, Douglas — 5D **18**)*
James Hogg Monument — 2B **12**
James Renwick Monument — 4E **11**
James Thomson Obelisk — 5E **21**
*(Jane Whyte Memorial, New Aberdour — 2D **50**)*
John Hunter Memorial — 2H **11**
John Macadam Monument — **Ayr**
King Edward VII Memorial — **Edinburgh**
*(Lady Hill Column, Elgin — 2F **49**)*
Leyden Obelisk — 2E **13**
Loch Nam Uamh Cairn — 5G **37**
McCaig's Tower — **Oban**
McDiarmid Memorial — 5C **12**
Macdonald Monument — 3E **31**
Macquarie Mausoleum — 5G **29**
Maggie Wall's Monument — 2B **26**
Mail Coach Memorial — 2H **11**
Martyr's Tomb — 1E **5**
*(Melville Monument — 1H **19**)*
Melville Monument — 1G **25**
Mercat Cross — **Edinburgh**
*(Merchant's Steeple, The, Glasgow — 2A **18**)*
Millholm Cross — 5D **12**
Murray's Monument — 1F **5**
National Monument, Edinburgh — **Edinburgh**
National Wallace Monument — **Stirling**
Nelson Monument, Edinburgh — **Edinburgh**
Nelson Tower — 3D **48**
Nisbet Stone — **Kilmarnock**
Ossian's Hall NTS — 4F **33**
*(Peach & Horne Memorial, Inchnadamph — 1H **53**)*
Prop of Ythsie — 5D **50**
Reformers Monument — **Kilmarnock**
*(Robertson Monument, Neilston — 3H **17**)*
Robert the Bruce Statue NTS — **Stirling**
*(Robinson Crusoe Statue, Leven — 3F **27**)*
*(Rob Roy's Statue, Peterculter — 3D **42**)*
Royal Scots Greys Memorial — **Edinburgh**
Royal Scots Monument — **Edinburgh**
Ruthwell Cross — 2E **7**
Scottish American War Memorial, The — **Edinburgh**
Scott Monument, Edinburgh — **Edinburgh**
Scott's Statue — **Glasgow**
Sir John Malcolm Obelisk — 5C **12**
Star Pyramid — **Stirling**
Stirling Mercat Cross — **Stirling**
Telford Memorial — 4C **12**
Temple, The — 2G **17**
*(Tolbooth Steeple, Glasgow — **Glasgow**)*
Wallace Tower — **Ayr**
Waterloo Monument — 2C **6**
Wigtown Martyrs' Monument — 3F **5**
Wigtown Martyrs' Stake — 3F **5**

Motor Racing Circuit

Knockhill Motor Circuit — 4B **26**

Museum

*602 (City of Glasgow) Squadron SS, Museum of the — 2A **18***
Abbot House Heritage Centre — **Dunfermline**
*Abbot's House, Arbroath — 4D **34***
Aberdeen Maritime Museum — **Aberdeen**
Aberdeenshire Farming Museum — 4E **51**
*Aberdeen, University Zoology Museum — 3E **43***
*(Albion Museum & Archive, The — 5F **19**)*
Alford Heritage Centre — 2A **42**
Alford Station Railway Museum — 2A **42**
*Almond Valley Heritage Centre, Livingston Village — 2F **19***
Alyth Folk Museum — 4H **33**
Andrew Carnegie Birthplace Museum — **Dunfermline**
Angus Folk Museum NTS — 4A **34**, S
Annan Museum — 2E **7**
Arbroath Museum — 5D **34**
Arbuthnot Museum — 4G **51**
Ardnamurchan Natural History Centre — 2G **29**
Argyll & Sutherland Highlanders Regimental Museum — **Stirling**
Atholl Country Collection — 2D **32**
Auchindrain Township Open Air Museum — 3H **23**
Auld Kirk Museum — 1B **18**
Avoch Heritage Centre — 3A **48**
Baird Institute History Centre & Museum — 2C **10**
Banchory Museum — 4B **42**
*Banff Museum — 2B **50***
*Bannockburn Heritage Centre NTS — 4G **25***
Barcloy Barn, The — 3B **6**
*(Barrhead Community Museum — 3A **18**)*
*Beatrix Potter Exhibition, Birnam — 4F **33***
Bennie Museum — 2E **19**
Bernera (Bearnaraigh) Museum — 1C **62**
Biggar Gasworks Museum — 5F **19**
Black Watch Regimental Museum — **Perth**
Boat of Garten Station Railway Museum — 2C **40**
Bo'ness Motor Museum — 5B **26**
Borreraig Park Museum — 3A **44**
Boswell Museum — 1C **10**
Braemar Highland Heritage Centre — 4E **41**
Brander Museum — 4A **50**
Breadalbane Folklore Centre — 5A **32**
Brechin Museum — 2D **34**
Brechin Station Railway Museum — 2D **34**
British Golf Museum — **St Andrews**
*Broughty Castle Museum, Broughty Ferry — 5B **34***
*(Buckhaven Museum — 4E **27**)*
*(Burns Cottage Museum, Alloway — 2A **10**)*
Burns House Museum — 1B **10**
*(Burntisland Edwardian Fair Museum — 5D **26**)*
*(Burrell Collection — 2A **18**)*
Bute Museum — 2D **16**
Bygones Museum — 1E **25**
*Callendar House, Falkirk — 1D **18***
Campbeltown Heritage Centre — 2C **8**
Campbeltown Museum — 2C **8**
*Carfin Pilgrimage Centre — 3C **18***
Carlyle's Birthplace NTS — 1E **7**, S
Carnegie Museum — 1C **42**
Castle House Museum — 1E **17**
*Childhood Heritage Centre & Toy Museum, Logierat — 3E **33***
Childhood Memories (The Toy Museum) — 2C **40**
Childhood, Museum of, Edinburgh — **Edinburgh**
*(Christian Heritage Centre, Largs — 3F **17**)*
Clan Armstrong Museum — 5C **12**
Clan Cameron Museum — 5C **38**
Clan Donnachaidh Museum — 2D **32**
Clan Gunn Heritage Centre & Museum — 5F **59**
Clan Macpherson Museum — 4A **40**
*(Clansman Centre, Fort Augustus — 3E **39**)*
Clydebank Museum — 1H **17**
*Clydebuilt, Renfrew — 2A **18***
Colbost Croft Museum — 4B **44**
*Coldstream Museum — 5F **21***
Commando Museum — 5D **38**
Crail Museum & Heritage Centre — 3H **27**
Crawfordjohn Heritage Museum — 1F **11**
Creetown Gem Rock Museum — 3F **5**
Creetown Heritage Museum — 3F **5**
Crichton Royal Museum — 1C **6**
Cromarty Courthouse Museum — 2A **48**
Cumbraes, Museum of The — 3E **17**
Customs & Excise Museum — 1F **17**
Dalbeattie Museum — 2B **6**
Devil's Porridge, The — 2F **7**
Dick Institute — **Kilmarnock**
Dingwall Museum — 3G **47**
Discovery Point — **Dundee**
Dollar Museum — 4A **26**
*('Dolly Mixture' Doll Museum, The, Langbank — 1G **17**)*
Doon Valley Museum — 3B **10**
Douglas Heritage Museum — 5D **18**
*(Drumin Country Museum — 5E **49**)*
Dumfries & Galloway Aviation Museum — 1D **6**
Dumfries Museum — **Dumfries**
*(Dunbar Town House Museum — 1D **20**)*
Dunbeath Heritage Centre — 5E **59**
Dunblane Cathedral Museum — 3G **25**
Dunrobin Castle Museum — 3F **55**
Easdale Island Folk Museum — 2E **23**
*Edinburgh University Collection of Historic Musical Instruments — **Edinburgh***
Elgin Museum — 2F **49**
Errol Station Heritage Centre — 1D **26**
*Eyemouth Museum — 2G **21***
Falconer Museum — 3D **48**
Farming Life, Museum of NTS — 1D **42**
Fife Folk Museum — 2F **27**
Findhorn Heritage Centre — 2D **48**
Fire, Museum of, Edinburgh — **Edinburgh**
Flight, Museum of — 1C **20**
*Fochabers Folk Museum — 3G **49***
Forest of Ae Plough Collection — 4G **11**
*Forth Bridges Exhibition, North Queensferry — 5C **26***
Fraserburgh Heritage Museum — 2E **51**
*(Gaelic Whiskies-Whisky Exhibition, Broadford — 2G **37**)*
Gairloch Heritage Museum — 1H **45**
Galloway Deer Museum — 1G **5**
Garlogie Mill Power House Museum — 3C **42**
Giant Angus MacAskill Museum — 4B **44**
*(Gladstone Court Museum, Biggar — 5F **19**)*
*Glasgow Museum of Transport — 2A **18***
*Glasgow Museums Resource Centre — 2A **18***
*(Glasgow Police Museum — 2A **18**)*
*(Glencoe & North Lorn Folk Museum — 3E **31**)*
Glendale Toy Museum — 4A **44**
Glenesk Folk Museum — 1C **34**
Glenfinnan Station Museum — 5H **37**
Glenluce Motor Museum — 3D **4**
Gordon Highlanders Museum — 3E **43**
Grampian Transport Museum — 2A **42**, S
*Grangemouth Museum — 5A **26***
Grantown-on-Spey Museum — 1D **40**
Groam House Museum — 3A **48**
Halliwell's House Museum — 1D **12**
Hamilton Toy Collection — 3F **25**
*Hawick Museum and Gallery — 2D **12***
HBOS Museum on the Mound, Edinburgh — **Edinburgh**
Highland Folk Museum (Am Fasgadh) — 3A **40**
*(Highland Folk Museum (Turus Tim), Newtonmore — 4A **40**)*
Highland Museum of Childhood — 3F **47**
*(Highland Sport, Museum of, Newtonmore — 4A **40**)*
*Hirsel Homestead Museum, Coldstream — 4F **21***
Hopetoun House Museum — 1F **19**
*(Hunter House Museum, Calderwood — 3B **18**)*
*Hunterian Museum, Glasgow — 2A **18***
Hynish Signal Tower Museum — 5A **28**
*Inveraray Maritime Museum — 3H **23***
*Inverkeithing Museum — 5C **26***
Inverness Museum & Art Gallery — **Inverness**
Iona Heritage Centre NTS — 3A **22**
Islay Life, Museum of — 3D **14**
*Isle of Arran Heritage Museum, Brodick — 5D **16***
Isles, Museum of The — 3F **37**
James Paterson Museum, The — 4E **11**
*Jane Welsh Carlyle Museum, Haddington — 1C **20***
Jedburgh Castle Jail & Museum — 2F **13**, S
Jim Clark Room — 3E **21**
J M Barrie's Birthplace NTS — 3A **34**
John Buchan Centre, The — 5G **19**
John Hastie Museum — 4C **18**
*(John Muir Birthplace, Dunbar — 1D **20**)*
Johnnie Armstrong Gallery — 3D **12**
John Paul Jones Museum & Visitor Centre — 3C **6**
*Jonah's Journey, Aberdeen — 3E **43***
Keathbank Mill Heritage Centre — 4G **33**
*Kelvingrove Art Gallery & Museum (Glasgow) — 2A **18***
Kilmartin House — 4F **23**
*Kinneil Museum, Bo'ness — 5A **26***
Kirkcaldy Museum & Art Gallery — **Kirkcaldy**
Kirriemuir Aviation Museum — 3A **34**
Laidhay Croft Museum — 5E **59**
Laing Museum — 2D **26**
Lanark Museum — 4D **18**
Largs Museum — 3F **17**
Last House Museum, The — 1G **59**
Lead Mining, The Museum of — 2F **11**
Liddesdown Heritage Centre & Museum — 5D **12**
Linlithgow Canal Museum — 1F **19**
*Linlithgow Story, The — 1E **19***
Little Treasures Dolls House Museum — 2C **42**
Lochcarron Museum — 5B **20**
*(Lochwinnoch Community Museum — 3G **17**)*
Lossiemouth Fisheries & Community Museum — 1F **49**
Low Parks Museum — **Hamilton**
Luib Croft Museum — 1E **37**
Maccrimmon Piping Heritage Centre — 3A **44**
McDouall Stuart Museum — 4E **27**
McKechnie Institute, The — 4G **9**
*McLean Museum & Art Gallery, Greenock — 1F **17***
McManus Galleries — **Dundee**
*(Maggie Law Maritime Museum, Gourdon — 1F **35**)*
Mallaig Heritage Centre — 4F **37**
Marischal Museum — **Aberdeen**
Mary-Ann's Cottage — 1F **59**
Matthew Architecture Gallery, The, Edinburgh — **Edinburgh**
*Maud Railway Museum — 4E **51***
Meigle Sculptured Stone Museum — 4H **33**, S
Melrose Abbey Museum — 5C **20**
Methil Heritage Centre — 4E **27**
Michael Bruce's Cottage — 3C **26**
*(Moat Park Heritage Centre, Biggar — 5F **19**)*
Moffat Museum — 3H **11**
Montrose Air Station Museum — 3E **35**
Montrose Museum & Art Gallery — 3E **35**
Monymusk Arts Centre — 2B **42**
*(Moonstone Miniatures, Kirkpatrick Durham — 1A **6**)*
Moray Motor Museum — 2F **49**
Motherwell Heritage Centre — **Motherwell**
Motoring Heritage Centre — 5C **24**
Mull Museum — 3G **29**
Museum of Ayrshire Country Life & Costume, The — 4F **17**
Museum of Edinburgh, The — **Edinburgh**
Museum of Scottish Country Life, The — 3B **18**
Muthill Village & Parish Museum — 2H **25**
Myreton Motor Museum — 1B **20**
Nairn Fishertown Museum — 3B **48**
Nairn Museum — 3B **48**
National War Museum of Scotland — **Edinburgh**
*Network Carradale Heritage Centre — 5A **16***
*Newhaven Heritage Museum — 1H **19***
*Newton Stewart Museum — 2F **5***
North Ayrshire Museum — 4F **17**
North Berwick Museum — 5G **27**
Northfield Farm Museum — 3D **50**
Northlands Viking Centre — 2G **59**
Oban War & Peace Museum — **Oban**
Old Blacksmith's Shop Museum — 2G **7**
Old Bridge House Museum, The — **Dumfries**
Old Byre Heritage Centre — 3F **29**
Old Gala House Museum and Scott Gallery — 5B **20**
Orcadian Stone Company — 3F **55**
Orkney Farm & Folk Museum (Corrigall) — 3C **64**
*(Orkney Farm & Folk Museum (Kirbuster) — 5J **65**)*
*(Orkney Fossil & Vintage Centre, Burray Village — 5D **64**)*
Orkney Wireless Museum — 5D **64**
Paisley Museum & Art Galleries — **Paisley**
Paisley Thread Mill Museum — **Paisley**
*(People's Palace, Glasgow — 2B **18**)*
People's Story, The, Edinburgh — **Edinburgh**
Perth Museum & Art Gallery — **Perth**
*(Peterhead Maritime Heritage — 4G **51**)*
Piping, Museum of, Glasgow — **Glasgow**
Pittencrieff House Museum — **Dunfermline**
Portpatrick Old Lifeboat House — 3A **4**
Prestongrange Industrial Heritage Museum — 1A **20**, S
Provand's Lordship, Glasgow — **Glasgow**
Provost Skene's House — **Aberdeen**
*Queensferry Museum, South Queensferry — 1G **19***
Queen's Own Highlanders Regimental Museum — 3A **48**
Raasay Heritage Museum — 5E **45**
*Renfrew Community Museum — 2A **18***
Robert Burns House — **Dumfries**
*(Robert D Clapperton Photographic Museum — 1D **12**)*
Robert Smail's Printing Works NTS — 5A **20**
Ross of Mull Historical Centre — 1A **22**
Royal Highland Fusiliers Museum, Glasgow — **Glasgow**
Royal Museum, Edinburgh — **Edinburgh**
St Andrews Cathedral Museum and Visitor Centre — **St Andrews**
St Andrews Museum — **St Andrews**
St Andrews Preservation Trust Museum — **St Andrews**
St Cecilia's Hall Museum of Instruments, Cowgate — **Edinburgh**
St Mungo Museum of Religious Life & Art, Glasgow — **Glasgow**
St Ronan's Wells Interpretive Centre — 5A **20**
St Vigeans Museum — 4D **34**
Sandaig Thatched House Museum — 4A **28**
Sanquhar Tolbooth Museum — 3E **11**
Savings Banks Museum — 2E **7**
*(Scotland, Museum of — 1H **19**)*
Scotland Street School Museum, Glasgow — 2A **18**
*(Scottish Agricultural Museum, Newbridge — 1G **19**)*
Scottish Country Life, Museum of — 1E **41**
Scottish Fisheries Museum — 3G **27**
Scottish Football Museum — 2A **18**
Scottish Horse Regimental Museum — 4F **33**
Scottish Industrial Railway Centre — 3B **10**
*Scottish Maritime Museum — 5G **17***
Scottish Mining Museum — 2A **20**
*Scottish Railway Exhibition, The, Bo'ness — 5B **26***
Scottish Skiing & Mountaineering Museum — 3F **31**
Scottish Vintage Bus Museum — 4B **26**
*(Seafield Collection, Fort George — 3A **48**)*
Shambellie House Museum of Costume — 2C **6**, S
Shawbost School Museum — 3G **63**
Shetland Croft House Museum — 5D **66**
*(Shetland Museum, Lerwick — 2D **66**)*
Shotts Heritage Centre — 2D **18**
Sir Walter Scott's Courtroom — 1D **12**
Skye Museum of Island Life — 1D **44**
Sma' Shot Cottages — **Paisley**

Smithy Heritage Centre — 4A **46**
Sophie's Puppenstube & Dolls House Museum — 2F **5**
Souter Johnnie's Cottage NTS — 3H **9**
Staffin Museum — 2D **44**
Stewartry Museum, The — 3H **5**
Stirling Smith Art Gallery & Museum — **Stirling**
Stonehaven Tolbooth Museum — 5D **42**
Strachur Smiddy Museum — 3H **23**
Stranraer Museum — 2B **4**
Strathnaver Museum — 2A **58**
Stromness Museum — 4B **64**
Summerlee Heritage Park, Coatbridge — 2C 18
Sunnyside Museum — 2E **35**
Tain Through Time (Tain & District Museum) — 5E **55**
(Tankerness House Museum, Kirkwall — 3D 64)
The Museum of Scottish Lighthouses — 2E **51**
(Thimble Museum, The, Biggar — 5F 19)
(Thomas Muir Museum, Bishopbriggs — 1B 18)
"Three Hills" Roman Heritage Centre, The and Trimontium Roman Fort
    — 5C 20
Thurso Heritage Museum — 2E **59**
Timespan Heritage Centre, Helmsdale — 2H 55
Tingwall Agricultural Museum — 2D **66**
Tomintoul Museum — 2E **41**
Torridon Deer Museum NTS — 3A **46**
Treasures of the Earth — 1D **30**
Tweeddale Museum & Gallery — 4H **19**
Ullapool Museum & Visitor Centre — 4G **53**
Verdant Works — **Dundee**
Village Store — 4F **49**
Weaver's Cottage NTS — 2G **17**, S
West Highland Museum — **Fort William**
Whithorn Story, The — 4F **5**
Wick Heritage Centre — 3G **59**
William Lamb Sculpture Studio, Montrose — 3E 35
Writers' Museum, The, Edinburgh — **Edinburgh**

Natural Attraction

Achness Waterfall — 3B **54**
Achriabhach Falls — 2E **31**
Allt Na Caillich Falls — 3D **38**
Ardessie Falls — 5F **53**
Arthur's Seat — 1H **19**
Balgy Falls — 3H **45**
Black Rock Gorge — 2G **47**
(Black Spout, Pitlochry — 3E 33)

(Bow Fiddle Rock, Portknockie — 2H 49)
Bracklinn Falls — 3F **25**
Bullers of Buchan — 5G **51**
Cape Wrath — 1D **56**
Carlingwark Loch — 2A **6**
Carsaig Arches — 2B **22**
Cauldron Linn — 4B **26**
Chia-aig Falls — 5C **38**
Clachaig Falls — 3E **31**
Clo Mor Cliffs — 1E **57**
Corra Linn — 4D **18**
Corrieshalloch Gorge NTS — 1D **46**
Culachy Falls — 3E **39**
Deil's Cauldron — 1G **25**
Devil's Beef Tub — 2H **11**
Dog Falls — 1D **38**
Dollar Glen — 4A **26**
Duncansby Stacks — 1G **59**
Dunnet Head — 1E **59**
Eagle's Falls — 2B **24**
Eas Coul Aulin Falls — 1H **53**
Eas Fors — 4F **29**
Fall of Bruar — 2D **32**
Falls of Acharn — 4C **32**
Falls of Clyde — 4D **18**
Falls of Cruachan — 1H **23**
Falls of Divach — 1F **39**
Falls of Dochart — 5A **32**
Falls of Edinample — 1F **25**
Falls of Falloch — 1C **24**
Falls of Foyers — 1F **39**
Falls of Glomach NTS — 1B **38**
Falls of Kirkaig — 2G **53**
Falls of Leny — 1E **25**
Falls of Lora — 5C **30**
Falls of Measach NTS — 1D **46**
Falls of Shin — 4C **54**
Giant's Chair — 5G **49**
Glenashdale Falls — 1F **9**
Glencoe Gorge — 3E **31**
Glen Lyon — 4A **32**
Glen Nevis Lower Falls — 2E **31**

Glen Nevis Waterslide — 2E **31**
Grey Mare's Tail (Kinlochleven) — 2E **31**
Grey Mare's Tail Waterfall (Moffat) NTS — 2A **12**
Grey Mare's Tail Waterfalls (Newton Stewart) — 1F **5**
(Hermitage, The, Dunkeld NTS — 4F 33)
Inchrigh Falls — 2D **30**
Inverlair Falls — 5E **39**
Invermoriston Falls — 2F **39**
Kelburn Glen — 3F **17**
Kilt Rock — 2E **45**
Lealt Falls — 2E **45**
Leap of Fintry — 5F **25**
Linn of Dee — 5D **40**
Linn of Quoich — 4E **41**
Loch Lomond — 4C **24**
Loch Morar — 4G **37**
Loch Ness — 1G **39**
Lowes Lochs — 1A **6**
Macleod's Maidens — 5B **44**
Mealt Falls — 2E **45**
Monessie Falls — 5D **38**
Mull of Galloway — 5C **4**
Old Man of Hoy — 4A **64**
Old Man of Stoer, The — 5B **56**
(Pass of Killiecrankie NTS — 2E 33)
Plodda Falls — 1D **38**
Quirang — 2D **44**
Randolph's Leap — 4C **48**
Reekie Linn — 3H **33**
Rocking Stone — 1E **31**
Rogie Falls — 3F **47**
Rumbling Bridge Gorge — 4B **26**
South Laggan Falls — 4D **38**
Steall Falls — 2E **31**
Stinchar Falls — 4A **10**
Victoria Falls — 1H **45**
Whangie, The — 5D **24**

Nature Reserve/Bird Sanctuary (RSPB, Wildfowl Trust, selected only)

See also Forest Walk

Aberlady Bay Nature Reserve — 5F **27**
Abernethy Forest National Nature Reserve — 2C **40**, S
Achmelvich Nature Reserve, Lochinver — 1F 53

Reflection in Loch

Addiewell Bing Nature Reserve — 2F **19**
Allt Nan Carnan Nature Reserve — 4H **45**
Arbroath Nature Trail — 4D 34
Ariundle Nature Reserve — 2B **30**
Balmaccan Woods Nature Reserve — 1F **39**
Balnaguard Glen Nature Reserve — 3E **33**
Balranald Bird Sanctuary — 3H **61**
Bankhead Moss Nature Reserve — 2F **27**
Barnyards Marsh Nature Reserve — 3F **27**
Baron's Haugh Nature Reserve, Motherwell — 3C 18
Bawsinch & Duddingston Nature Reserve — 1H 19
Beinn Eighe Nature Reserve — 2A **46**
Belmaduthy Dam Nature Reserve — 3H **47**
Bemersyde Moss Nature Reserve — 5D **20**
Ben Lawers National Nature Reserve NTS — 5B **32**
Ben Mor Coigach Nature Reserve — 3F **53**
Birnie Loch Nature Reserve — 2D **26**
Birsay Moors & Cottasgarth Bird Sanctuary — 2C **64**
Bishop Loch Local Nature Reserve, Glasgow — 2B 18
Black Wood of Rannoch Forest Nature Reserve — 3A **32**
(Bogburn Flood Lagoons Nature Reserve — 2E 19)
Bo'mains Meadow Nature Reserve — 1E 19
Braehead Moss Nature Reserve — 3E **19**
Brighty Wood Nature Reserve — 5B **34**
Caenlochan Nature Reserve — 1H **33**
Caerlaverock National Nature Reserve — 2D **6**
Caerlaverock Wildfowl & Wetlands Centre — 2D **6**
Cairn Gorm Nature Reserve — 3D **40**
(Cairngorms Nature Reserve, Aviemore — 2B 40)
Cairnsmore of Fleet Nature Reserve — 2G **5**
Calingnose Point Nature Reserve — 5C **26**
Cambus Pools Nature Reserve — 4H **25**
Cameron Reservoir Nature Reserve — 2F **27**
Carron Dam Nature Reserve — 5H 25
Carstramon Wood Nature Reserve — 2G **5**
Clachtoll Nature Reserve — 1F 53
Clyde Valley Woodlands Nature Reserve — 4E **19**
Coll Bird Sanctuary — 3C **28**
Corrieshalloch Gorge National Nature Reserve NTS — 1D **46**
Corstorphine Hill Local Nature Reserve — 1H 19
*Craigellachie National Nature Reserve — **Aviemore***
Creag Meagaidh Nature Reserve — 5F **39**

Culbin Forest Nature Reserve — 2C **48**
Culbin Sands Bird Sanctuary — 3C **48**
Cullaloe Nature Reserve — 5C **26**
Cumbernauld Glen Nature Reserve — 1C **18**
Dells Wood Nature Reserve — 2D **40**
Den of Maidencraig Local Nature Reserve, Aberdeen — 3D 42
Doire Donn Nature Reserve — 1D **30**
Donmouth Local Nature Reserve — 3E **43**
Doune Ponds — 3G **25**
Dunnet Links Nature Reserve — 2F **59**
Duns Castle Nature Reserve — 3E 21
Eden Estuary Nature Reserve — 2F **27**
Eigg Nature Reserve — 5D **36**
Eilean Na Creige Duibhe Nature Reserve, Plockton — 5H 45
Fair Isle Bird Sanctuary NTS — 1J **65**
Fairy Glen Bird Sanctuary — 3A **48**
Falls of Clyde Wildlife Reserve — 4D **18**
Fetlar Bird Sanctuary — 3J **67**
Fife Ness Muir Nature Reserve — 2H **27**
Findhorn Nature Reserve — 2D **48**
Forsinard Bird Sanctuary — 3B **58**
Fowlsheugh Bird Sanctuary — 5D **42**
Gartmorn Dam Local Nature Reserve — 4A **26**
Glen Affric Forest Nature Reserve — 1D **38**
Glenborrodale Bird Sanctuary — 2G **29**
Glenmore Forest Nature Reserve, Aviemore — 2C 40
Glen Moss Nature Reserve — 2G **17**
Glenmuick & Lochnagar Wildlife Reserve — 5G **41**
Glen Nant Nature Reserve — 1H **23**
Glen Roy Nature Reserve — 5D **38**
Glen Tanar Nature Reserve — 4H **41**
Gordon Moss Nature Reserve — 4D **20**
Grey Mare's Tail Nature Reserve NTS — 2A **12**
Handa Island Nature Reserve — 4C **56**
Hobbister Bird Sanctuary — 4C **64**
Inchnadamph Nature Reserve — 2H **53**
Insh Marshes Bird Sanctuary — 3B **40**
Invernaver Nature Reserve — 2H **57**
Inverpolly Nature Reserve — 2G **53**
Inversnaid Bird Sanctuary — 2C **24**
Isle of May Nature Reserve — 4H **27**
Isle Ristol Nature Reserve — 2E **53**
Keltneyburn Nature Reserve — 3C **32**
Ken-Dee Marshes Nature Reserve — 2H **5**
Killiecrankie Bird Sanctuary — 2E **33**
Kilmining Coast Nature Reserve — 3H **27**
(Kincorth Hill Local Nature Reserve — 3E 43)
Knockman Wood Forest Nature Reserve — 2F **5**
(Lein & Speymouth Nature Reserve, The, Kingston — 2G 49)
Leiterfearn Forest Nature Reserve — 4E **39**
Linn of Tummel Nature Reserve, Killiecrankie NTS — 2D 32
Lochaber Loch Forest Nature Reserve — 2C **6**
Loch Fleet Nature Reserve — 4E **55**
Loch Gruinart Bird Sanctuary — 2D **14**
Loch Leven Nature Reserve — 3C **26**
Loch Lomond Nature Reserve — 5D **24**
Loch Maree Nature Reserve — 1H **45**
Loch of Kinnordy Bird Sanctuary — 3A **34**
Loch of Lintrathen Nature Reserve — 3H **33**
Loch of Spiggie Bird Sanctuary, Scousburgh — 5C 66
Loch of Strathbeg Bird Sanctuary — 3F **51**
Loch of the Lowes Nature Reserve, Dunkeld — 4F 33
Lochore Meadows Nature Reserve — 4C **26**
Loch Ruthven Nature Reserve — 1H **39**
Lochwinnoch Nature Reserve — 3G 17
Longhaven Cliffs Nature Reserve — 5G **51**
Loons Bird Sanctuary, The — 2B **64**
Lower Nethan Gorge Nature Reserve — 4D **18**
Marwick Head Bird Sanctuary — 2B **64**
Mersehead Nature Reserve — 3C **6**
Miley Nature Reserve, The — 5A **34**
Mill Dam Bird Sanctuary — 3D **64**
Moine Mhor Nature Reserve — 4F **23**
Montrose Basin Wildlife Reserve — 3D 34
Morrone Birkwood Nature Reserve — 4E **41**
Morton Lochs Nature Reserve — 1F **27**
Muir of Dinnet Nature Reserve — 3H **41**
Mull of Galloway Nature Reserve — 5C **4**
Munlochy Bay Nature Reserve — 3H **47**
Naver Forest Forest Nature Reserve — 4H **57**
Nigg Bay Nature Reserve — 1A **48**
North Hill Bird Sanctuary — 2G **65**
North Hoy Bird Sanctuary — 4B **64**
Noup Cliffs Bird Sanctuary — 3F **65**
(Paisley Moss Local Nature Reserve — 2H 17)
Possil Marsh Nature Reserve — 1A **18**
Rahoy Hills Nature Reserve — 3H **29**
Rannoch Moor Nature Reserve — 3H **31**
Rassal Ashwood Nature Reserve — 4H **45**
Retreat Oakwood Forest Nature Reserve — 2H **5**
Rùm Nature Reserve — 4C 36
Rough Island Bird Sanctuary NTS — 3B **6**
St Abb's Head National Nature Reserve NTS — 2G **21**
St Cyrus Nature Reserve — 2E **35**
Sands of Forvie Nature Reserve — 1F **43**
Scotstown Moor (Perwinnes Moss)
    Local Nature Reserve — 2E **43**
Seaton Cliffs Nature Reserve — 4D **34**
Silver Flowe Nature Reserve — 5B **10**
(Southwick Nature Reserve, Caulkerbush — 3C 6)
Stenhouse Wood Nature Reserve — 4E **11**
Stormont Loch Nature Reserve — 4G **33**
Strathfarra Nature Reserve — 5D **46**
Sumburgh Head Bird Sanctuary — 6D **66**
Talich Nature Reserve — 1B **48**
Taynish Nature Reserve — 5E **23**
Tentsmuir Point Nature Reserve — 1G **27**
Threave Wildfowl Reserve NTS — 2A **6**
Trumland Bird Sanctuary — 2D **64**
Tummel Shingle Islands Nature Reserve — 3E **33**
Tynron Nature Reserve — 4F **11**
Udale Bay Bird Sanctuary — 2A **48**
Vane Farm Bird Sanctuary — 4C **26**
Waters of Philorth Local Nature Reserve — 2F **51**
West Quarry Braes Nature Reserve — 3G **27**
Wigtown Bay Nature Reserve — 3F **5**
Wood of Cree Nature Reserve — 1E **5**
Yetholm Loch Nature Reserve — 1H **13**

Place of Interest (General)

Aberlemno Sculptured Stones — 3C **34**
Achiltibuie Smokehouse — 2E **53**

Achray Forest Drive — 3E **25**
(Acre Wood Nursery, Stirling — 4H 25)
Andrew Elliot Ltd. Factory & Mill Shop — 1D **12**
Annait — 3B **44**
(Archaeolink (Prehistory Park), Oyne — 1B 42)
Ardclach Bell Tower — 4C **48**
Aros Experience — 4D **44**
Auchterarder Heritage Centre — 2A **26**
Badbea — 1H **55**
Balnain House NTS — **Inverness**
(Banff Town Cross — 2B 50)
Beheading Stone, The — **Stirling**
(Ben Nevis Exhibition, Fort William — 1E 31)
Beveridge Park — 4D **26**
Biggar Fountain — 2B **50**
Biggar Puppet Theatre — 5F **19**
Bod of Gremista — 2D **66**
Brandsbutt Symbol Stone — 1C **42**
Brough of Birsay — 2B **64**
Brow Well — 2D **6**
Bruce's Stone NTS — 1G **5**
Buckie Drifter — 2H **49**
Burghead Well — 2E **49**
(Burns Heckling Shop, Irvine — 5G 17)
Cairngorm Whisky Centre — 2C **40**
Calton Hill — **Edinburgh**
Campbeltown Cross — 1C **8**
(Captain Scott & Dr Wilson Cairn, Dykehead — 2A 34)
Carfin Grotto — 3C **18**
Carrick Forest Drive — 4B **10**
Carsphairn Heritage Centre — 4C **10**
Castle Garrison Encounter — **Inverness**
Ceramic Experience, The — 3B **18**
City Observatory — **Edinburgh**
Clach a Charridh — 1B **48**
Clachan Bridge — 2E **23**
Clach Ard Symbol Stone — 4D **44**
Clach-na-coileach — 2G **33**
Claverhouse Stone — 2E **33**
Coats Observatory — **Paisley**
(Conoco Natural History Centre, Aberdeen — 3E 43)
Cove Conservation Park — 5B **24**
Craft Daft — **Ayr**
Craft Daft on a Raft — 1B **18**
(Crail Mercat Cross — 3H 27)
(Cross of Lorraine, Greenock — 1F 17)
Crow Stone — 1H **41**
Cruachan Power Station — 1H **23**
Cullen Market Cross — 2A **50**
Culsh Earth-house — 3A **42**
Dalton Pottery — 1E **7**
(David Livingstone Centre, Blantyre — 3B 18)
Dee Valley Confectioners — 4G **41**
(Denny Tank, Dumbarton — 1G 17)
Dinnet Oakwood — 4H **41**
Dogton Stone — 4D **26**
Doonhill Homestead — 1D **20**
Drinnie's Wood Observatory — 4E **51**
Dumfries Camera Obscura — **Dumfries**
(Duncrub Standing Stone, Dunning — 2B 26)
Dunfallandy Stone — 3E **33**
(Dunning Thorn Tree — 2B 26)
(Dunnottar Woodland Park, Stonehaven — 5D 42)
Dyce Symbol Stones — 2D **42**
Eagle Rock — 1G **19**
Eagle Stone — 3F **47**
Earl's Bu — 4C **64**
Eassie Sculptured Stone — 4A **34**
East Links Family Park & Narrow Gauge Railway — 1D **20**
Edderton Symbol Stone — 5E **55**
(Edinburgh Brass Rubbing Centre — Edinburgh)
Edinburgh Camera Obscura & World of Illusions
— **Edinburgh**
Edinburgh Dungeon, The — **Edinburgh**
Electric Brae — 2H **9**
Falkirk Wheel — 5H **25**
Findhorn Foundation — 2D **48**
Floral Clock — **Edinburgh**
Fortviot Cross — 2B **26**
Forth Bridge — 1G **19**
Fortingall Yew Tree — 4C **32**
(Fossil Grove, Glasgow — 2B 18, S)
Fowlis Wester Sculptured Stones — 1A **26**
(Fraserburgh Lifeboat Shed — 2E 51)
(Fraserburgh Mercat Cross — 2E 51)
(Galloway Country Style, Gatehouse of Fleet — 3G 5)
Glasgow Necropolis — **Glasgow**
(Glasgow Science Centre, The — 2A 18)
Glenholm Wildlife Project — 5G **19**
Glen Roy Parallel Roads — 5D **38**
Globe Inn — **Dumfries**
Highland Aromatics — 4G **47**
(Holyrood Park, Canongate — 1H 19)
Homeston Farm Trail — 2B **8**
(House for an Art Lover, Glasgow — 2A 18)
Innerpeffray Library — 2A **26**
Inveraray All Saints' Church Bell Tower — 3H **23**
Inveraray Jail — 3H **23**
Inverawe Smokery — 5D **30**
Islay Woolen Mill — 2E **15**
Isle of Skye Brewing Company (Leann an Eilein) — 2C **44**
James Hamilton Heritage Park — 3B **18**
Kagyu Samye Ling Monastery — 3B **12**
Kartstart — 4D **26**
Kelburn Country Centre, Fairlie — 3F 17
Kempock Stone — 1F **17**
Kilberry Sculptured Stones — 2A **16**
Kildalton Cross — 3F **15**
Kilmartin Sculptured Stones — 4F **23**
Kilmodan Sculptured Stones — 5G **23**
Kilpatrick Dun — 1E **9**
King's Knot — **Stirling**
Kinnoull Hill Woodland Park — 1C **26**
(Kintore Kirkyard — 2C 42)
Kirkmadrine Memorial Stones — 4B **4**
Kirriemuir Camera Obscura — 3A **34**
Kirroughtree Forest Drive — 2F **5**
Knocknagael Boar Stone — **Inverness**
Ladies Rock — **Stirling**
Landmark Highland Heritage & Adventure Park — 1C **40**
(Lands of Finderlie, Milnathort — 3B 26)
Latheronwheel Whalebone Arch — 5E **59**
Leadhills Miners' Library — 2F **11**
Leighton Library — 3G **25**
Lindean Mill Glass — 5B **20**
Macculloch's Fossil Tree NTS — 1B **22**
Maclean's Cross — 3A **22**

Magnum Beach Park — 5G **17**
Maiden Stone — 1C **42**
Meikleour Beech Hedge — 5G **33**
Merkland Cross — 1F **7**
(Mess John's Well, New Aberdour — 2D 50)
Midlothian Ski Centre — 2H **19**
Miller House Museum and Hugh Miller's Cottage
NTS — 2A **48**, S
Mills Observatory — 5A **34**
Mitchell Library, Glasgow — **Glasgow**
Moffat Woollen Mill — 3H **11**
Mutiny Stones — 3D **20**
National Flag Heritage Centre — 1C **20**
National Library of Scotland, Edinburgh — **Edinburgh**
Nevis Range Cable Cars — 1E **31**
Newton Steeple — **Ayr**
Noah's Ark Activity Centre — 1B **26**
North Kessock Lifeboat Station — 4H **47**
Ormiston Market Cross — 2B **20**
Our Dynamic Earth — **Edinburgh**
(Pannanich Wells, Ballater — 4G 41)
Parliament House, Edinburgh — **Edinburgh**
(Peel Farm Trail, Lintrathen — 3H 33)
Picardy Symbol Stone — 5B **50**
Pictavia — 3C **34**
(Pitlochry Fish Ladder — 3E 33, S)
Polmaddy Settlement — 5C **10**
Port Askaig Lifeboat Station — 2F **15**
(Preston Market Cross — 1A 20)
Quarrelwood Woodland Park — 2E **49**
Raiders Road Forest Drive — 1H **5**
Rispain Camp — 5F **5**
Robertson Museum & Aquarium — 3E **17**
Rob Roy's Grave — 1E **25**
Rodney's Stone — 3C **48**
Rosal Deserted Township — 4H **57**
(Rouken Glen Park, Giffnock — 3A 18)
Royal Highland Showground — 1G **19**
Royal Yacht Britannia — 1H **19**
St Andrews West Port — **St Andrews**
St Columba's Island — 4D **44**
(St Drostan's Well, New Aberdour — 2D 50)
(St Erchard's Well, Kincardine O'Neil — 5A 26)
St Orland's Stone — 4B **34**
Sandy Knowes Lake — 2C **26**
Sanquhar Post Office — 3E **11**
*(Satrosphere Science & Technology Centre,
Aberdeen — 3E 43)*
Scolty Woodland Park — 4B **42**
Scotch Whisky Heritage Centre, The — **Edinburgh**
Scotland's Larder — 3F **27**
Scotland's Secret Bunker — 3G **27**
Scotlandwell Well — 3C **26**
Scottish Borders Art Glass — 2E **13**
Scottish Crannog Centre — 4C **32**
(Scottish National War Memorial, The — Edinburgh)
(Scottish Parliament — 1H 19)
Sculpture Walk — 1H **41**
(Secret Forest, The, Fairlie — 3F 17)
Seven Men of Moidart — 1A **30**
Sharmanka Kinetic Gallery & Theatre — **Glasgow**
Skelmorlie Aisle — 3F **17**
(Skyeskyns, Portree — 3B 44)
(Smillie Centre, The — 3E 17)
Speyside Cooperage — 4F **49**
Spey Viaduct Walk — 2G **49**
Stirling Old Town Jail — **Stirling**
Stuart Crystal — 1H **25**
Sueno's Stone — 3D **48**
(Tall Ship at Glasgow Harbour, The — 2A 18)
Tam O'Shanter Experience — 2A **10**
Tartan Weaving Mill & Exhibition, Edinburgh — **Edinburgh**
Tarves Medieval Tomb — 5D **50**
(Time Capsule, The, Coatbridge — 2C 18)
Tomintoul Peat Moss — 1E **41**
Trial Stone, The — 2B **44**
Tugnet Ice House — 2G **49**
(Turriff Mercat Cross — 4C 50)
Ugie Salmon Fish House — 4G **51**
Ullapool Village Clock — 4G **53**
Valley International Park — 4D **18**
(Vikingar, Largs — 3F 17)
Waltzing Waters — 4A **40**
Well of Seven Heads (Tobar Nan Ceann) — 4E **39**
Well of the Dead (St Mary's Well) NTS — 4A **48**
Well of the Lecht — 2F **41**
(White Horse Close — Edinburgh)
Willow Tea Rooms, The — **Glasgow**
(Witches' Stone, Forres — 3D 48)

Prehistoric Monument

See also Earthwork, Hill Fort

Achany Chambered Cairn — 3C **54**
Achavanich Standing Stones — 4E **59**
Achnabreck Cup & Ring Marks — 4F **23**
Aiky Brae — 2D **42**
An Corran Shell Midden (Carn Ban) — 2D **44**
Ardestie Earth-house — 5C **34**
Auchagallon Stone Circle — 5B **16**
Ballygowan Cup & Ring Marks — 4F **23**
Baluachraig Cup & Ring Marks — 4F **23**
Balvraid Chambered Cairn — 2H **37**
Blackhammer Chambered Cairn, Brinian — 2D 64
Borve Standing Stones — 4D **44**
Broch of Gurness — 2C **64**
Cairnbaan Cup & Ring Marks — 4F **23**
Cairn Holy Chambered Cairns — 3G **5**
Cairn O'get — 4G **59**
Cairnpapple Hill — 1E **19**, S
Caisteal Grugaig Broch — 1H **37**
Caiy Stone NTS — 2H **19**
Calanais Standing Stones — 1D **62**
Capo Long Barrow — 2D **34**
Carlungie Earth-house — 5C **34**
Carn Ban — 1E **9**
Carn Liath — 2C **44**
Carn Liath — 5C **44**
Carn Liath Broch — 3F **55**
Clach Mor — 5F **47**
Clach na h'Annait — 1E **37**
Clachtoll Broch — 1F **53**
Cladh Chiaran Chambered Cairn — 2G **29**
Claigan Souterrain — 3B **44**

Clava Cairns — 4A **48**
Clickhimin Broch — 2D **66**
Cnocan Nan Gobhar Chambered Cairn — 2E **37**
Cnoc Freiceadain Long Cairns — 2D **58**
Colmealie Stone Circle — 1C **34**
Corrimony Chambered Cairn — 5E **47**
Cullerlie Stone Circle — 3C **42**
Cup & Ring Marks — 4F **23**
Cuween Hill Chambered Cairn — 3C **64**
Drumtroddan Cup & Ring Marked Rocks — 4E **5**
Drumtroddan Standing Stones — 4E **5**
Dun an Ruigh Ruadh Broch — 4G **53**
Dun Ard an t-Sabhail — 5C **44**
Dun Ardtreck — 5C **44**
Dun Beag — 5C **44**
Dun Borrafiach — 2B **44**
Dun Borreraig — 3A **44**
Dun Carloway Broch — 3F **63**
Dunchraigaig Cairn — 4F **23**
Dun Dornaigil Broch — 4F **57**
Dun Fiadhairt — 3B **44**
(Dun Flashader — 3C 44)
Dun Gearymore — 2B **44**
Dun Grianan — 2E **45**
Dun Grugaig — 2E **37**
Dun Grugaig — 2H **37**
Dun Hallin — 3B **44**
Dun Kearstack — 2E **37**
Dun Lagaidh — 4G **53**
Dun Osdale — 4B **44**
Dun Ringill — 2E **37**
Dun Telve — 2H **37**
Dun Troddan — 2H **37**
Dwarfie Stane — 4B **64**
Easter Aquhorthies Stone Circle — 1C **42**
Edin's Hall Broch — 2E **21**
Fortingall Standing Stones — 4C **32**
(Garmouth Standing Stones — 2G 49)
Gask Ring Cairn — 5H **47**
Glebe Cairn — 4F **23**
Glenrothes Standing Stones — 3D **26**
Grain Earth-house — 3D **64**
Grey Cairns of Camster — 4F **59**
Hill O'many Stanes — 5F **59**
Hinnisdal Hut Circle — 3C **44**
Jarlshof Prehistoric & Norse Settlement — 6C **66**, S
Kensaleyre Cairn — 3D **44**
Kensaleyre Standing Stones — 3D **44**
Kilmarie Stone Circle — 2E **37**
Kilmuir Hut Circles — 2C **44**
Knap of Howar — 2G **65**
Knock Earth House — 1E **41**
Knowe of Yarso Chambered Cairn — 2D **64**
Laggangairn Standing Stones — 1D **4**
Lairg Broch — 3C **54**
Latheron Standing Stones — 5F **59**
Liveras Chambered Cairn — 1F **37**
Loanhead Stone Circle — 1C **42**
Loudon Wood Stone Circle — 4E **51**
(Lundin Links Standing Stones, Leven — 3F 27)
Machrie Moor Stone Circles — 5C **16**
Maeshowe Chambered Cairn — 3C **64**
Memsie Cairn — 2E **51**
Midhowe Broch — 1C **64**
Midhowe Chambered Cairn — 1C **64**
Midmar Kirk — 3B **42**
Moss Farm Road Stone Circle — 5C **16**
Mousa Broch — 4D **66**
Ness of Burgi — 6C **66**
Nether Largie Cairns — 4F **23**
New Kinord Settlement — 3H **41**
Nine Stanes Stone Circle — 4C **42**
Ord Hill Chambered Cairns — 3C **54**
Orwell Standing Stones — 3C **26**
Ousdale Broch — 2H **55**
Papa Westray Chambered Cairn — 2H **65**
Quoyness Chambered Cairn — 4J **65**
Rennibister Earth House — 3C **64**
Ri Cruin Cairn — 4F **23**
Ring of Brogar Stone Circle & Henge — 3B **64**
Rudh an Dunain Chambered Cairn — 2C **36**
Skara Brae Prehistoric Village — 3B **64**
South Yarrows Broch — 4G **59**
South Yarrows North Long Cairn — 4G **59**
South Yarrows South Long Cairn — 4G **59**
South Ythsie Stone Circle — 5D **50**
Stanydale Temple — 1B **66**
Steinacleit Cairn & Stone Circle, Siadar — 2H 63
Stones of Stenness Stone Circle & Henge — 3C **64**
Strichen Stone Circle — 3E **51**
Suardal Chambered Cairn — 1F **37**
Suardal Hut Circle — 3B **44**
Sunhoney Stone Circle — 3C **42**
Taversoe Tuick Chambered Cairn, Brinian — 2D 64
Tealing Earth-house — 5B **34**
Temple Wood Stone Circles — 4F **23**
Tomnaverie Stone Circle — 3H **41**
Torhouse Stone Circle — 3E **5**
Torrylin Cairn — 1E **9**
Tungadal Souterrain — 4D **44**
Twelve Apostles Stone Circle — 1C **6**
Uig Standing Stone — 2C **44**
Ullinish Lodge Chambered Cairn — 5C **44**
Unstan Chambered Cairn — 3B **64**
Urquhart Stone Circle — 2F **49**
Vatten Chambered Cairns — 4B **44**
Whitehill Stone Circle — 2B **42**
Wideford Hill Chambered Cairn — 3D **64**

Railway (Heritage, Narrow Gauge, Miniature)

Alford Valley Railway — 2A **42**, S
Bo'ness & Kinneil Railway — 5A **26**
Brechin Castle Miniature Railway — 2C **34**
CairnGorm Funicular Railway — 3C **40**
Caledonian Railway, The — 3D **34**, S
Craigtoun Miniature Railway — 2F **27**
Fraserburgh Mini Railway — 2F 51
Glen Line (Dufftown & Keith Railway) — 4G **49**
Jacobite, The (Fort William - Mallaig Steam Service) — **Fort William**
Kerr's Miniature Railway — 5D **34**
Leadhills & Wanlockhead Railway — 2F **11**
Mull Rail (Mull & West Highland Railway) — 5A **30**
(Ness Island Miniature Railway, Inverness — 4H 47)
Strathspey Railway, The — **Aviemore**, S